Making Your Mind: Communication & Social Influence

Tim Thompson
Communication Studies
Edinboro University

Making Your Mind: Communication & Social Influence
Tim Thompson
© 2015, August Learning Solutions

Published by August Learning Solutions
Cleveland, OH

August Learning Solutions concentrates instructor's efforts to create products that provide the best learning experience, streamlining your workload and delivering optimal value for the end user, the student.

www.augustlearningsolutions.com

Cover Image: Andrey_Kuzmin/iStock/Thinkstock

All rights reserved. This book or any portion thereof may not be reproduced or used in any manner whatsoever, including but not limited to photocopying, scanning, digitizing, or any other electronic storage or transmission, without the express written permission of the publisher.

ISBN-13: 978-1-941626-04-7
ISBN-10: 1-941626-04-1

Printed in the United States of America
18 17 16 15 14 1 2 3 4 5 6 7 8 9 10

To my family, friends, students, and colleagues—you are all sunshine for the soul. Thank you.

Contents

About the Author *vi*

Preface *vii*

Chapter 1
Communication in Evolving Social Systems   1

Social Systems *3*

Relationships, Power, and Interdependence *6*

Homeostasis and Feedback Loops *8*

Social Evolution *9*

Stochastic Process *10*

Creative Moment *11*

Exercise *14*

Chapter 2
The Drama of Social Interaction   15

Kenneth Burke's Definition of Humans *16*

Symbol-Making, Symbol-Using, Symbol-Misusing *16*

Inventor of the Negative *17*

Separate from our Natural Condition *18*

Goaded by the Spirit of Hierarchy *18*

Acquiring Foreknowledge of Death *19*

And Rotten with Perfection *20*

The Drama *22*

Creative Moment *25*

Exercise *25*

Chapter 3
Mind   27

Mind Is More Than Brain *28*

Brain Is Physical—Mind Is Metaphysical *28*

Brain Is Individual—Mind Is Social *28*

Brain Is Time Bound—Mind Is Transcendent *28*

Brain Is Processor—Mind Is Information *29*

The Nature of Consciousness *29*

Freud's Model of Mind *30*

Jung's Model of Mind *32*

Mead's Model of Mind *34*

Gardner's Intelligences *35*

Creative Moment *37*

Exercise *38*

Chapter 4
Minding Your World: "MAPs," Abstraction, and Critical Thinking   39

Memory *40*

Attitude *41*

Perception *43*

The Abstracting Animal *46*

Creative Moment *50*

Chapter 5
Making Meaning   53

Coordinated Management of Meaning *57*

Summary of Meaning *62*

Creative Moment *62*

Exercise *63*

Chapter 6
What Moves You? 65

Order, the Secret, and the Kill *66*

Motivation à la Maslow *68*

Choice Theory *70*

Being, Doing, and Having *71*

Murray's Motivations *72*

Murray's Map of Motivation: Psychogenic Needs 73

Creative Moment *74*

Exercise *75*

Chapter 7
Personality 77

Factors of Personality *78*

Myers-Briggs Personality Types 82

Interpersonal Personality *84*

What Is Personality? *86*

Creative Moment *87*

Chapter 8
Who Moves You? 89

The History of Rhetoric in Five Minutes *90*

Schopenhauer's Stratagems 91

Persuasion and Identification *93*

Advertising and Identification *94*

Compliance-Gaining Strategies *96*

Persuasion and Postmodern Mind *98*

Creative Moment *100*

Chapter 9
Media and Mind 103

The Medium and the Message *104*

The Media and the Message *105*

Media Effects *106*

Bobo Dolls and Beyond 108
Who Sets the Agenda? 109
Cultivating Minds 110

Creative Moment *112*

Another Moment *112*

Chapter 10
Getting Past Fear 113

Categories of Communication Apprehension *114*

Where Is Fear From? *115*

The Impact of Apprehensiveness *116*

Letting Go of Fear *118*

Creative Moment *120*

Chapter 11
Communication Competence 123

Learning to Listen *126*

Becoming a More Competent Communicator *128*

Creative Moment *133*

Chapter 12
Creating Your Social Reality 135

Summarizing the Story So Far *136*

Ithaka *138*

Connecting Patterns *140*

Be Here Now *142*

Tree of Being *143*

References *145*

Index *147*

About the Author

Timothy Neal Thompson, PhD, Bowling Green State University, is a professor in Communication Studies and founding director of the Edinboro Highland Games at Edinboro University. Tim and his wife Dee Dee live in Edinboro, Pennsylvania, where they raised five children.

Preface

**What is Mind?
No Matter.
What is Matter?
Never Mind.**

We can question that wisdom—is mind not matter and matter never mind? Is there some kind of *thought* going on, other than in brains, in the nature around us? Is mind made of physical stuff?

We might not answer that here, but we will certainly have a go at it. It's not just matters of mind but also the relations between minds, how it all interacts, that is of interest. Your mind is made by interactions with many others. Your thoughts are encoded with words, images, and information you took in from various people and groups. Mind evolves in relation to many groups, like family and friends.

My friend said "don't think here" (pointing to his head), "think here" (pointing to his heart). Now what in the world could that mean—think with your heart? Can you think with your heart? Where's mind, then?

How is mind influenced in social systems and the dancing ideas between us? And how does a mind become mindful?

Chapter 1

JupiterImages/liquidlibrary/Thinkstock

Communication in Evolving Social Systems

"Mind gleams in every atom of the universe."
—*Lisa Mason*

2 Chapter 1 Communication in Evolving Social Systems

Mind is created in communication. Throughout this book we will be making models of mind and social influence. When we discuss and sketch how communication works, we are essentially making models. A model is a small- or large-scale abstract version of the real thing. The interesting thing about our models of communication is that they are communication themselves, because they communicate something. Life's full of multi-layered meanings.

Typically, communication has been modeled as linear, interactive, and transactional. The linear model of communication was developed in the 1940s by Claude Shannon, a Bell Laboratories scientist and professor at MIT, and then revised when he worked with Warren Weaver, a consultant with the Sloan Foundation. Their model depicted the source sending a message over a channel to a receiver with noise along the way. The model, as seen in Figure 1.1, was originally applied to telephone messages then to human action.

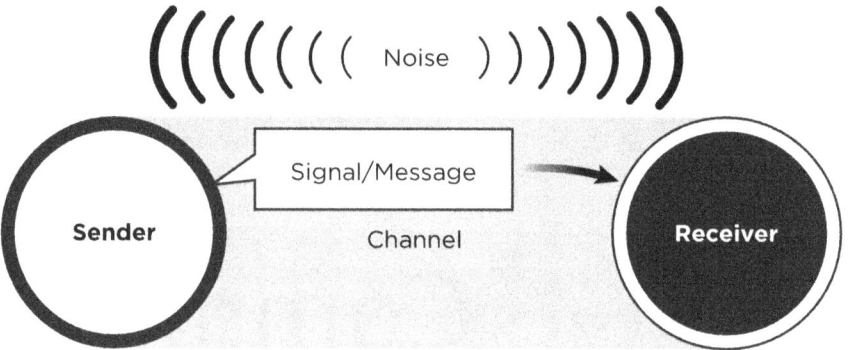

FIGURE 1.1 Linear model of communication

That linear model (communication traveling in a line) was enhanced by adding a loop of feedback from the receiver to the source. Norbert Weiner's (1948) work on cybernetics (systems) suggested the need for feedback in communication models, and from those thoughts Wilbur Schramm (1954) developed an interactive model of communication shown in Figure 1.2.

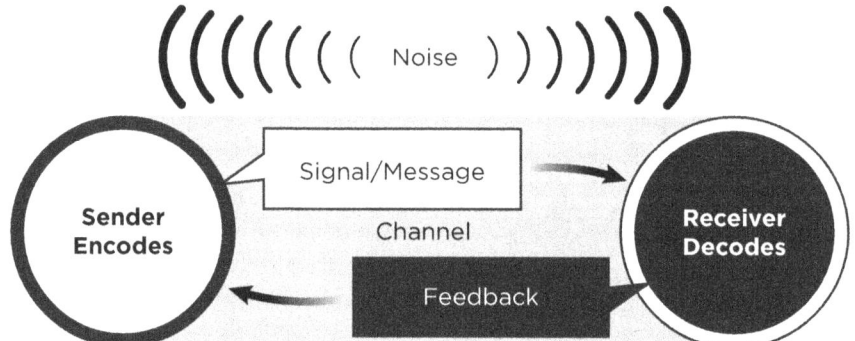

FIGURE 1.2 Interactive model of communication

This interactive model shows feedback: messages and responses flowing between participants. The interactive model does not, however, depict the simultaneous messages being sent and received by each person.

Think of a simple conversation between you and another. Each of you exchanges messages and responds to previous messages. But you are also aware of the other's nonverbal responses even as you speak, so both of you are simultaneously a source and a receiver of information.

Transactional implies the source is simultaneously a receiver and more. It also implies that past behaviors and goals for the future feed into present communication, so the influences in the communication process transcend the current situation; past and future impact our present communication, as shown in Figure 1.3. As you engage in conversation with a friend, your past interactions affect the meaning of present words and gestures, and you may have an idea of where you're trying to go with the discussion in the near or distant future; that is, some communication is goal-directed.

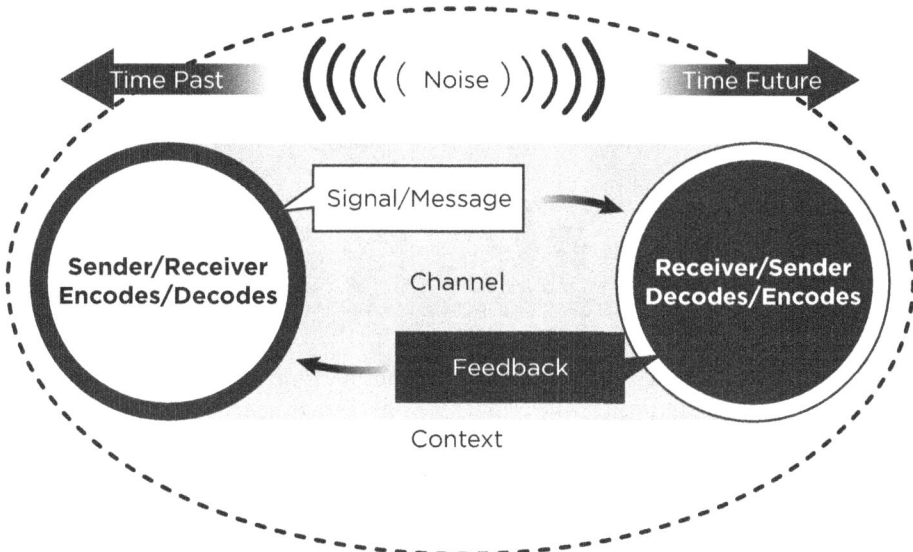

FIGURE 1.3 Transactional model of communication

Notice that Person 1 and Person 2 are simultaneously encoding messages (converting ideas into words and gestures—into a *code* that might be understood by the receiver) and decoding meanings (translating the code, such as words and gestures, into ideas). They are also communicating within various contexts: physical, social, and time, to name a few.

These models are helpful for getting started as we begin to make our own maps of the communication process. They are simplified abstractions—all models are. One way to begin complicating our models is to put them in motion and look at the wider social systems in which they operate.

Social Systems

You were born into a family, you hang out with certain friends, you've learned in various schools, and you listen to various musicians. Each of these groups is a social system, and your mind has been made by interaction in social systems. Your thoughts are the products of social systemic interactions swimming in memory—from your parents/guardians, friends, teachers, preachers, and others.

Social systems are the essence of societies. Each of us helps to shape some systems and we are shaped by them. You and I are a part of families, peer groups, organizations, and other sets of people. We are part of what makes these groups and they play into who we are. We make social systems and they make us.

Understanding social systems is one of those foundational bits of knowledge that will help in understanding other disciplines. The same concepts that apply to communication from a systems perspective will provide insight into other fields

4 Chapter 1 Communication in Evolving Social Systems

Social systems are groups of people interacting and making meaning together. YanLev/iStock/Thinkstock

from business to biology. In fact, borrowing terms from one domain to think about another may help you strike it rich, even if the riches are "mere" knowledge.

Can you think of any thought you have that is *not* influenced by a social system (groups of people interacting through words and other ways)? Everything you think has origins somewhere else, and much of that somewhere is found in the social sphere, whether it be the influence of the news, your family, friends, or other social groupings. Your life is contextualized by many groups—that's what systems are—like the club you're considering, or the group of people who like the same authors, or the group of people who meet after midnight to continue the party, or that group of people who text each other. We are members of multiple social systems.

The idea of social systems extends from General Systems Theory, developed by Ludwig von Bertalanffy (1968) and others. Systems theory views the universe as interconnected levels or layers of interacting parts. You are from a family that resides in a town or city, encircled by a subculture and a culture and so forth, as illustrated in Figure 1.4.

FIGURE 1.4
Systems diagram of you

Or rather, that's what it doesn't look like! That systems diagram looks nothing like you. It is an abstract map of your social relations (and a very rough map, at that). It's kind of like when you were in kindergarten and you learned that your address was on a street, in a town, in a state—and you can take that farther to country, world, Milky Way, universe. Each is a different system level.

Another way to say that is you are a *subsystem* of a family system that exists within wider social environments. That's typically the way the levels are separated: subsystems within systems within environments. Of course, you are a subsystem within many other social systems simultaneously. Your group of friends, workplace, clubs, church, and even your target demographic group for that marketing executive wanting a share of your wallet—all are subsystems within wider social systems.

Where we draw the line for what constitutes the system and subsystems is arbitrary. Social systems are people interacting in various groupings at different levels, but how we name the levels is a matter of preference. So, for instance, I am an individual in a college classroom—a subsystem within that classroom system. But we can also consider the classroom as a subsystem within the university system, or the university as a subsystem within the higher education system, and so on. What we name as the system or subsystem level is an arbitrary decision.

The same is true of the body as a biological system. We can think of the body as the system, made up of various subsystems (cardiovascular, musculoskeletal, dermal, neural, and others), and operating within an immediate environment. Or we could think of each of those inner parts as a system, operating within the "environment" of the body. And we could go another step downward—as in *The Fantastic Voyage*, to see your heart as an environment that contains various systems (auricles, ventricles, and such) that are made up of subsystems. As we go further into the subatomic realm we see whole communities thriving in each speck of tissue—very much like Dr. Seuss's *Horton Hears a Who*. In that story, Horton the elephant realizes there is an entire community of little "whos" living on the speck of dust he comes across in the jungle. It is indeed fantastic, that voyage into the wonderland of your body! It is likewise fantastic to journey into the interconnectedness of all systems, biological and social.

Where you draw the line between the system and the subsystems depends on the level of analysis. There are social systems inside of social systems inside of social systems. You may be a part of a group of friends. Within that group exist groupings, cliques. Within those cliques there may be further alliances, and those alliances shift, change across time. Social systems are not simple.

Not only are there many groups within groups, but the complexity multiplies when we consider the boundaries of social systems. Consider you. You are part of a family, a town, a state, and a nation, and perhaps a school, a religion, a political party, a club or team, and other organizations. You hang with different friends. You are a part of many social systems. Some call this the law of partial inclusion: each of us is a member of many social systems simultaneously.

You are a part of many social systems and you interact with others who are also a part of many different systems, each of you crossing boundaries that are more or less apparent. For example, let's say I am politically independent and I'm at a garden party talking to my friends, Tom the democrat and Sue the republican. Our discussion, social systems-wise, could be mapped as shown in Figure 1.5.

Each of us crosses boundaries, talking to friends in this context who might be labeled as enemies in another context. Our lives are full of such boundaries, crossings, and interactions. Social systems have boundaries that are more or less open or closed. Remember that sixth or seventh grade science class, when you looked at an amoeba on a slide under the microscope? Then you put something on the slide—an acid or something—to see if it would permeate the cell wall. You investigated the permeability of the cell wall. Likewise, we can discuss the *permeability* of social systems. But this kind of permeability is different because there is not necessarily a physical wall to penetrate. The "walls" of social systems are defined by a person's talk, dress, and mannerisms more than bricks and mortar.

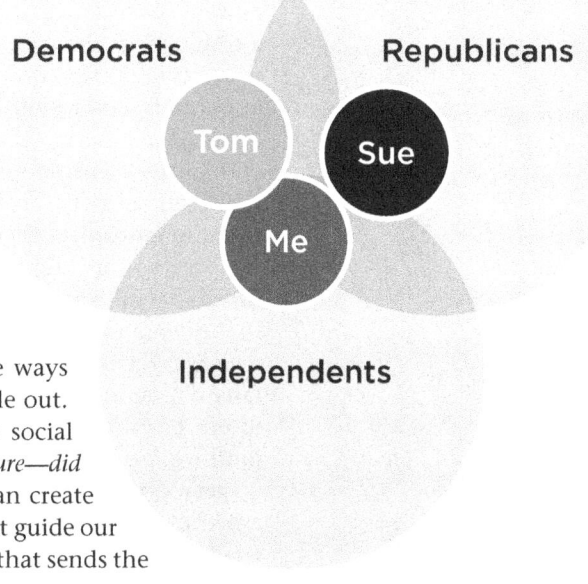

FIGURE 1.5 Social system boundaries and parties

Think of a clique of girls in high school. They have ways of determining who "belongs" and ways of keeping people out. Rather than the cell wall of an amoeba they have the social boundary created by talk and other actions. *Like, I'm so sure—did you see what she said . . . Oh my god, what a ditz . . .* Talk can create walls. The ways we name people can establish attitudes that guide our actions, and those actions may include a certain aloofness that sends the signal "you're not one of us." The divisions we feel in our thoughts often grow out of talk, especially the ways we name "us and them."

Boundaries are found at the edges and inside of social systems. Inside of each group—be it a family, an organization, church, or whatever—there are clubs within the club. Let's say you come into a large amount of money. You decide to join the Club, an exclusive golf, tennis, and recreational organization that protects its boundaries through high membership fees, a vote of existing members, and rules. You pay the dues, they vote to let you in, and you join. You quickly discover that membership in the Club does not necessarily gain you entry into the inner clubs within the Club. You find there the group of rich guys who party hard, the super-rich CEOs and such, the wanna-be-rich pretenders, and other groups. Each social system has subsystems that have ways of protecting their membership—what some have called "boundary maintenance." If you want to gain membership in the clubs within the Club you will need to form relationships, and *relationship* is a key term in the study of social systems.

Relationships, Power, and Interdependence

Social systems are made of relationships between people. Relationship refers to the degree of interdependence, power, and history of interactions between people. Consider a simple social system: two people in love, Jack and Diane, an intimate dyad. Let's go back to a time before the two lovers met, back to a time when they had "zero" history. Jack shows up as a new kid at Diane's high school. Jack plays football and Diane is a cheerleader. They become aware of each other during the football season, and through friends they learn that each is interested in the other. In one magical moment at the Tastee Freeze, Jack asks Diane if she wants to go to a party after the game Friday night. She goes, they meet there, and they hit it off. Next week they go to a movie together, and soon they are eating meals together. They later discuss how they like each other, and consider themselves "steady" or "going out." Jack and Diane have formed a relationship, and it may go on to take the form of friends, lovers, ex-lovers, marriage partners, or whatever.

As we see in the potential arcs of Jack and Diane's relationship curve, relationships change over time. And different aspects of the relationship change over time, as well. For instance, the power-sharing arrangement between parties involved in a relationship changes. Power refers, in part, to who's doing the controlling and who's being controlled. Many intimate relationships start with a kind of equal power and then morph into more one-sided power. Perhaps Jack and Diane start out on equal footing, but then later on in the relationship, Jack suggests and Diane obeys, or vice versa. You can probably think of many marriages or friendships where one person controls and the other defers to that control—and their relationship probably didn't start out that way. Relational power evolves.

Power is apparent in all relationships and all interactions. Gregory Bateson noted that all communication has a report-and-command aspect. "Report" refers to the denotative meaning. "Command" refers to the power move evident in each message. For instance, if I say, "Go get us a pizza," I am referring to that round, tasty object; but the message is also inferring that I have the right to tell you what to do. But notice we don't really know about the power operating between us until we see your response and subsequent moves. If in response to my order to go get a pizza, you say, "Okay—what do you want on it?" that demonstrates one aspect of power operating. If instead you say, "Go to hell; get your own pizza," that would show an entirely different power dimension. We don't know how power is operating in social relationships until we see how the responses play out in a sequence of interactions.

Another way of looking at that relational power dimension is to say the power is part of the context of relationships, and the relationship contextualizes messages. Let's say you and I are friends, have been for quite a while, and we like to playfully swear at each other. So, we're playing a drinking game, and you try to cheat, and I say, "F—you," and you say, "F—you" back to me. In the context of our friendship, this swearing at each other means "I like you." In another context, with someone different, those same words might mean "I despise you!" Words and other symbolic interactions take on meaning within the context of our social systems, our networks of relationships.

You are interconnected with others in the various relationships of different social systems. You affect and are affected by others. That is to say, you are interdependent with others. Interdependence is an important concept for understanding relational social systems, and refers to the extent to which people need each other and affect each other. It can refer to the strength of the bond between people in social systems. Those bonds, or linkages, can be loose, tight, or uptight. Think back to Jack and Diane. Before they met they had no relationship and no (or very little) interdependence. After they met and began going out on dates, their lives became intertwined. They were loosely interdependent. With time they might grow more dependent on one another, as together they decide things to do and influence each other's feelings. Their romance might grow to the point where one or both "can't live without" the other. That's a strong interdependence. And sometimes romance can evolve into various dysfunctional relational patterns where the participants become overly dependent—the linkage, or coupling, between the partners becomes uptight. For instance, some cases of extreme jealousy show an uptight coupling, like when a boyfriend beats up a girlfriend for talking to another boy. That's a bit uptight.

Relationships change across time—but what is it that changes? The people change, yes, but also the very nature of the relationship changes. As social systems evolve, relationships change across time, and the ways that relationship contextualizes the participants' interactions changes. You might playfully pinch your lover after a year in the relationship, but if you had pinched on the first date, the act would have had a different meaning. The pinch may be okay at one time, not okay at another. Saying "I love you" after six months has a whole different meaning than saying it when you just met someone.

Subsystems are interdependent with systems, and they're all interdependent with the wider environment. For example, a parent and child affect one another, and each is affected by and affects the wider family. And that family is further affected by wider systems like the community, educational system, political system, technological systems, solar system, and others. Think about how family social gatherings have changed with the invention of various technologies; from video games to cell phones and television, the technological system is intertwined with family systems. Technology, as we will discuss in later chapters, has changed interpersonal dynamics.

Social systems are dynamic, ever-changing, yet stable. Systems, from your physical body to the cosmos, are almost the same as they were yesterday. You've aged since yesterday, but not too much. (Why, I can't even tell by looking at you.) Different from bodies, though, social systems have structure through the network of relationships and interactions. Rules within relationships are one of the things that help maintain that structure or stability. We'll talk more about that under the concept of order.

The links of people in social systems are dynamic, changing. Those interdependencies between you and the rest of your social world are in motion. Your drama is a motion picture.

Homeostasis and Feedback Loops

The structures of social systems are somewhat stable and yet fluid and dynamic. Systems demonstrate dynamic steady states, and often show a tendency to try to stay in balance. Systems try to maintain equilibrium, or *homeostasis*. Within social systems, people develop a sense of what is okay and what is not okay. The rules and norms for behavior take shape as relationships grow and change. Homeostasis is the term used to refer to the normal operating range or the balancing of that dynamic steady state for systems. Just as our bodies have a certain normal operating range—pulse, blood pressure, body temperature, and other vital signs—social systems develop normal operating ranges. So, your family or intimate relationships can have times when things feel okay, or everything's cool—homeostasis.

Your body is a natural system. Your connection with others is a social system. Your body tries to achieve and maintain balance with the environment in several ways. Heart rate, body temperature, and other leading indicators of life get adjusted moment to moment as the body regulates itself, adjusting to changes in activity and environmental influences, all the while attempting to stay within acceptable limits. In social systems—families and friendships, for example—those acceptable limits are set by *expectations* and *rules*. In Jack and Diane's case, they may have reached that time where they labeled their system—we're "going out" or "steady" or "dating." That co-defining of "we're not going to date others" becomes a rule or expectation that helps govern the relationship. Note that that agreement between the two is a social concoction—they make it up and then believe in it. In a sense, then, social reality is make-believe. Yet, it's very real. To say we reach agreements and make rules that help regulate our relationships (help maintain homeostasis) is not to say that people in the relationship think alike. Each person is a subsystem within the system of the relationship. The rules are being interpreted differently by different actors in the relationship, and a large amount of communication goes into reaching agreement about rules. Still, we usually manage meanings between us without having exactly the same interpretations. Rules and expectations give social systems structure and stability amid the constant change.

Part of the change going on in systems, social and otherwise, is constant disintegration. That is the concept of *entropy*—systems are constantly coming apart. Systems also demonstrate *negentropy*, a reintegration or putting-back-together process. Like our bodies, heading back to dust, social systems tend to break apart. From intimate lovers, to families, to corporate giants, nations, and world empires, all systems disintegrate, exhibit entropy, and there are fixes going on—reintegrating forces, or negentropy.

For instance, let's say you're "going steady" with someone, and you come across several conflicts, from disagreements about how to spend money to disagreements about proper party etiquette. There is a tendency for such relationships to break up, a tendency toward entropy. But you do things to keep it together, like talking, going places, giving gifts, and just enjoying each other's company. Entropy and negentropy are continually in a swirl surrounding the relationship and all social systems.

Social systems have hierarchical levels (subsystem, system, environment), interdependencies, homeostasis, and disintegrating and reintegrating (entropy/negentropy). Relationships, the glue of social systems, depend on rules and expectations to maintain stability and structure amid change. Those balancing acts are accomplished through *feedback loops*. To look at how systems work their way toward homeostasis, toward "everything's okay," we look at positive and negative feedback loops. Positive and negative feedback in systems theory may be a little different than what we're used to thinking. You may think of positive feedback as "good boy" or "nice job," and negative feedback as "you suck." In systems theory, however, positive feedback refers to loops of interaction that move the system away from homeostasis. Negative feedback refers to loops of interaction that move the system back toward homeostasis; they "correct" the system.

Positive feedback loops are sometimes called "deviation-amplifying" loops because they carry the system away from normal. Say, for example, a family is sitting down to dinner. Two of the family members start to argue. The rest of the family may see this as a deviation away from normal—the back and forth argument of conflict would represent positive feedback, deviation-amplifying loops, taking the family away from their normal calm. And if some of the family members make moves to try to resolve the conflict, those moves would represent negative, or correcting, feedback. Notice in this case that the positive feedback loops could be construed as "bad" and the negative loops "good."

For other families argument is an art form. They see it as normal and perhaps even encourage it. Some families—like some interpersonal relationships—thrive on argument, and so their point of homeostasis would be at a more combative level than the family that prefers calm. Different strokes for different folks. *Homeostasis*—when the various "vital signs" of a system are in the normal range—is different for each system.

Systems establish different senses of what is normal and what is not. For one loving couple a lot of conflict might be normal. For another couple the conflict might signify something is terribly wrong. Each system establishes its expectations of normal, equilibrium or homeostasis, over time and operates according to those expectations. If you're a member of the Wild Ass Rock Music Group, then it might be perfectly normal to party until you can't find the door and throw furniture out hotel windows; it may even be expected. If you're a socially conservative fellow playing checkers on a small-town drugstore porch, then you probably define *fun* differently. Different people, different social circles, have different ideas of what's normal, right, and fun. And those ideas will change throughout people's lifetimes as their systems evolve.

Social Evolution

Social systems are evolving. Think about the United States as a large social system. It has evolved since 1776. Think of your family through the years from when you were young to where you are now. It has evolved. Think about the nature of mediated and computerized interactions now with cell phones, computers, and music at the tap of a finger. Human-technology interactions have evolved.

Social evolution includes variation, selection, and retention. *Variation* refers to something new. It could be a new idea, new technology, new fashion, new way of behaving, new anything. *Selection* refers to choosing and using those variations. As we become aware of variations, we try some of them and not others. Those new things, ideas, or behaviors we try have a chance of becoming part of our routines. *Retention* refers to what is held on to, gets retained, or becomes routine and a part of the system. Retention is related to memory and the habits a system gets into.

Consider the social evolution in your life as you lived through your teen years. You came across many variations—new ideas and things to do, new fashions and friends. From that array of new things in your life, you acted on, that is, selected, some variations (new things to do, think, and say) but not others. And some of those choices (selections) led to your acquiring your habitual ways of doing and thinking (retention).

When I was eleven years old my mother let me go into a large department store to buy a pair of pants on my own for the first time. Things had been changing in our culture throughout the 1960s, and clothing styles were changing as well. Up to that point I had been wearing straight-legged black pants and shiny black regal shoes, just like my older brothers. That day in the May Company I saw a pair of gold bell-bottom pants. They were a variation, something new, to me. I tried them on and glanced in the mirror and marveled at how cool I was. That was selection—choosing and using the variation. I bought the pants and wore them, and from that day I wore bell-bottom jeans and brown leather earthy shoes for the next few years. Wearing bell-bottoms became routine, habituated. That's retention; the selected variation became a part of the ongoing system of my wardrobe. Around the country, millions of youth were going through the same change process, as the bell-bottom and blue-jean fashion waves echoed through our change-loving culture. People interact about new things, choosing and using some of them, and acquiring new habits and new ideas of normal. That's social evolution. All systems are evolving.

We will explore ideas about evolution throughout this book. Note for now, however, that within that process of variation/selection/retention, sometimes the parts work at odds with the whole. Most notably, retention (the habits of the system, the "way things are done") works at odds with variation, the system's ability to recognize new things and ideas. The habits a system gets into can inhibit exploration and creativity. Our mind, as part of social and psychological systems, can get into habits and routines that discourage new thoughts and new paths of action. A mind, like any system, can grow stale.

Stochastic Process

While systems are evolving they are also proceeding along stochastic paths. Stochastic process is formally defined as "a system that evolves in time according to probabilistic equations." This means that there are probabilities associated with each potential course or direction a system might take as it changes. Some changes, directions, are more likely than others to lead to success. Business managers will sometimes look at stochastic models to help in determining the likelihood that a given course of action will lead to success.

We can also define stochastic process as *choosing the best potential path among an array of choices, as those choices branch into other possibilities*. This is more in line with how Gregory Bateson (1972, p. 255) used the term to discuss learning in evolving systems. At each moment in your life you stand at the doorways to several decisions, from "what shall I eat for lunch?" to "what will I do in my career?" As you choose actions, certain pathways become more likely and others become less likely. For instance, when you chose a college to attend, that choice opened up possibilities for where you would live, who you would meet, how you would eat, and other future paths. When you choose a major, certain probabilities come into play about how your studies will proceed, what you'll learn, and so on. Choosing a major in medicine creates different future pathways than a major in communication. After deciding on a major, you might need to choose an area of specialization, and that area will present an array of decision pathways. The stochastic process is like a branching decision tree, and as people decide on certain branches—pathways in life—new branches grow ahead of that decision. In a sense you actually create new pathways by the decisions you make. And had you decided differently, you would have been presented with a different array of choices. Figure 1.6 shows how we might illustrate it—start reading from the bottom and continue up.

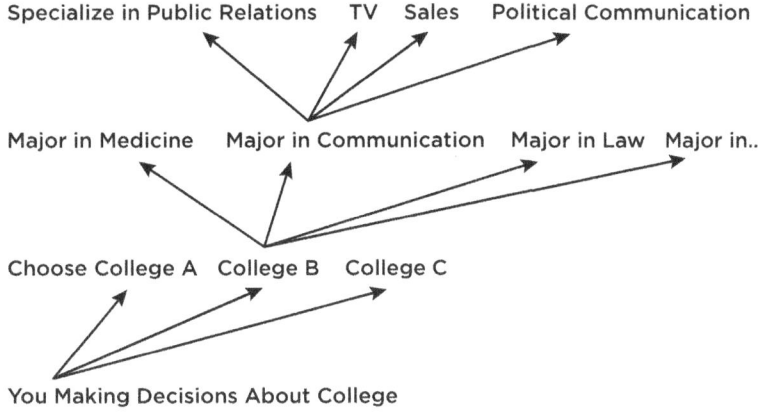

FIGURE 1.6 Stochastic process as branching decision tree

In that illustration, each of those decisions leads toward certain social systems and not toward others. Thus, your stochastic choices will bring you into contact with social interactions and opportunities down the road.

What makes the dynamic interesting is that as you are making choices on your "decision tree of life," so too are other people and whole social systems making decisions. So, as you decide on college, major, relationships, and lunch, other people are making their choices, and social systems from families to countries are making choices that will open some doors and close others. As you head down the paths of decisions you made, you "bump into" others heading down their paths. Some of the friends you've made, teachers you've learned from, and clubs you've joined were made possible by the paths you chose. And as you interact with other people and social systems met on your path, randomness is born. That is, there is a kind of unpredictability that results as people and systems interact. You might've had your major all figured out, knew exactly where you were going. Then you met a friend (your stochastic pathways crossed) who introduced you to a different major with a different way of thinking, and you decided to change direction. That change could not be predicted before you bumped into that new friend.

Social systems are continually changing, where decisions are made that present an array of opportunities, leading people in different directions than originally planned. Each system is evolving within wider evolving systems.

Creative Moment

Journal writing is an evolving loop of action-reflection. Doing breeds ideas, and those ideas set the course for more doing. The importance of action cannot be overstated. Action is exercise that helps maintain the fluidity of mind and flexibility for future actions. Viewing creativity as an evolutionary process, action produces variations.

The creative process is evolutionary. Evolution includes variation, selection, and retention. Variation is something new. Selection is the process of choosing and using variations. Retention is what gets kept for the future. In the creative process, we want to encourage variations (new ideas, techniques, materials, meanings) and loosen the grip retention often holds on attempting something new. Retention works at odds with variation. Retention is the habits a person or system gets into (and habits do have their place). Recognizing and using variations, then, helps break habits. Gregory Bateson noted the same tension in the closing words of *Steps to an Ecology of Mind*:

It used to be said that "Nature abhors a vacuum," and indeed something of the sort seems to be true of unused potentiality for change in any biological system.

In other words, if a given variable remains too long at some middle value, other variables will encroach upon its freedom, narrowing the tolerance limits until its freedom to move is zero. . . .

In other words, the variable which does not change its value becomes *ipso facto* hard programmed. Indeed, this way of stating the genesis of hard-programmed variables is only another way of describing *habit formation*.

As a Japanese Zen master once told me, "To become accustomed to anything is a terrible thing."

From all of this it follows that to maintain the flexibility of a given variable, either that flexibility must be *exercised*, or the encroaching variables must be directly controlled. (1972, p. 511)

The creative process—whether it is writing a journal, planting a garden, or changing your life—becomes one of exercising options and controlling encroaching habits.

Exercising options to diminish the impact of habits and finding variations to break free of retention are both parts of the essential *dialectic* at work in the creative process. The dialectic can be viewed in various forms as we study the art of creative communication.

For the ancient Greeks, dialectic was a conversation involving question and answer, where the participants explored different aspects of a topic while searching for truth. Plato and Aristotle would walk about in their peripatetic way while debating the nature of truth and beauty and love. In Hegel's sense of the word, dialectic was the ever-emergent conflict between thesis and antithesis as they give way to the synthesis. The bourgeois would clash with the proletariat, giving rise to the new middle class. The Chinese terms *yin* and *yang* present another view of dialectic. Yin and yang are the opposing yet interdependent forces that continually swirl in a dynamic balance. The symbol for yin and yang can be seen in Figure 1.7.

FIGURE 1.7 Yin & yang

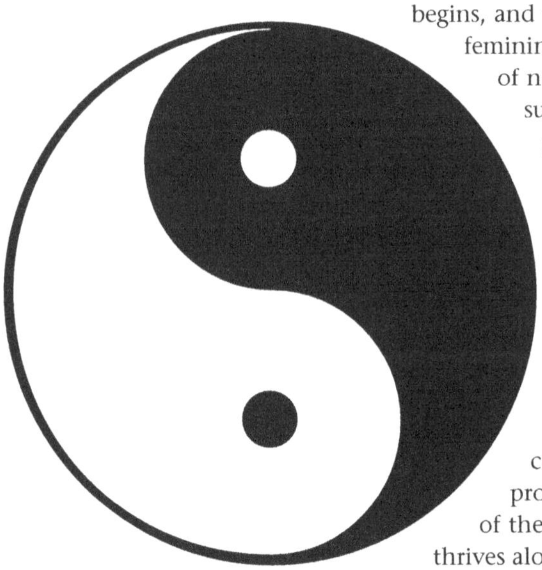

They are opposites that complement each other, need each other. Yin is dark, flexible, yielding, flowing, and of the night. Yang is light, hard, forceful, solid, and of the day. As the two opposites turn, each reaches its highest potency as the other begins, and the seed of the other is in each. Yin and yang can be conceived as feminine-masculine qualities and as the decomposition-composition in all of nature and the universe. For instance, the composition of spring and summer yield to the decomposition of fall and winter, and so on it goes, the circle unbroken. Life gives way to death gives way to life. . . .

The yin-yang dialectic, listed in Table 1.1, applies to the creative process as well. Certain qualities complement each other, and those opposites often work together. Motion needs stillness; activity needs rest. Divergent paths are helpful for exploring and wandering and moving outward into new realms of meaning; but you need to converge at some point, giving structure and order to ideas. Awareness of variety is essential in the search for variations, but a single-minded focus can be productive at times. Training can enhance creative potential in any domain, but sometimes training can actually get in the way of discovery, and a curious naïveté might prove more fruitful. Social interaction can be the source of ideas, one of the best contexts for variations to be born; but the creative spirit also thrives alone with one's thoughts.

TABLE 1.1 The Yin & Yang of the Creative Process

Yin	Yang
Rest	Activity
Divergence	Convergence
Awareness of Variety	Single-minded Focus
Naïveté	Training
Aloneness	Social Interaction

We can also think of the creative dialectic as forces that enhance versus those that inhibit creativity, as shown in Table 1.2. For instance, exercise enhances creativity—whether it is exercises within the domain of interest (practicing for your profession) or sheer physical exercise, which can help in maintaining the energy necessary to create. Laziness can inhibit creativity, and it may become a habit that saps your energy.

Constructive argumentation can enhance your creative efforts. It helps to test ideas in the forum, to push toward better through critique and disagreement. Groupthink, where group members avoid conflict and agree with one another out of mindless habit, is not often conducive to creative action.

Relaxation generally enhances the creative process, while uptightness will tend to block creative energy. Later on we'll discuss some yoga and relaxation techniques, from breathing to stretching and meditation, to enhance mindfulness. Now, we should note that it is possible to become too relaxed, to the point where you lose motivation or the drive to create. And a little uptightness may be good for your creative drive. Dissatisfaction with the current state of affairs has been the mother of many inventions. So a little uptight can be good, but a whole lot of uptight will tend to bind and limit creative potential.

Freedom of mind, a certain flexibility, and not-yet-housebroken playfulness of thought enhances inventiveness. When the mind feels imprisoned, immobilized through fears, anxieties, addictions, or other inhibitive influences, the creative process can lock. Freeing the mind is the key, but how?

TABLE 1.2 Enhancing and Inhibiting Creativity

Enhance Creativity	Inhibit Creativity
Exercise	Habitual Laziness
Argumentation	Groupthink
Relaxation	Uptightness
Mind Freedom	Mind Imprisonment

This book is about freedom and fluidity in social relations, and awareness of how social systems are influencing mind. There is no one single answer to the question, how can I be free? In fact, the quest might only lead us to further questions. Is that where the fun is?

Exercise

You will be encouraged throughout this book to make maps of your ideas. Tony and Barry Buzan's idea of "mind mapping" can be helpful in your creative process. *The Mind Map Book* (1993) encourages the use of "radiant thinking" to explore how ideas can expand outward from a center. Essentially, you start with a central idea then radiate outward with connected ideas. These maps can take on a branching, fractal form—similar to the branching form of ideas in mind.

> Map your social systems. Start with a circle with your name or just "Me." From there, work your way outward with circles showing the various social systems with which you are connected. Of course, there are immediate and extended family, friends, schools, communities, religious beliefs, and other obvious social systems in which you interact. Then there are social systems related to your hobbies and interests, music preferences, political parties, media habits, and any other connection that influences your mind.
>
> You can add lines to show connections between systems. Should you feel the need for artistic enhancements, add sketches or symbols or colors to the map.
>
> Map your social systems. Then think about how they are all evolving.

Chapter 2

Thinkstock Images/Stockbyte/Thinkstock

The Drama of Social Interaction

"And though she feels as if she's in a play, she is anyway."
—The Beatles, "Penny Lane"

Your social systems define your drama. Who you hang out with, who you work with, who you play with, and so many other social systems make up your drama, your story. Your drama is happening within a wider, overarching Drama, your story a chapter within the larger Story of humankind.

Humans are symbol-making, symbol-using, symbol-misusing animals. Ridofranz/iStock/Thinkstock

Each of our social systems—family, friendships, workplace, church, teams—has its drama: actors, scenes, stories, motivations. Kenneth Burke wrote about this drama, and the nature of communication and persuasion within it, throughout the twentieth century. Burke was a literary critic, philosopher, and poet who redefined the nature of rhetoric (the art of persuasion) in his time. He provided us with a language for talking about the ways we use language. Let's begin with Burke's definition of humans and proceed to some of his other ideas. *His definition provides a starting point for understanding the social construction of reality* through language and its connection to mind. The definition starts with a preamble and then describes us as the symbol-using animal. What follows is Burke's definition with my interpretation.

Kenneth Burke's Definition of Humans

being bodies that learn language,

thereby becoming wordlings.

Humans are

symbol-making, symbol-using, and symbol-misusing animals,

inventors of the negative,

separated from our natural condition

by instruments of our own making,

goaded by the spirit of hierarchy,

acquiring foreknowledge of death,

and rotten with perfection.

Burke begins by noting we are bodies (natural world) that learn language (social world)—what he also called the realms of motion and action. Our biological bodies are part of the realm of sheer motion, no conscious thought. Language is part of the realm of conscious, purposeful, willful action. It's kind of like the distinction between matter and mind, but with Burke's emphasis on language as key to our motivation.

Symbol-Making, Symbol-Using, Symbol-Misusing

Language is central to understanding human social and cultural evolution and motivations. Symbols (anything that stands for something else, such as language and logos) are the stuff of our social realities. Everything we have learned comes from words and images. We use symbols to teach our young. Everything we know about math, science, geography, and so on has been taught to us through words and pictures and other symbols. Humans created those symbols. We (our ancestors) have created all of the alphabets and definitions and meanings of things. From words like *cow* and *tree* to (dare I say?) *piss* and *fuck* and on to swastikas and McDonalds' golden arches: humans make symbols and load them with meaning.

Not only do we make all of our symbols, but we also use them to communicate, to convey thoughts from one mind to another. You can read these words and thus think about later what I am thinking about now. That's awesome, if you ask me. We also use symbols, said Burke, to "induce cooperation" amongst each other. That is, we use symbols to persuade, to get people to act with us, to influence beliefs and attitudes. For instance, marketers out there want you and me to buy that car, those clothes, this high-tech device—and they are using symbols, advertising words and visuals, to persuade us. We use symbols to convey meanings and persuade. Symbols move us.

We are also the symbol-misusing animal. Misuse can be conceived in a few ways. We misuse symbols when we deceive. When a person lies, knowingly says something that is untrue, that's a misuse of symbols. You can also misuse symbols by making mistakes when using them. Misspellings, grammatical gaffes, and problems with pronunciation could be counted as misuses of symbols. But Burke was more concerned with the deceptive, dissembling aspects of symbol misusage. That's where most of our ethical dilemmas are born. Think about that for a moment: a person can actually misrepresent reality by naming it as it is not. So I could make up a lie about my past or about the present and tell it to you, and you might think it was true. I might say, "Hey, did you hear what Bill said about you? He said you're a frigging idiot." And I might've made that up entirely, but maybe you believe me. So I have manufactured something out of nothing through the deceptive misuse of words. Poor Bill—he doesn't even know I'm telling you this!

We make our symbols, from alphabets to alpha and omega. We use symbols to communicate, to connect our minds and make meaning. And we misuse symbols, from making mistakes to telling outright lies. So far as we know, we are the only species to use symbols to tell stories and talk about past, present, and future. We interact through symbol-using, and that interaction is the key to understanding mind and human action.

Inventor of the Negative

Burke learned from Henri Bergson that everything in the universe positively exists; there is no such thing as nothing. For instance, these words are right here in your line of vision, and the only way we can say these words are *not* over there in the other room is by our human invention of "not." The negative—"no," "not," "thou shall not," "don't you dare!" and so on—was invented by us. It does not exist in nature, where everything is positively what it is.

Beyond the philosophical fun we can have discussing the implications of our invention of "do not," Burke notes further that we are "moralized by the negative." From our earliest experience in life we are taught right from wrong, how to behave properly, and the nature of someone's understanding of good and evil through the negative. Infants hear "No," "Don't do that," "Don't touch that," and other forms of the negative all the time. In other words, the negative is *hortatory*—it provides instructions on how to live, what to do and not do. We are raised, nurtured, on a healthy dose of "no" in its many forms. From "don't take cookies from the jar" to "don't have sex before marriage," our minds are made from many directives in the negative form. Much of what moves you, motivates you, is likely rooted in some negative you picked up along the way. For a quick exercise in the negatives that shape your life, jot down some of the rules that guide you that start with "Do not _____."

Poet Shel Silverstein wrote a great sort of rebuttal to the negatives we hear in our childhood. His poem is called "Listen to the Mustn'ts" and was published in his book *Where the Sidewalk Ends*:

> Listen to the Mustn'ts, child, listen to the Don'ts.
>
> Listen to the Shouldn'ts, the Impossibles, the Won'ts.
>
> Listen to the Never Haves, then listen close to me.
>
> Anything can happen, child. Anything can be.

Separate from our Natural Condition

The third idea in Burke's definition of humans assumes that our natural condition would consist of living naked in the woods digging roots and eating berries. We are *a part of* nature and yet *apart from* it. We've invented a number of things that separate us from our original state of being. Our technologies—tools, computers, cars, bombs, phones, and more—make us different from other animals. Autos, trains, planes, and rocket ships give us unnatural modes of transportation. Our houses and buildings are quite different from what the birds and bees make. Burke referred to technology as "counter-nature" because it often works at odds with the natural cycles of Mother Nature. For instance, the pollution we've created in the air, water, and earth has exceeded the earth's abilities to cleanse itself in some cases. So the "greenhouse gasses" that eat away at the ozone layer work counter to nature's apparent intent to maintain the ozone. Dr. Seuss's story of *The Lorax* was all about that.

Not only are we separate from nature by the hard technologies and pollution we've made, but also by words as well. Words are instruments, things we use for getting things and getting ideas across. Symbols are tools, and those tools often rend a separation between us and nature. Here we can look at the various ways in which we name nature negatively and the implications of those names. Some people grow up to despise dirt, making efforts to keep it off clothing, remove it from houses, and chase it out of their lives. A good bit of time is spent dealing with dirt, and some beliefs are built around dirt as negative. After all, "cleanliness is next to godliness," isn't it? Dirt is imbued with negative associations and people may actually grow to fear it. In some ways, dirt really can be bad, in that it might contain germs that hurt you. But much of our hang-up with dirt is entirely created by people and the brilliance of marketers such as advertisers for cleaning products. They're trying to get into our heads with a fear of germs—from symbols/words/visuals to our thoughts—further separating us from nature. We are separated from nature by technologies and ideas of our own making.

Goaded by the Spirit of Hierarchy

Burke said we are moved by a sense of order. We make up the various hierarchies we live within, from the priorities in our shopping lists to the rules for living a good life, and on to the many ladders we climb. All of our social systems have an order, a hierarchy to them. Think about the hierarchies you belong to. On the job there is an order from entry level to top dog. In families, clubs, schools, organizations, and any social grouping there is order, with people moving up, down, in, and out. Perhaps you're attempting to move up within a hierarchy at this time, trying to move on to the next level, be it a promotion or the next grade. Or perhaps you're trying to be regarded more favorably by friends. We attempt to "move up" in so many hierarchies: working toward graduation (moving up in the classes); trying to get promoted (up the organizational ladder); trying to influence community decisions (up the local political ladder); trying to live our lives more like Jesus or Buddha or some other religious role model (up the spiritual ladder); trying to win the game (up the athletic ladder); and so on in so many hierarchies we move in.

You're striving toward something, trying to achieve within some order, and as part of that striving there are rules for what you do and what you don't do—rules of the order. It is people's sense of right and wrong, their pieties that build the order. Burke said piety is a system builder. It is our sense of right/wrong, good/bad, what we do or don't do that establishes the orders we live in. Piety guides our actions from moment to moment. But note that different people interpret the rules differently, and we could even say people within the same order are operating in different hierarchies. Let me give you an example: Pat is involved in a year-round athletic competition called the QUAD Games with about four hundred to five hundred athletes competing in swimming, biking, running, and skiing races held in the spring, summer, fall, and winter. Order and hierarchy are woven throughout the games, and each person is involved in many others, including family, friends, work, worship, and whatnot. As you get involved in the games you see different subsystems of competitors, from those in it just to have fun to those who train hard all year and take it very seriously, and a whole range of competitors in between.

Pat tries to improve his times for each event each year. Faster times represent something good, defined by this order, and the fastest time becomes the "principle of perfection" toward which some strive. Not only might Pat strive toward a faster time, but toward the idea of what a faster time means. As Burke said, we are moved by a sense of order. Your ideas of order and mine actually cause us to act in certain ways. We'll discuss this more when we talk about motivation.

While Pat is out there running or biking, someone else in this country will be getting fired from his job; a heroin addict will be readying for her next fix; a romantic couple will be playing under the sheets; a boy will be petting his dog; and a dying mother will be saying goodbye to her child. All are involved in their dramas, their orders, that have hierarchies built upon what they do and what they don't do, what to say, and how to play.

We create various orders, our hierarchies, and then act within them. Each order has winners and losers, some doing what you're supposed to do, and some doing what you're not supposed to do (let's gossip about them). One of the rules for several orders—from Mama telling her child not to run in the street to the pharmaceutical company telling us to lead a healthier life—is the rule that you should try not to die. Ideas about death influence our lives.

Acquiring Foreknowledge of Death

Burke inserted this part of the definition later in his life. In a film, shot by his grandson Harry Chapin, Burke claimed it wasn't the fear of death that made him include it so much as a fascination with our fascination with death. So far as we know, we are the only species that can sit around and discuss death and what might happen after we die. This foreknowledge—knowing we're going to die—has implications for living.

Religious systems, for instance, are very much based on beliefs about the afterlife, and those beliefs may guide us toward certain prescriptions for how to lead a right and good life. Whether you believe in heaven or you are trying to earn karmic points for your next go around, and even if you don't believe and don't care, ideas of the hereafter can influence your beliefs and behaviors.

The idea of impending death impacts people differently. Some see it as horrific, and some see it as a blissful release. Some are afraid, some not. Many come to a time in their lives when they wonder what will be their legacy: What will I leave to future generations? What will I be remembered for? Some will spend time and money figuring out the best way to leave an inheritance to their heirs. Some will leave donations to charities. Some will leave money to their dog or cat. Some will have memorials made, and some will plan to be dust in the wind or sprinkled on a meaningful place. Different folks have different ideas about how to die properly, and what it all means. Each of us faces the certainty of death in our way, with varying results in the way it impacts our lives.

And Rotten with Perfection

Finally, Burke says we humans are rotten with perfection. This was a playful oxymoron that can be taken in different ways. People try to perfect the order of production, and yet in doing so we pollute the environment. In the perfecting of petroleum products, for instance, we have seen concomitant polluting of water, earth, and air. Pollution represents rottenness in the perfecting of the productive order.

Another way of looking at that is our notions of economy are at odds with ecology. Our ideas about how an economy should be, which are supported by and motivated by our language about the economy, goad us to produce more and more. The automobile industry, for instance, is expected to produce and sell more cars each year. If sales go down, that's a bad thing. If sales go up, that's a good thing. Sales make money for people. The sale of more and more cars has contributed to the growth in pollution over the years. The ideas (the hierarchy, order, principles of perfection) that drive the economies of the auto industry have led to problems in the earth's ecology. So in this sense the earth has become rotten with technological perfection. The human race is getting better, becoming more aware of our impact on future sustainability. Reducing pollution hurts profitability, however, so production systems remain somewhat at odds with the ecosystem.

There is another way in which we are rotten with perfection, referring to one of the grand ironies of our life's purpose. Our whole life might be spent trying to perfect—learn more, plant a better garden, practice music to master it, get promoted in various hierarchies, and so forth. But then we die, and perhaps rot—dust to dust. So, while we are perfecting certain aspects of our life, we are also on the way to the rottenness of death (assuming you get buried in the ground).

Burke's definition of humans provides a good starting point for looking at the ways we use symbols and create our social systems, our dramas. I tried to capture the essence of Burke's definition in this poem written in his honor. It was written in 1987, while I drove from western New York back home to Michigan, with my mind on teaching a lesson in Burke, and anticipating the birth of my first child, evident in the first line. The original title was "Logos Dialecticus" but I think I will rename it "Grand Old Dialectic":

A satisfied sperm's striving
    has been worth the struggle.
Near-perfect information exchanged in an
    orgasm of fertilization.
And nine moons cycle till
    another birth into
    a world of words and
    The Word.

The symbol-using animal
>is a curious sort.
Ever pondering the mystery
>of the first message.
Explaining the beginning
>and talking of telos
>as now becomes then in
>The Drama.
Talking of borders and baubles and
>the price of dirt,
We toil forth rewriting the scripts
>and laying down the laws.
We inventors of the good and bad,
>the shall and shall not,
>the system of pieties born in
>The Negative.
Unsatisfied souls yearn to conform with
>the source of all being.
Hence the conspiring
>to preserve the covenant;
All keeping the secret while
>the king's order remains clothed
>in the perfecting of fear we call
>Hierarchy.
Separate from each other
>by name and by number;
Divided by the doings of our
>rage for order;
We seek some simplicity
>in weaving our meanings
>in the mazes of manna in
>The Mystery.
Through this fog of symbolocity
>we come a-court'n the unknown;
Imperfectly imitating the communion
>of the original message.
And so on we trudge
>in the life by death journey
>in the rotting perfection of
>Grand Old Dialectic.

A critical theme in Burke's work is his emphasis on language as motivation and literature as "equipment for living." *We pick up attitudes and strategies for handling situations through the language we incorporate into mind.* In so many ways, we learn how to live our lives through the words of others, and learning "the language" is critical equipment for fitting into life's social circles and understanding the drama.

Learning the lingo of any social scene is part of the secret to success. In every drama, every social game, players are trying to learn the language and use it to their advantage. This "fitting in" function of language relates to Burke's key concept—identification—which refers to the process and product of associations we create through symbols. Your identity is very much dependent on associations to others and the terms by which you define yourself. Are you a golfer, a prayerful person, a game lover, a lover, a traveler? What are the terms and associations that define you? That is part of the meaning of identification. Another meaning is the process of persuasion by which we associate ourselves. We identify, associate, with many systems. The drug company wants you to feel a need for their product, so they devise advertising that first convinces you of your inadequacy then shows how their products fulfill that need. That process of persuasion is an identification process connecting your mind to their way of minding the world. The identification process is very much a part of those interactions that make up our mind.

The Drama

Burke was a dramatist. As Shakespeare said in *As You Like It*,

> All the world's a stage,
>
> and all the men and women merely players.
>
> They have their exits and their entrances,
>
> and one man in his time plays many parts . . .

Burke viewed human action and interaction through the use of a critical tool called the dramatic pentad. The pentad focuses on *act, scene, agent, agency,* and *purpose.* The *act* is what is happening, the action or behavior. For instance, I am writing these words. This is my act at the moment. Your act might be sitting there reading. The *scene* refers to the place and the context or situation in which the action occurs. I'm in my office, the place, but I'm also acting within a certain context of "these times," and my particular situation within these times. The country's in a recession—that's part of my scene now. The *agent* is the actor, the person playing the role(s). For instance, when the president comes on TV and says, "Everything's fine; we're not in a recession," he's an agent. *Agency* refers to the means by which we act—what facilitates the action. I am acting as a professor at Edinboro University, and that job allows me to do things like write and teach—it plays a part in the means by which I act. The *purpose* is the motivation. It is the answer to *why*? Why do we do what we do? We'll discuss that later.

Burke mentioned the ratios between the elements of the pentad are important for understanding the drama. That is, how do the elements interact with or affect each other? For instance, the scene-act ratio looks at how the place or situation can influence what people do. When you're in class, your behavior might be different than when you're at a party. Behaviors at a wedding are typically different than behaviors at a funeral. Thus, the scene influences action. The agency-purpose ratio would look at how the way something is done influences motivation. Let's say you're a high school football player who plays for a certain team and coach (agency), who get you fired up tremendously before the game. Thus, the agency influences motivation. We could look at ratios between all the elements to draw more thorough insights into human action, but let's move on.

Erving Goffman was a sociologist who also drew upon dramatic metaphors to explain social interaction. Borrowing a bit from Burke, Goffman (1967) developed a "dramaturgical perspective," which focused on symbolic interaction and the influences of time, scene, and audience. *Symbolic interaction is a perspective that assumes people act according to the meaning they hold, and those meanings are developed through social interaction.* So, for example, the way I feel about Burke and Goffman is based on the meanings I have of them, and those meanings have been developed through reading and discussions with teachers, students, and friends. Now you are a part of those social interactions, this social influence a part of your mind, more or less.

Goffman's notions of impression management and his distinctions between front stage and back stage action are helpful here. We each try to manage the impressions other people have of us, with varying levels of skill and success. One key insight of Goffman's is that other people help us to manage impressions. We coproduce images and impressions with each other. Here's how it works: In any given situation, we have roles we play. For instance, my role might be teacher, father, friend, competitor, or a mix in any given situation. Those roles have certain expectations and social value attached to them. In my role as father I'm expected to act in certain ways, and in my role as teacher I'm expected to act certain ways, and sometimes those roles might mix, as when a father teaches his child. Now, when I'm in my role as teacher, I am somewhat dependent on my students in order to pull off a "good show," to manage impressions of my performance. If students don't cooperate—for instance, if they disrupt the class or ignore me or cast doubt on my facts, and so on—it makes it harder for me to put on a "good show." We coproduce our impressions of each other in social situations.

Action in social situations is occurring in the front stage and back stage. The front stage is action that is evident to all the players and the audience. The back stage is behind-the-scenes action that is not evident to all the players and audience. Let's say you're with a group of friends—Dave, Sarah, John, and Mary—talking about a party you all were at the other night. You're talking about all the fun and silliness, but no one in the present conversation (the front stage) is talking about how John got roaring drunk and said those nasty things to Mary. You, Dave, and Sarah had been discussing it earlier, and your private conversation would represent the back stage to John and Mary.

In all social situations there are front-stage and back-stage elements at work, and some skillful social actors (and all of us are social actors) work the back-stage interpretations in order to better manage their front-stage impressions. Note that the front stage and back stage don't really have to be physical places; you could be in a discussion with someone in the conscious front stage while you held information back in the subconscious back stage. You might be talking with a co-worker, saying "wow, that's interesting" (front stage), but you are thinking "man, this guy is an idiot" (backstage). The front stage is available to all actors, the back stage is not; all dramas are unfolding simultaneously on the front and back stages.

Ernest Bormann's (1972) dramatic theory also adds insight to human action. His fantasy theme analysis, as part of *symbolic convergence theory*, looks at the ways people co-create meanings in the stories that are told and retold. Bormann studies group communication, and his basic unit of analysis is a fantasy theme. Before going on, we should note that he is not treating fantasy as some purely imaginative or wishful phenomena, but rather talking about the nature of groups' social realities. Fantasy themes may be socially constructed, but they are very real and have real implications.

Fantasy themes are the stories and dramatic elements found in communication between people—the characters, plots, and motivations present in our conversations. Bormann borrowed the term *fantasy theme* from Robert Bales (1970), who noted that group communication is not so much about here and now as about there and then. Group members tend to talk about people, characters, often placing them into storylines with good or evil intent and deriving morals from their story. Take the same activity and look at how it gets interpreted differently by different groups, for example. Let's say you have a boy who jumps off of a train trestle into a river from ninety feet up. His friends talk about how gutsy and awesome that was, and they repeat the theme of that story for years to come. The boy's parents talk about how careless and dangerous the jump was; a different fantasy theme. Our fantasy themes are present in everyday stories, gossip, and even intellectual conversation.

Different fantasy types get repeated in human dramas. Oftentimes we relate our own experiences to lessons in literature metaphorically. So, when a friend continues to worry and get you agitated over a perceived threat that is really nothing at all, your situation shares qualities with the "boy who cried wolf"; it is a "crying wolf" fantasy type. The Horatio Alger story is still alive and well, wherein the hero is born into adversity, but through hard work, perseverance, and a little luck he finds his way to prosperity. In many stories we find quests, conflicts, trials, and successes—all story lines that get recycled through human dramas.

Bormann calls it "chaining out," as stories spread outward and diffuse between group members and across social systems. As news spreads about some hero or villain, groups share stories and meanings. Note that stories are not met with the same interpretations across different groups. One group's villain is another group's hero. In the 2004 presidential election campaign democrat John Kerry was relying on his heroics in the Vietnam War to reflect well on his "tough on defense" image. He had skippered a swift boat in the war. Kerry's record was questioned over and over in commercials produced by "The Swift Boat Veterans for Truth," (a group opposed to Kerry, supported by his opponents) who successfully made Kerry's Purple Heart and other medals seem undeserved. Each of the political sides put out numerous ads and stories about "Kerry is a hero" versus "Kerry is a liar." The fantasies quickly chained out among the party faithful and then to the general voting public. In the end those stories, those fantasies constructed by small groups of people then diffused (chained out) into the general public, impacted an election. In 2014 different fantasy themes are taking root for the next presidential election, each side constructing their heroes and villains, including Hilary Clinton, Jeb Bush, and a whole host of other characters who may run.

When we weave a group's fantasy themes together into a composite worldview, we get what Bormann calls a "rhetorical vision." Different social systems have their particular angle on reality, their coproduced interpretations and meanings. Conservatives and liberals tend to weave together different political fantasy themes, creating different rhetorical visions about what motivates people, political priorities, and other differences in naming reality and a vision for how things should be. Different groups construct and *live in* dramatically different realities with meanings and context provided by their language and repeated fantasy themes. Depending upon the fantasy themes and rhetorical visions that you buy into, literally and figuratively (with your money and your beliefs), you will be influenced in that direction. This is not to say you are persuaded by things unreal, but *you are persuaded by socially constructed realities, and those realities are very real*.

So, where are we? We are each a part of social systems that are forever moving, changing, coming together, and falling apart. Continual loops of interaction help to maintain the systems, from friendships to families to nation states, and keep the systems hovering around homeostasis. Those systems are our dramas, our social realities, which we build and maintain through language and other symbols. Within those social orders, we follow rules created by the negative—"do not" and "thou shall not"—and our codes of right and wrong: pieties. All of this unfolds while striving toward certain principles of perfection that we also have created within our particular drama. In our various dramatic productions, we manage impressions of ourselves and others, with action occurring on the front stage and in the back stage. It is critical to remember that humans create these dramas. We make them up and then believe them. That is the essence of social reality, and that which allows us to even conceive and connect the stories of social reality is Mind.

Creative Moment

If you were to create a brief video about the story of your life, your drama, what would you include?

What would you be striving for—what is your quest?

What words, phrases, lyrics, quotes, or poems capture the essence of your story?

Are there forces of good and evil? How would you depict them?

Is there a moral to your story—a lesson to be learned?

Your story, as with much of your life, is a social construction.

Exercise

Create your "Coat of Arms." Think of seven symbols that define you—mainly visual images, but you can include words. Maybe it's the image of a heart, or a clover, or an animal, or a recliner if you think of yourself as lazy. Include what best represents your life or aspirations: musical symbols, religious icons, sports images, or words like "carpe diem," or letters like "YOLO." Take seven symbols that define you and arrange them into a shield—your coat of arms.

Chapter 3

Eyecandy Images/Thinkstock

Mind

"Wonder is the beginning of wisdom."
—*Socrates*

Mind is a mystery. We often refer to mind as a mental process or frames of thought, and we can discuss it in so many other ways. Consider, as Plato and Aristotle did, whether mind is separate from body. Is mind physical, chemical, or something more? Is there mind without human brains?

What happens when we think of something new, when we learn? How do neurons get connected in novel combinations? And does that new idea exist in a physical place, or is it only alive in the interactions among and between nerve networks? Further, is mind only possible in the interactions—the cycles or loops or patterns of communication—between people?

We can think about mind as the software that zips across the hardware of brains. We can ponder mind as it relates to soul and other supernatural subjects. Is there a soul that transcends death? Does it think? Or consider Mind as a more universal phenomenon—Mind with a big M—that is the larger system or universe of thought; the Mind that is beyond human thought, a grand intelligence.

Mind Is More Than Brain

We can differentiate mind from brain along several lines: physical/metaphysical, individual/social, time bound/transcendent, and information processor/information. There are, of course, more distinctions, but these will do for now. Keep in mind that even though we can make distinctions, mind is interrelated with brain. Brains bring the thoughts of human minds into being.

Brain Is Physical—Mind Is Metaphysical

Our brains are physiological organs composed of water and tissue that run on chemicals and electricity. They physically exist in the here and now, a part of the material world. Mind is more like information that's drifting around in the dance between physical nerves and brains. Your thoughts, for instance, are symbols that move about your brain's electrochemical networks. As such, they may have some physical properties, but they definitely have a "beyond physical" property that is born in the interactions (chemicals, electrical impulses). Thoughts have a metaphysical and somewhat spiritual quality. Gregory Bateson once said, "My idea of a pig is not a pig." Your thoughts stand for something, they are symbolic, but they are *not* the physical thing they stand for. Mind is not a thing so much as an interaction between things and ideas. You can touch a brain, but it is much more difficult to get our hands on mind.

Brain Is Individual—Mind Is Social

Your brain is yours. It's an organ stuck inside your gourd. Mind is not just yours. Your mind came through interaction with people and symbols (e.g., words) and ideas. It is the product of interaction and is still interacting, even as you read these words. Right now your mind is interacting with mine and relying on the structures of ideas that others have given you to help you make sense of my words. Mind comes from interacting with Mama and teachers and preachers and others; it is social.

Brain Is Time Bound—Mind Is Transcendent

Your brain is stuck within the time frame of your lifetime; it is born with you and dies with you (unless you have it cryogenically frozen in the hopes that it might be revived some day with its thoughts still intact, which is very doubtful. Some say Walt Disney did that. Do you believe it?). Mind transcends time. The thoughts in your head are in the here and now, but they're a product of the past and can think about the future. Some of the ideas in our heads have come from ages past, from

Jesus or Plato or the Phoenicians or the Puritans. For instance, some people do not believe sex should be discussed in public and may believe that nudity is dirty or socially unacceptable. Those ideas are not new; the Puritans espoused them to the early American settlers, just as others had before them. Beyond Puritanism, every subject in school has its earlier origins, and the ideas develop and get passed along through the years. Ideas—the stuff of mind—transcend time.

Brain Is Processor—Mind Is Information

The brain is an information storage and processing device. Mind is information. This idea of mind as information is beginning to unfold in interesting ways. Some information theorists and physicists, mentioned in James Gleick's book *The Information* (2011), conceive the universe as a vast web of information. It used to be that we distinguished between matter and energy. Then it was popularly theorized that all is energy of one form or another. Well, now these thinkers are thinking that not only is the universe all energy, but also all information. For instance, take a deep breath and let it out. That breath just initiated many interactions throughout your body, perhaps triggering trillions of information exchanges between cells, atoms, and other small stuff. If ALL is made of information exchanges, then there again we can conceive the universe as Mind with a big M—and our own mind is but a microcosm, seeking connection within the vast interconnectedness of the universal web of information.

Brain is the hardware, and mind is the software package that gets programmed. Brains are somewhat similar to computers, and as our technologies mutate the two become more similar. Brains are built for electrical and chemical charges to flit about. Mind is the messages in those charges.

Mind is a wide-open subject. Thinkers have wondered about it since the beginning of wonder, and we still don't understand completely what it is. When we address questions about mind we are inevitably led to questions about consciousness.

The Nature of Consciousness

Burke said we are "bodies that learn language"; we are biological organisms who use symbolic interaction to think, learn, and share ideas. Our biology is our nature, while symbolic interaction represents the better part of our nurture. Mind is a product of nature and nurture and both play into making us conscious beings.

We are aware, conscious of the world around us and our self. Is our awareness purely created by our brain? Or is there something more, a soul, for instance, that illuminates the conscious mind? Plato argued back in the fifth century B.C.E. that the only reason we can think about our self and the world around us is that we have a soul that is immaterial (not made of anything physical) and immortal (it goes on forever). Christian thought grew out of this belief, as St. Thomas Aquinas and others claimed the soul creates consciousness and is of divine origin. The question was debated outside religious circles as well. René Descartes, the seventeenth-century philosopher, said humans have a dual nature: a physical body and a mind, which emanates from the spiritual nature of the soul. This is essentially the "substantial view" of mind, understanding it as something that exists, has substance.

The "functional view" of mind, promoted by 19th-century scientists like Charles Darwin and Thomas Huxley, considers mind as a function of the mental processes in the brain. In this view, mind has no separate existence of its own but is a function of cognitive processes such as reason and memory. In this functional view, mind can be reduced to physical, electrical, and chemical processes—and mind has no existence without brain—when the brain dies, so does mind.

Those arguments revolve around individual consciousness. What if we open the concept up to consider consciousness in a wider sense, such as the possibility that nature or the universe might be conscious?

What if consciousness is woven into all the fabric of the universe and our brains merely tap into that wider consciousness? Gregory Bateson said as much in his notes on *Mind and Nature*. Bateson discussed the inherent intelligence in all systems. From simple examples like phototropic plants that track the sun to more complex examples like a disease mutating to develop immunity to antibiotics, there is evidence of a kind of consciousness in nature. Now, you could argue that those events in plants and diseases are "purely biological"; they're not thought. But we would argue that at some point in the cycle of events there is symbolic interaction—"take this to mean that" or "if sun, then turn this way"—that looks very much like thought. Or take the example of a tree shooting its sap up in the spring. Is that a purely physical occurrence, or is there an *idea* imbedded in the process? Even our own bodies demonstrate subconscious intelligence in the ways they automatically monitor and adjust to environmental cues. Perhaps there is a wisdom that pervades the universe that is very much like human intelligence and consciousness.

Consciousness is an interaction. We become self-aware through interaction with others. We are able to consider our self only by way of the symbols and images incorporated into our thinking through social interaction. Three prominent models of mind—Freud's, Jung's, and Mead's—consider interaction as crucial to development.

Freud's Model of Mind

Our conscious mind has been mapped in many ways. Sigmund Freud (1923/1949) offered his structural model of the psyche, which included the ego, id, and superego. Ego is consciousness. The ego is mostly conscious (perceptual consciousness, receiving sensory information from the outside world and aware of the self), but it includes preconscious and unconscious thoughts. Preconscious refers to ideas in memories that are not being consciously considered but can be easily accessed (that is, made conscious). Unconscious refers to that vast store of ideas that are buried, not readily available to your conscious mind, and could include anything from a deep-seated painful experience from long ago to an unexplainable fear you feel. Ego acts on the "reality principle," continually assessing implications and deciding the best course of action for any given situation. Ego is the moderator between id and superego, which tend to be at odds with one another. Much of the symbolic action that makes up the psyche, as shown in Figure 3.1, resides at the unconscious level.

Id is that aspect of the psyche guided by the hedonistic pleasure principle—to seek pleasure and avoid pain. The id is a human's inner "wild child," driven by sexual and aggressive instincts. The id is selfish and childish and wants instant gratification. It may manifest in the desire to have sex with a stranger (or a friend, for that matter) or in a strong need to punch your boss in the nose. The id is the animal aspect of the human psyche. It is instinctive, programmed in from birth. It is, according to Freud, part of our nature.

The superego is developed in nurture, programmed into mind during the socialization process. It is the psychic governor that keeps the id in check. It is your moral fiber and the parental controls in mind. The superego includes internalized standards of right and wrong, good and bad behavior. Your "conscience" stores ideas about what is bad and what you should not do in order not to be punished. Going back to Burke, this is the individual's internalization of "the negative"—the many variations of "no" and "do not" that you learn through interaction. The "ego ideal" is that aspect of the superego that tells you what is good and what you should do. For example, let's say you are an eighteen-year-old male looking with lust at the female seated next to you. Ego is aware of her and aware of yourself ("Man, she's nice . . ."; "I wonder what she thinks of me?" . . .). Id is saying, "Sex would be nice." Superego is saying "You can't have sex with her. You don't even know her, you're not protected, you're not married, you'll get a disease, God won't like it. . . ." Ego is moderating between the two, consciously making choices based upon "the reality" of the situation, which may include rewards and punishments for whatever choice is made.

The internalized commandments of the superego are formed through social interaction. Throughout a child's development, the dictates of parents and teachers and preachers and others get considered, and some become part of internal rule sets. It's interesting to note what happens when nature is in conflict with nurture. In the case of the teen feeling sexual desire (what some call the instinctual "urge to merge"), that drive is natural, arising in most animals as they become capable of copulation. But the rules in mind that say "don't, because _____," were put there by social interaction in the nurturance process. Put simply, id is a part of our nature and superego is developed in nurture. Sometimes our natural drives conflict with socially constructed rules and those conflicts get resolved by the ego, often by using "defense mechanisms."

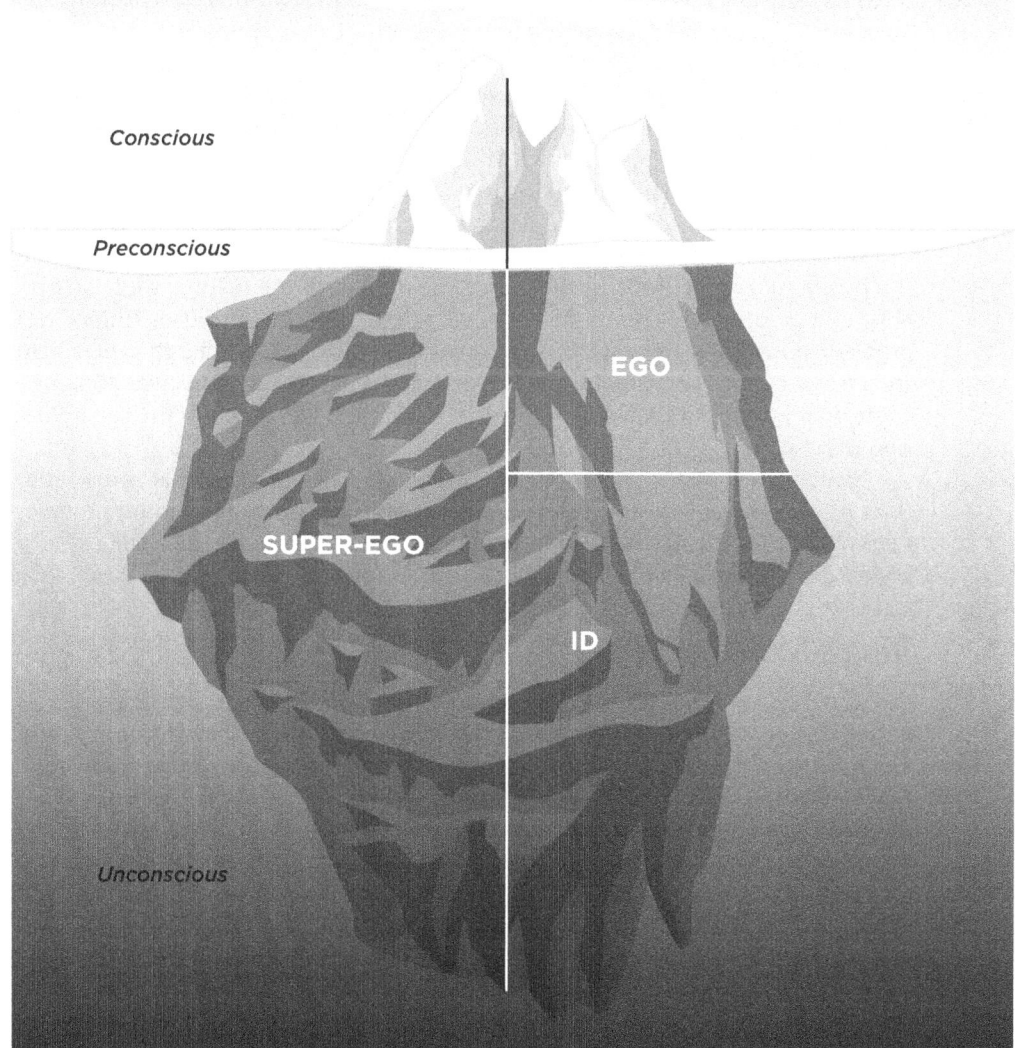

FIGURE 3.1 Freud's model of the psyche

The tension between the wild id and the subjugating superego produces anxiety, and when that anxiety goes beyond an acceptable limit, the ego resorts to defense mechanisms to protect the individual. Those defense mechanisms were initially theorized by Freud and later developed by his daughter, Anna Freud, in her *Ego and Mechanisms of Defense* (1937). Defense mechanisms are psychic processes that either distort an individual's ideas of reality or drive anxiety-producing ideas into the unconscious. There are many defense mechanisms, ranging from dysfunctional and pathological to those used by emotionally healthy and mature adults. We'll just look at a few of the more common, including repression, denial, and projection.

Repression is the process of pulling thoughts into the unconscious and preventing painful or dangerous thoughts from entering consciousness. For instance, we might repress the memories of certain traumatic experiences from childhood. Some therapies (of debatable success) in the latter part of the twentieth century focused on recovering repressed memories then working out the initial problem that produced them.

Denial is the refusal to accept reality as it is. This may be in the form of claiming an anxiety-producing stimulus does not exist or a refusal to consciously acknowledge an unpleasant aspect of reality. For instance, sometimes after the death of a loved one the person in grief might not believe, or deny, that the deceased is gone. Or in the case of a lover who has found information that the loved is cheating, the lover may refuse to believe it in order to protect his or her emotional equilibrium.

Projection is found in attributing one's own unacceptable thoughts and feelings to another—seeing in other people those negative impulses that are actually present in our own thought and action. For instance, perhaps we see another person as psychotically competitive when the over-competitiveness is our own trait. Or how about this: a person is talking to you about Sally, saying "I can't stand how Sally always talks about other people; she's such a gossip." That's projection.

As mentioned, there are plenty of other defense mechanisms, ranging from the psychotic and neurotic to the mature. Examples of the mature, more acceptable, and emotionally correct defenses include humor and altruism. Humor can provide comic relief from distressing situations. Altruism, service to others, can sometimes be used as a shield against seeing a seedier reality. This was Melanie's strategy in Margaret Mitchell's (1936) *Gone with the Wind*, much to the consternation of Scarlett.

Freud's ideas have certainly run their course, more in fashion at some times than others. His theory serves as the foundation for psychoanalysis and provides helpful tools for therapists. Keep in mind that his model represents social psychological development in the clash of nature and nurture.

Jung's Model of Mind

Carl Jung (1947, 1966, and 1981) was influenced by and shares some perspectives with Freud on concepts related to mind. Both believed human thought and action are influenced by conscious and unconscious forces. But Jung diverges from Freud in several important ways, including his theory of types, psychological complexes, the collective unconscious, and individuation.

Whereas Freud saw the psyche as a dynamic interplay between id, ego, and superego, Jung divided the human psyche into ego, personal unconscious, and collective unconscious. Ego is the conscious, thinking self. Personal unconscious is the collective personal experiences unique to each individual. Collective unconscious is a reservoir of experiences and behavior patterns common to all people. This is one of Jung's most memorable concepts and we will explore it in greater detail below.

Carl Jung conceptualized conscious and unconscious aspects of the psyche, including the shadow, a mysterious part of mind. Stockbyte/Thinkstock

Within his theory of personality types, Jung suggested four functions of consciousness (sensation, intuition, thinking, and feeling) that operate within two main personality types—extraversion and introversion. Sensation involves the use of our sense organs in conscious perception, for instance, as we see and hear in the here and now. Intuition is perception that occurs through unconscious means, as when we become aware of something but are not quite sure where that awareness originated. Thinking is related to formal cognition, as when we arrive at conclusions through logic or rational thought. Feeling is more guided by emotion, a subjective way of knowing. Sensation and intuition are modes of perception, the process of taking information into mind. Thinking and feeling are modes of judgment, making decisions about the information brought to mind. Those modes of perceiving and judging are at work in the two basic personality types, extraversion and introversion. Extraverts, who tend to be focused on and seek gratification from outside the self, are outgoing, talkative, and generally sociable. Introverts are focused more on their own mental life, and tend to be more introspective, reflective, and nonsocial. We will expand on these in a later chapter on personality.

"Complex" refers to a constellation of memories, emotions, perceptions, and wishes that organize around a common psychic theme and operate mainly at the unconscious level. We have certain sets of memories and emotions that are knotted together in the unconscious that affect our experience. For instance, an "inferiority complex" may include deep-seated ideas of low self-worth that resulted from experiences and interactions across a lifetime. Maybe mother got the idea going through degrading remarks, and the complex grew through sarcastic and mean-spirited comments from peers during the socialization process, and was perhaps further developed through failed attempts in some aspect of life. Memories of all those lessons about one's inferior nature then coalesce into a complex, where unconscious influences are woven together. Jung's initial formulation has evolved into all kinds of complexes—ego, guilt, persecution, and many others—that represent psychic activity percolating below the conscious level.

There are psychic forces operating below the level of consciousness. We have sets of fears, desires, memories, and other baggage—functional and dysfunctional—impacting our thoughts and behavior. Some of those unconscious influences are personal, picked up along the way in our individual experiences. But Jung also hypothesized a "collective unconscious," which is a more universal set of images and patterns of experience that impact all humans in one way or another. It is kind of like psychic "instinct" as it is programmed into the human mind before birth and somehow transferred and evolved across generations. It is an inherited pool of wisdom—shared knowledge and experience passed down through human history. The collective unconscious is illustrated more deeply in Jung's notions of "archetypes," which are forms and images that recur in human experience across time. Jung did note that such theorizing set him up for critics to accuse him of mysticism, but his ideas have withstood the tests of time, and can be expanded upon in consideration of mind and universal Mind.

Archetypes are recurring themes in human action and thought, a pattern in our awareness through time. They are kind of like stories that are programmed into the species. For instance, anima and animus are two archetypes lurking in the unconscious that affect our conscious lives. Anima is a feminine image in the male psyche and animus is a male image in the female psyche. So as a man, you truly have your feminine side and so do women have their inner man, albeit mostly unconscious. For Jung, the interplay of anima-animus represents the true self, different from the image (or persona) we present to others.

Many archetypes, recurring images in our collective unconscious, are identified: The mother archetype is our nurturing, comforting, female image. The father is the male authority figure, powerful and stern (and we note that many conceptions of God make use of the father archetype). The child is an archetype, found in our longing for innocence and quests toward rebirth. The wise old man is the archetype, like Gandalf from the *Lord of the Rings* trilogy, of that person who leads us toward wisdom, providing knowledge and guidance. There are many more, including the maiden archetype (so pure, so innocent), and the trickster archetype (that devious troublemaker!). These archetypes are images that recur through literature, art, and other aspects of the ever-unfolding human drama. They are in our lives and also dance through the unconscious mind.

Jung also discussed the "shadow," which is somewhat similar to Freud's "id." The shadow is the mysterious, deep unconscious animal nature that could be conceived as the dark side of our psyche. As with the id, the shadow is partly instinctive (programmed into the organism) and procreative, oriented toward sex. The shadow may be a cauldron of innate drives, fears, desires, repressed ideas, and unconscious impulses. The shadow, says Jung, will appear in dreams in the form of snakes, monsters, demons, or dark and exotic figures. Because it is by definition mysterious, it is not easy to describe or pin down. Suffice to say the shadow lurks in the depths of our unconscious mind, perhaps a mixture of the personal and collective unconscious.

Individuation is the transformational process of integrating the conscious with the personal and collective unconscious (Jung, 1962, p. 301). In this formulation, ego is our conscious mind. The personal unconscious includes buried or suppressed memories from our personal life. These may be integrated with the collective unconscious (our store of archetypes and wisdom of the ages) via several paths, including psychoanalysis, spirituality, meditative techniques, and other adventures into higher planes of awareness. Individuation, for Jung, is that process by which we become an individual, or as some might say: "Coming into your own." It is the process of becoming our true self, and we will explore that a little more under personality.

Mead's Model of Mind

Another model of mind comes to us from George Herbert Mead. Mead's book *Mind, Self, and Society* (assembled after his death by students and friends from his articles and lecture notes) is about how each of those three aspects influences the others. Mind is a product of self and society interacting; self develops as a co-creation of mind and society; and society is a collection of minds and selves.

Mead believed that mind develops through the social process of communication, where people interact by means of symbols and gestures. His ideas laid the foundation for the "symbolic interaction" school of thought, which is very much at the roots of such fields as sociology, social psychology, and communication studies. Mead looked at how humans develop through stages of social interaction.

We enter the social world and begin understanding it through "play" and "game" stages, said Mead. Play comes first. The child takes roles that she or he observe in adult society and acts them out. For example, I remember acting like I was an electrical engineer at age seven, modeling my behavior after Mr. K, the electrical engineer down the street. Part of my role was to stick a piece of copper wire in an electrical outlet in our family room and get shocked and burned, ignoring my mother's command not to do that. As girls and boys play with dolls or action heroes, they take on an adult role and begin to develop social awareness.

As children mature, they begin to play games together, and they must learn the rules in order to relate to others and play properly. This is when people enter the game stage, where they begin to understand rules and norms, and become aware that other people are aware of them. In T-ball at age eight, I began to see that parents and coaches and other players were aware of me and had expectations. My father asked after a game, "Why are you grabbing yourself there? Do you have to pee?" That threw a switch in my self-awareness. When we begin playing games that include roles where others depend on us, we start to develop a wider social awareness.

A child's journey into the game stage brings an awareness of what Mead called the "generalized other." The generalized other is the summation of a given group's expectations (implicit rules, norms) as they get into an individual's thoughts through social interaction. So Mama's rules for the dinner table, teacher's "don't chew gum," and preacher's "thou shall not ____" become part of the generalized other in people's minds. As the generalized other becomes more developed within people, they become more attuned to what is expected for different social settings and circles. The rules in your head for proper behavior in dating, sporting events, family parties, funerals, weddings, and other situations have come to you from interactions with others. And those interactions continue to reverberate in your memory and your mind.

Of course, the internalization of others' expectations is not a simple "open your head and dump it in" process. One reason the development of your generalized other is so complex is that there are so many competing models to take roles from. Are we more likely to learn the rules for dating and mating from parents, teachers, friends, television, or chat on the Internet? Likely from a mix of those influences, and that mix will be different for different people and will change over the course of a lifetime. At one time, the influence of parents might be high; at another time, friends may be the central models for our behavior. It is important to note that thinking in terms of the generalized other marks our capacity to look at ourselves from the perspective of others—taking the role of others in becoming aware of what's expected of our self. Our "self" is very much a product of what we think others think.

Mead distinguished between the "I" and the "me" as separate aspects of self. The "me" is the summation of an individual's generalized others, including thoughts about appropriate behaviors, norms, and proper patterns of social response. This "me" is the community in mind, it's "what *they* say." The "I" is the unique, idiosyncratic side of the self. The "I" is your individual opinions and the reflector or observer of the social world. It is your unique perspective, different from all others.

You are unique in many ways, genetically and socially. What distinguishes you from all other people is that you have grown and developed within a unique social matrix. You were nurtured by different parents or guardians, had fun with different friends, and were socialized by a different mix of teachers and preachers than anyone else. You also read different publications, watched different videos, and played different games. Even if you are an identical twin, you have had interactions with friends, family, and others that your sibling did not have. All of these interactions through your lifetime add to the uniqueness of your "I."

Mind is an interaction between "I" and "me," with constant communication between your unique perspective and the community of expectations. The thought process itself, for Mead, is a kind of internal discussion between you and others. Even thinking about your self is an internal discussion. Consider looking in the mirror: are you thinking about you from your own point of view, or thinking what others might think? Mead would say both, in the sense that you have incorporated "they" into your mind, which communicates with "I."

Gardner's Intelligences

We have different minds, different propensities, different areas where our particular kind of thinking can excel. Creative mind and brain are domains of interest for Howard Gardner (1982, 1999). Mind is at the heart of creative change. Gardner's *Multiple Intelligences* is an adventure into the processes and products of mind and brain.

Each area of intelligence suggested by Gardner represents an area for creativity that can flourish if we find it. Much like Joseph Campbell's advice to "follow your bliss," Gardner advises us to discover and develop the areas of intelligence in which we excel. Creativity is most likely to blossom in the domain best fitted to our mind. He outlines the kinds of intelligence and some of the career paths most fitting:

Linguistic intelligence involves sensitivity to the spoken and written language, the ability to learn languages, and the capacity to use language to accomplish certain goals. Lawyers, speakers, writers, and poets are among the people with high linguistic intelligence.

Logical-mathematical intelligence involves the capacity to analyze problems logically and carry out mathematical operations, and investigate issues scientifically. Mathematicians, logicians, and scientists exploit logical-mathematical intelligence.

Musical intelligence entails skill in performance, composition, and appreciation of musical patterns.

Bodily-kinesthetic intelligence entails the potential for using one's whole body or parts of the body to solve problems or fashion products. Obviously, dancers, actors, and athletes foreground bodily-kinesthetic intelligence.

Spatial intelligence features the potential to recognize and manipulate the patterns of wide space (those used, for instance, by navigators and pilots) as well as the patterns of more confined areas (such as those of importance to sculptors, surgeons, chess players, graphic artists, or architects).

Interpersonal intelligence denotes a person's capacity to understand the intentions, motivations, and desires of other people and, consequently, to work effectively with others. Salespeople, teachers, clinicians, religious leaders, political leaders, and actors all need acute interpersonal intelligence.

Intrapersonal intelligence involves the capacity to understand oneself, to have an effective working model of oneself—including one's own desires, fears, and capacities—and use such information effectively in regulating one's own life.

Natural intelligence (one who understands natural organisms, a "green thumb" for instance) and *spiritual intelligence* (one who understands the supernatural) are also mentioned, and then developed in his later works. (Gardner, 1999, pp. 41–43)

Minds are creative when areas of intelligence are identified and ignited by inspiration. People have combinations of intelligences that can open pathways. A blend of musical and interpersonal talents can open doors for musical agents; a combination of naturalistic and spatial intelligence would make a good landscape architect; and the linguistic-interpersonal combination makes for an effective communicator. This would also suggest that better journals will be produced by those who prospect in the various veins of intelligence to find what areas hold the most potential for them. Creative acts become much more likely for those who are actualizing—exploring potential paths, discovering bliss, finding vision.

Mind and self develop through interaction, via symbols, between you and others. Your mind might have a little bit of Plato, Puritan, or Playboy cycling about in the neural nets. You may have ideas borrowed from Vladimir Lenin about equality or John Lennon about giving peace a chance. You have a few math facts, historical figures, geography lessons, and driving directions mixing it up with how to act properly and memories of Mama—and so much more. Mind is amazing.

I once heard someone say, "What is mind? No matter. What is matter? Never mind." At the time, in a communication conference presentation back in the 1980s, I thought it was kind of cute. The more I think about it, though, the more I believe that brief remark hits on the central question we are considering. Is there mind beyond brain, beyond sheer physical existence?

Combining Bateson's idea of the unity between mind and nature—Mind with a large "M" that is a superordinate system surrounding our individual minds—with Jung's concept of the collective unconscious, we can begin thinking of a consciousness that pervades the universe. Perhaps that universal mind, or consciousness, is the "pattern which connects," in Bateson's terms. Perhaps it is a grand frequency or patterns of vibrations, or the *information matrix* that permeates everything. Perhaps it is God. Whatever the ultimate answer to this mystery of a universal mind that pervades the universe, we can be fairly certain that our mind is but a subsystem within the system.

Understanding mind and the deeper levels of consciousness is a primary concern for persuaders. Researchers and practitioners (such as advertisers) build their models of mind and motivation then create their messages accordingly. Understanding mind will help us in our attempts at persuasion and to become critically aware of those trying to persuade us.

Creative Moment

Our minds have grown accustomed to seeing the world around us in certain ways. We develop habits of thought, and at times those habits can include one side of the brain more than the other side. Betty Edwards argues that it is often the left side that hampers the right. Borrowing from the seminal work of Roger Sperry, she proposes ways to enhance our right brain. She quotes Richard Bergland's *The Fabric of Mind* (1985, p. 1) to lay out the difference: "You have two brains: a left and a right. Modern brain scientists now know that your left brain is your verbal and rational brain; it thinks serially and reduces its thoughts to numbers, letters, and words. . . . Your right brain is your non-verbal and intuitive brain; it thinks in patterns, pictures, composed of 'whole things,' and does not comprehend reductions, either numbers, letters, or words." Edwards built a practical program for exercising the right brain (R-mode) that plays down the dominance of the linguistic left brain (L-mode). In *Drawing from the Right Side of the Brain* (1979/1999) she suggests the following:

> In order to gain access to the subdominant visual, perceptual R-mode of the brain, it is necessary to present the brain with a job that the verbal, analytic L-mode will turn down. For most of us, L-mode thinking seems easy, normal, and familiar (though perhaps not for many children and dyslexic individuals). The perverse R-mode strategy, in contrast, may seem difficult and unfamiliar—even "off-the-wall." It must be learned in opposition to the "natural" tendency of the brain to favor L-mode because, in general, language dominates. By learning to control this tendency for specific tasks, one gains access to powerful brain functions often obscured by language. (1999, p. xx)

Beginning with her experiments in upside-down drawing, Edwards created exercises that enhance R-mode and downright trick the left side of the brain to keep it from seeing the world in familiar ways. One of the best ways to develop it is to draw, sketch, play with pictures—illustrate and doodle.

Exercise

Try looking at a picture upside down and drawing it. You might be amazed at how good an artist you are when your assumptions and habits of perceiving the world are flipped on their head.

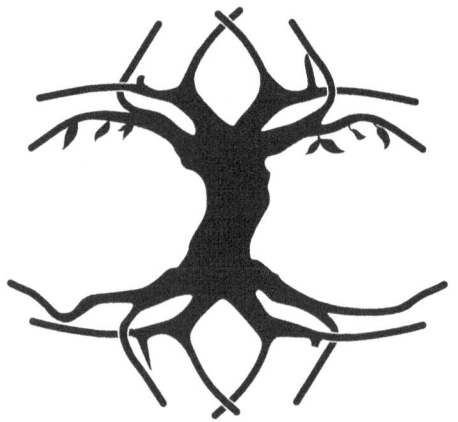

Chapter 4

Fuse/Thinkstock

Minding Your World: "MAPs," Abstraction, and Critical Thinking

"... still, a man hears what he wants to hear
and disregards the rest..."

—*Simon and Garfunkel, "The Boxer"*

In the last chapter we considered a few maps of the mind. You probably know we only scratched the surface. Ideas about mind go much deeper and wider, branching into psychological, medical, philosophical, and other pathways. This chapter will consider mind as an active form, asking how we *mind* the world. What comes into play as we become aware and explore levels of consciousness? We'll approach the question with a MAP—Memory, Attitude, and Perception. These three are intimately woven into our outlook, the ways in which we come into contact with and process our world. In fact, they are a good part of our maps of the reality out there. Keep in mind Korzybski's bit of wisdom that our maps are *not* the territory. We'll study more of Korzybski later in the chapter.

Memory

The concept of memory is still somewhat mysterious. It affects just about every moment of our lives—from reading these words to lifting a spoon—but it is not fully understood. Memory is the core of your consciousness, yet much of it is subconscious. It is the storeroom of your nurturance and the path to your personality. It acts in the here and now and allows you to travel across time to yesterday and long ago. Memory is a key process and product of mind.

Memory is a *process*, a dynamic information storage and retrieval system. And it is a *product*, though many scientists agree we do not know exactly what that product is. Like the concept of mind, memory is tough to "place." Is there a physical space where memories reside (like a neural-chemical bubble)? Or do memories exist more as an interaction between parts of the brain and nets of nerves (a trace), not so much having a residence as "coming alive" in the interaction?

Memory, simply defined by Eric Kandel (2006, p. 441), a Nobel Prize-winning neuroscientist, is "the storage of learned information" and much more. Memory can be short term, long term, explicit, or implicit. Some memories are with us for only moments. In your head, add five and six. Now, take the answer and add seven to it. There, you just used short-term, working memory. What's one of your earliest memories of childhood? I remember my brother trying to convince me to take the blame for ink he spilled in the bathroom, telling me I wouldn't get in trouble because I was too young to know better. I didn't buy it. That's a long-term memory.

Short-term memory is typically measured in minutes to hours, whereas long-term memory is days to weeks or even a lifetime. When you memorize someone's phone number for a few moments before calling, or if you remember we called memory a *process* and a *product* above, those are short-term memories. A special type of short-term memory is "working memory," which integrates moment-to-moment perceptions and combines them with past experiences. You're using working memory right now as you make sense of these words. You are connecting these perceived marks on paper or screen with memorized meanings, associations for the words. You use working memory in a conversation as you match the spoken words to memories of what they stand for or mean. When you subtract the amount of the check you wrote from the balance in your checking account, you are using working memory. If you are thinking, you are using memory.

Long-term memories are the bits of information that stay with you, sometimes for a few weeks (until you can take that test and do a memory-dump) and sometimes for a lifetime. As you rehearse the lyrics of a song or the lines of a poem, those symbols might go from short-term working memory to long-term when you get them memorized. Those who know say our brain's hippocampus has something to do with encoding long-term memories. In the case of reading a song or a poem, the visual cortex (occipital lobe), the prefrontal cortex (frontal lobe)—where your working memory operates—and other parts of the brain will be involved with the hippocampus in making the memory. The parts of the brain involved go through continual circuits, or cycles of communication, as they create a memory and when it is retrieved. Memory is an interaction between stimuli that trigger and systems of associations that are stored.

Memories can also be *explicit* or *implicit*. Explicit memory is storage of information about people, places, things, and contexts that can be recalled consciously. It's also called "declarative memory" because we can state those memories with words. For instance, I remember the day at age eight that my mother showed me how to create a sense of perspective on the drawing I was doing of the Washington Monument. I remember giggling with excitement as I learned it, there in our kitchen with its cool and colorful 1960s flowers on the wallpaper.

Whether it is flowers you can visualize or a strong smell brought to mind, memories often have sense impressions, and are sometimes triggered by the senses, as when a smell takes you to a time past. Explicit, declarative memory is probably what most people are thinking of when they talk about memory.

Implicit memory is the storage of information that does not require conscious attention for recall. Habits we get into, motor skills we develop, and the ways we perceive the world around us all rely on implicit memory. Implicit memory is often automatic. For instance, once you learn to ride a bike you can do it without consciously considering the muscle movements, pressure on the pedals, or balance required. You just do it because your *body knows* how to do it. That's implicit memory. Or as you tell a story, you do not consciously consider what order to put words in ("Let's see, does the subject come before the verb?"). You just say it. As I practice the fiddle, I learn to associate certain fingering and bowing with notes on a printed page. At first it is a very conscious effort, but once the notes are learned, the finger placement and bowing becomes an implicit memory. Implicit memories get formed by repetition in our language and behaviors, of body and mind.

Memory is central to the way you mind your world; all meaning you get from or give to the world comes from stored associations between symbols and referents. (The word *tree* is a symbol, and the thing it refers to is the referent.) Whether it is conscious or subconscious, you draw upon memory to make sense of your world, and your sense-making is full of attitude.

Memory is always at work while we communicate, from explicit memories like "remember the time when we..." to implicit memories, such as the connection between mind, music, and fingers. Fuse/Thinkstock

Attitude

Memory is packed with attitudes. Attitude, according to Fishbein and Ajzen, is "a learned predisposition to respond in a consistently favorable or unfavorable manner with respect to an object" (1975, p. 6). When they say object, it could be a thing, a person, a group of people, a place, or anything you can think of. Attitudes are *learned*, coming to us through social interaction. We learn them from people. Attitudes are *predisposed*, involving a readiness to think about the object in a certain way. Attitudes are *consistent*, somewhat stable across time, though they can be changed. Attitudes are *evaluative*, judging the object on a continuum from positive to negative, favorable to unfavorable. Attitudes are the value judgments we hold in mind ready to be triggered by symbols or situations.

Kenneth Burke once said attitude is an "incipient act," a behavior waiting to happen. You would think that most behaviors would act according to a person's attitude. So, if I think so-and-so candidate is a buffoon (my attitude), then you would expect that I won't vote for him (my behavior). But not all behaviors do follow attitudes. For instance, let's say Mary is John's boss. John despises

Mary. He thinks she doesn't deserve her place in the company. He thinks she's mean and she's even "a bitch" sometimes. His attitude is quite negative. John is in the conference room and Mary passes by. John waves and says, "Hey, how you doin'?" with a big smile on his face. His behavior doesn't agree with his attitude. In this case the behavior can be explained by Mary's ability to affect John's job and future—she has power. Typically those "down" in power relationships do not always treat those "up" according to their true attitudes.

That "attitude-behavior discrepancy" was noted by Richard LaPierre in his 1934 study that tried to gain understanding into attitudes and prejudice against Asians at the time. He traveled around the United States for three months with a Chinese couple, checking into various hotels and restaurants. Only one out of 250 hotels and restaurants refused to serve them. LaPierre was perplexed, expecting much more prejudicial action. So he wrote a letter to the owners of those same hotels and restaurants asking if they allowed Chinese to enter. Ninety percent of those who replied said they would not allow Chinese customers. Of course this threw social psychologists into a tizzy for years, as they tried to understand the relationship between what the owners said and what they did, between their attitude and their behavior. I think it's pretty easy to explain: money talked and attitude walked.

Attitudes are attached to memories, and often those attitudes are complex clusters, not simple favorable or unfavorable predispositions. For instance, you might have a friend whom you simultaneously love, loathe, and fear, depending on which attitude is triggered in a given situation. Or consider a complex issue like your attitude toward the president's stance on the environment. You may have a cluster of competing attitudes on the topic rather than just simply favorable versus unfavorable.

Attitudes are tied to emotions. Some like to distinguish between thinking (cognition) and feeling (emotion). The two are not separate, though they do seem to be based in different parts of the brain, with thinking in the cerebral cortex and emotions in the midbrain and earliest evolved "reptilian brain." Emotion and cognition are tied together, they interact, as when you watch a tragic drama and think about its meaning and cry. Gregory Bateson often quoted William Blake: "A tear is an intellectual thing."

Susan Greenfield—the brain researcher, baroness, and former director of Britain's Royal Institution—claims that emotion is a different animal than cognition, based in a different part of the brain and more primitive and automatic than deeper conscious thought. Emotions, she argues, are the most basic form of consciousness, and the constellations of neurons that get formed in the amygdala and elsewhere as a result of our unique life experiences are what shape emotion and individuality. Moreover, Greenfield shows evidence of certain cognitive circuits getting bypassed when we have an emotional response to a situation, supporting her argument that the more intense our emotions, the less we engage in critical, self-reflective, conscious thinking. Perhaps we could further argue that attitudes, which are built upon emotional/affective information, can override critical thought in certain situations. Many attempts to persuade us are based on emotional appeals that attempt to bypass reasoned thought.

Attitudes are built upon emotions, beliefs, and past experience. Beliefs are ideas we have about what is true or false. Is the earth flat? Are women better than men at nurturing children? Does God exist? Your answers to these questions indicate beliefs, ideas you have about what is true or false, and those beliefs weave with emotions and past experience in creating your attitudes. Past experience plays a role in attitude formation, especially in the ways positive or negative experiences shape your thinking. For instance, my youngest daughter once got ill after eating some food from a certain fast-food restaurant. For three years she would not eat anything from that restaurant. Her experience created a negative attitude. Her attitude has since changed, as attitudes sometimes do, and we will discuss changing attitudes later.

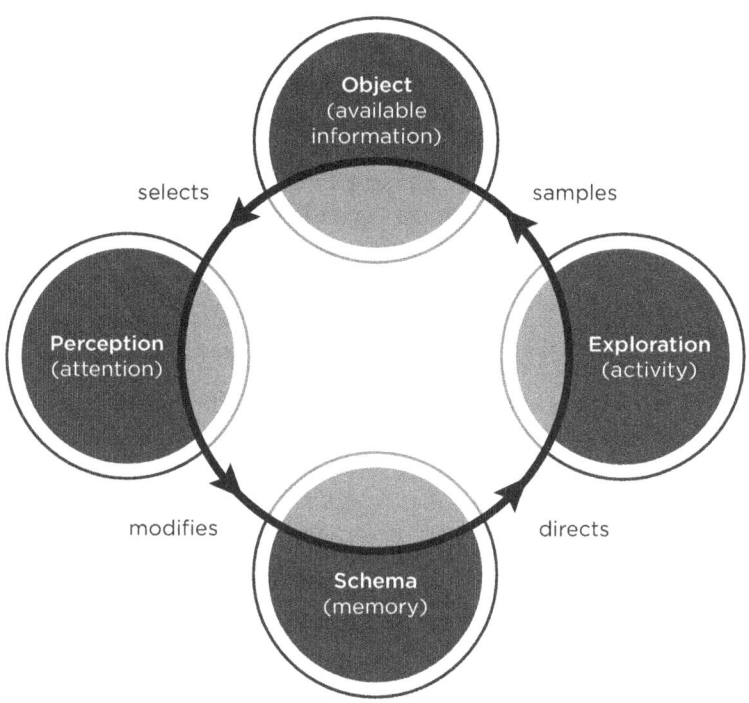

FIGURE 4.1 Neisser's model of the perpetual cycle

Perception

Your memory and attitudes play into the way you perceive the world around you. Perception is your point of contact with the world; it is the organism sensing its environment. Ulrich Neisser (1976) claimed perception is a process, depicted in Figure 4.1.

Perception is a process of actively exploring, or sensing, our surroundings and those explorations are guided by cognitive schemata. Schemata, or schema, are sets of memories about the object of our perception. Neisser also referred to those clusters of memories as expectancies and "anticipatory sets," because once a perception-directing memory becomes habitual we tend to expect and anticipate what we will sense.

We develop schema about people, places, things, or anything we perceive. I have schemata, cognitive maps, about my wife. After living with her for years, I've developed expectancies about how she will behave in given situations, how she will respond to me, and how she will respond to our children's behavior, among many other maps. I also have schemata (memories, cognitive maps) of the layout and décor of my house, where things are in town, how my colleagues tend to act, where a doorknob tends to be located on a door, and where the light switch is. You have schemata—anticipatory sets of memories about many of the same—your family, friends, teachers, home, and other things you perceive.

Those schema direct exploration of our perceptual field, that which is in range of our senses. Sensing is an activity, whether it is eye movement, sound creating vibrations on an eardrum, moving fingers across a surface, or any other sensual experience. *In exploring our environment we collect "samples," bits of information. We do not perceive all of the information available, only pieces of it.* For instance, I'm writing this while sitting in a doctor's office. Typically, I wouldn't be writing in a doctor's office, I'd be reading *National Geographic* or something. But today I'm in the mood to be productive. As I look around this room—at the woman tapping away on her laptop computer (she's feeling the need to be productive too) or the child whining to his mother—I am only getting bits of information from this environment. I'm attending to some bits of information and not to others.

As we attend to a particular object, we select bits of information to be perceived. Note that we can only attend to the available information. As I perceive you, I can only sample bits of information about your outward appearance and such. I cannot perceive your food being digested or the thoughts inside your head. All information is not available to perception.

As we sample bits of our environment we match those samples to our schemata, either confirming or rejecting what we expect to perceive. *We tend to confirm existing schemata. There is a tendency to see what we believe we are going to see.* For example, let's say you have a negative attitude toward a particular person, Tad. You think that Tad is cunning, deceitful, and downright mean. There is a good chance that when you observe Tad behaving, you will perceive him as cunning, deceitful, or downright mean. Even if he is acting saintly, you may take that to be an instance of just how cunning he is. Karl Weick (1979, p. 135) once said "believing is seeing." What a simple, eloquent turn of phrase. We often see what we believe we will see.

We've discussed how perception works, but what is it we perceive? What are we sensing when we sense our world? Over one hundred years ago, William James remarked that we not only perceive things but relationships. Everything we perceive is in relation to other things and the surrounding context. The first relationship we can distinguish is *figure and ground*. A figure-ground relationship is one in which something stands out against a background. If you are looking at one tree in a forest, that tree is the figure and the rest is ground. Look at the back of your hand. That hand is the figure and everything else in your perceptual field is ground.

FIGURE 4.2 Figure-ground relationships

Sometimes we experience shifts in the figure-ground relationship, where what was in the background becomes the figure and vice versa. Edgar Rubin showed this with his classic drawing representing an ambiguous figure-ground relationship. What do you see when you view Figure 4.2? The black and white could either be the figure or ground. This figure-ground shift happens in our day-to-day experience as we change perceptual levels. Perhaps you are watching a cute caterpillar climb a twig; then you notice the twig is a milkweed plant; then you notice the whole field and edge of the woods is awash in beautiful fall colors, surrounded by a crisp blue sky. At each level what was the ground becomes the figure in a new perspective. Or maybe you're looking at a tree (figure) at the edge of the woods (ground), and then you see a squirrel running up the tree, a new figure on the ground of the tree.

When you perceive a gorgeous fall forest or breathtaking sunset, it's likely that you not only notice individual details but also take in the view as a whole, all at once. This holistic aspect of perception is known as the principle of gestalt, which grew up to be a whole school of thought within psychology. Gestalt psychology is a domain interested in the way we perceive order in our experience, and gestalt psychologists have developed a number of laws about perception, including the law of closure, law of similarity, law of proximity, law of symmetry, law of continuity, and the law of common fate. The laws are all guided by what gestalt theorists call prägnanz, a German term which roughly means we seek regularity and pattern in the way we perceive.

FIGURE 4.3 Closure

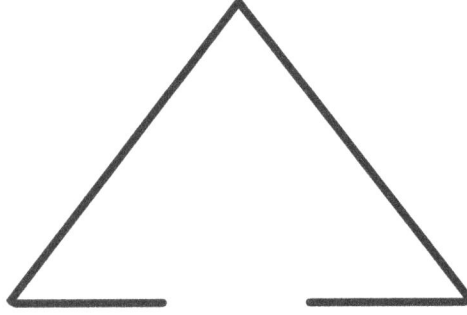

The law of closure states that the mind will tend to experience elements not perceived through sensation in order to complete a regular figure. So, for instance, even if Figure 4.3 is not a triangle, your mind will tend to fill in the blank to make it a triangle.

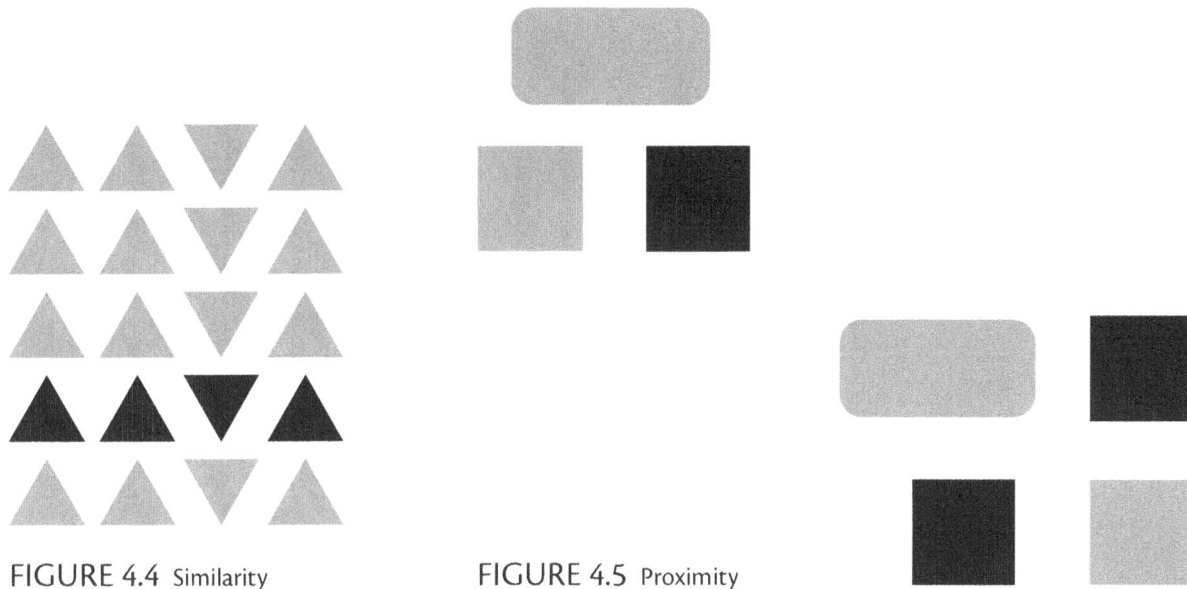

FIGURE 4.4 Similarity

FIGURE 4.5 Proximity

The law of similarity states that the mind will tend to group similar elements into collective entities or totalities. The similarity could be based on form, color, size, brightness, texture, or any other perceived aspect. For instance, you can find similarity in direction in Figure 4.4. You might also tend to perceive similarities in people of the same size, color, wardrobe, and so forth, even if no such similarity exists.

The law of proximity states that spatial or temporal nearness may influence the mind to perceive a relationship. For instance, in Figure 4.5 the shapes near each other might seem related, or in a group together, due to their proximity. Likewise, you might perceive people who live in the same neighborhood to share certain qualities, or if someone grew up in the same time frame as your parents you might perceive certain shared qualities to be due to temporal proximity.

The law of symmetry states that symmetrical images are perceived collectively, even if distance separates them. Look at the image in Figure 4.6, for example. The law of symmetry would guide us to perceive three sets of closed brackets.

The law of continuity states that the mind perceives the continuation of visual, auditory, and kinetic patterns. For instance, you will tend to perceive the lines of the poor caged baby in Figure 4.7 as continuing even though you cannot see them behind the bars. Or perhaps you hear part of a familiar phrase and your mind fills in the rest as though it will continue: "Whatever goes up, _____ _____ _____."

The law of common fate states that elements that are moving in the same direction are perceived as a collective or a unit. I've noticed that whenever I'm driving to a big event, a game or a concert or the beach, I tend to imagine that others on the road are going there too.

These gestalt laws often do apply as we perceive the world around us. Most importantly, we tend to perceive relationships. Gestalt is the relationship between parts as they interact in making the whole. "The whole is greater than the sum of its parts." That's a good old gestalt phrase. So as you perceive another person, you might notice a few details, but you will also perceive him or her in relation to the scenery, situation, other people, and other aspects of the whole. When you perceive a cityscape or the countryside, you might see individual aspects, but you also perceive the totality of many parts interacting.

FIGURE 4.6 Symmetry

[ ][ ][ ]

FIGURE 4.7 Continuity

Cold hearted orb that rules the night
Removes the colours from our sight
Red is gray and yellow white
But we decide which is right
And which is an Illusion

~ The Moody Blues, "Knights in White Satin"

We "map" our experience through memory, attitude, and perception. These are key factors in how we *mind* the world, from our self-concept to our outlook. And as we mind the world, looking inward and outward, we inherently abstract.

The Abstracting Animal

Gregory Bateson said, "My idea of a pig is not a pig. Alfred Korzybski said, "The map is not the territory," and "the word is not the thing." The way we perceive the world through clusters of symbols—through associations of "this will mean that and that will mean this"—is full of abstractions.

Korzybski is sometimes called the father of general semantics. He liked to look at the meaning of things, especially the meanings people create that are not necessarily the dictionary or denotative meaning. In his classic *Science and Sanity* (1933), Korzybski developed his model of the "structural differential," which at once differentiates the various levels of reality as we think and talk about it, and differentiates humans from other animals. His model addresses consciousness and the various problems presented by abstraction in our conscious thought. Let's look at an illustration of the model then discuss its various parts.

The structural differential starts with the *event* level at the top. The event is the *real* reality, which we are aware of but understanding most of it is beyond our knowing, and much of it is beyond our ability to comprehend. Korzybski said this level is the "mad dance of electrons," which at the time was the smallest hypothesized subatomic particle. Now we could call the event level the mad dance of neutrinos, quarks, photon packets, strings, or whatever other bits of energy are moving in our midst. This physical world has a reality, and it is all energy and all moving, all the time, in theory. Even that hard desk and wall are vibrating or moving, according to current ideas of matter. It was S. I. Hayakawa's belief that everything is moving—a fluxist notion—that drove him to rename the event level as the *process*.

FIGURE 4.8 Korzybski's structural differential

Event (Process) level

Object level

Descriptive level

Inference level

Generalization level

Et cetera

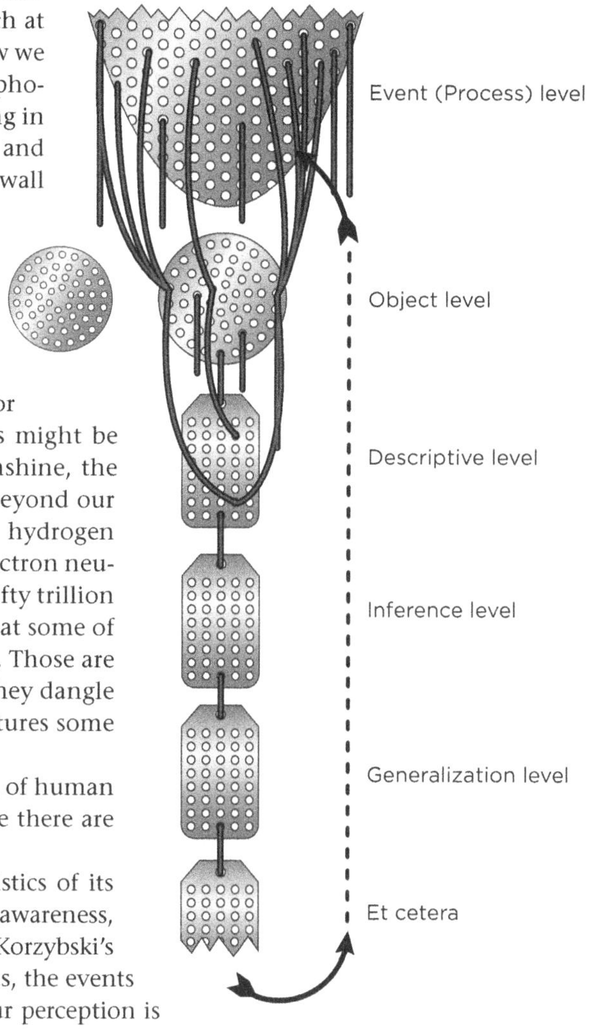

Notice in Figure 4.8 there are lines coming from the colander-looking contraption at the top. Those lines represent characteristics of the event, aspects of the reality. So, for instance, if the event is a sunset, some of the characteristics might be the color of the sun, the color of the sky, clouds, rays of sunshine, the horizon, and much more. There are so many characteristics beyond our senses as well, such as the inner explosions of helium and hydrogen going on in the sun. One product of those explosions, solar electron neutrinos, are theoretically passing through our body right now (fifty trillion per second!), well below our threshold of awareness. Notice that some of the lines in the diagram are connected to the next level below. Those are characteristics abstracted. Some of the lines do not connect; they dangle in the air. Those are characteristics left out. Our attention captures some characteristics and misses others.

The next level down is the *object* level, and this is the level of human perception. Korzybski called this the "silent level" too, because there are no words yet, just perception.

As we perceive an event, we sense some of the characteristics of its reality but miss most. Some aspects are abstracted, brought to awareness, but most are left out. This is a critical map to take away from Korzybski's model, because it means that as we perceive the world around us, the events and processes of reality, we are missing most of that reality. Our perception is imperfect and only abstracts a few aspects from the totality. So as I perceive you, I can sense a few characteristics—your hair color, clothes, height, and such. But I miss most of the characteristics that comprise the total reality of you—your thoughts, feelings, history, food digesting, blood sugar levels, favorite flavors and colors, and so much more. Again, going back to Neisser's perceptual cycle, we only sample a few bits of information in the process of perceiving.

As our gaze moves down from the object level to the *descriptive* level, notice there are some characteristics abstracted (connected lines) and, again, some characteristics left out. The descriptive level is talking and writing, where humans start applying words to the perceived world. But our words cannot capture all that is perceived. As I look at the beautiful sunset and try to describe it, my words can't quite name the grandeur of my perceptions, or the interactions of light and atmosphere and energy I'm seeing. Our language is limited. The average "active" vocabulary (words a person actually uses) for Americans has been estimated between five hundred and two thousand words per day. Some people use far more words in their vocabulary, their repertoire of word choices, and some use fewer. Most use very few words to represent a wide range of perceptions, and those words miss most of what is perceived.

As we abstract—that is, we lose characteristics from the reality through the perception of the event and on to the description of the event—we move from real to representation of real. At the descriptive level, we should note that there are different kinds of descriptions, some closer to the reality of the event. First-order descriptions are those based on actual experience. If I am running my hand over the surface of a desk and say, "This is smooth," that's a first-order descriptive statement, based on my direct experience. If I say, "I smelled a skunk on the road today," that too is based on direct experience. But if I say, "Mary told me John smelled like a skunk," that is not based on direct experience. I can only infer that what she said is true.

Moving down the structural differential we come to the *inference* level. Inferences are thoughts or claims that are not based on direct experience. Of course, gossip and hearsay and "he said, she said" are examples of inference. If I tell you that your best friend was saying bad things about you, you should probably withhold judgment, because you don't know if what I say is true. Plenty of conflicts and angry moments have been made worse by such inferences. Yes, these blatant examples of inference are out there in the social circles and social media all the time. But most of us are unaware of the degree to which our thinking is filled with inferences.

You watch the news, getting a story about violence in some hot spot around the world. You may believe the story, but you cannot be sure. All you can do is infer because you did not experience the violence directly. Rather, you saw it on an edited, packaged piece of news that a producer created for you. You read your history and geography books about faraway times and places, but you can only infer that what you're told is true because you did not experience it for yourself. You're told stories of your ancestors and extended family. You can only infer that what you're told is true. Korzybski suggested that most of what we know is based on inference. Most of what I know about history and science, the here and the hereafter, is built upon what I've been told by others. I have not verified it all with my own senses through my own experience.

Korzybski was adamant about trying to fix the fallacies of thinking and problems with perception in human action and interaction. His theory of general semantics was aimed at such, and the road to recovery for us inferential animals began with "consciousness of abstracting." We need to become aware that our maps are not the territory; words are not the things they represent.

S. I. Hayakawa, one of Korzybski's most celebrated students, popularized the cause of general semantics in 1949 with the publication of his book, *Language and Thought in Action*. The book was an updated version of his 1941 publication, from which Figure 4.9 below is borrowed. Hayakawa flips the model to start from the ground up, as reality is more grounded and our abstractions and inferences carry us further away from that grounding. Hayakawa uses his example of Bessie the cow to discuss how language and thought carry us away from reality.

It begins again with the reality. Bessie is a dynamic process, a "perpetual dance of electrons," ingesting food and air, creating energy and waste, and constantly transforming, even down to the smallest particle. Bessie exists within a context that is also very real, a part of the totality of Bessie. The next level, where human perception enters the picture, finds Bessie as an object of experience—"an interaction between our nervous system and something outside of it," says Hayakawa. Keep that in mind: perception is an interaction between us and our environment. Here's where Hayakawa diverges a bit from his teacher's model. Now he looks at the way various words and categories carry us further from the reality of the process that is the cow. When we say "cow," we group Bessie with other like animals. When we call her "livestock" we group her with other farm animals, abstracting

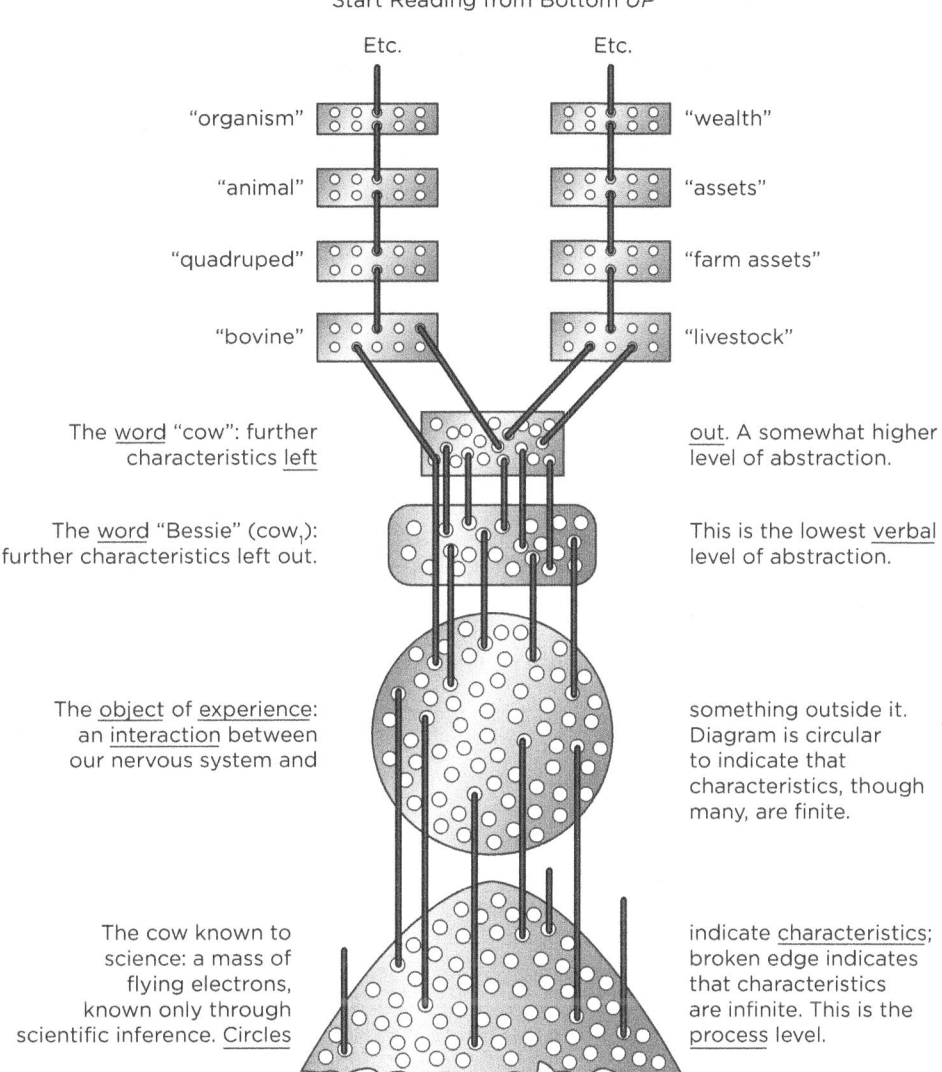

FIGURE 4.9 Hayakawa's abstraction ladder

higher. Then we can start talking about her as a farm asset, or an asset in general, or as "wealth," which is extremely abstract. Wealth blends in with so many other things that the individuality of "cow process" gets entirely lost. But it's also abstract in the sense that humans have invented the notion of wealth and ownership. That I can say "that cow is mine" is made possible by our logical, linguistic, and belief systems.

Korzybski and Hayakawa taught us to be aware of our inferences. Consciousness of abstracting means knowing our map does not necessarily match the territory. Our maps are flawed. *Awareness of abstracting is crucial to critical thinking, encouraging us to rethink our perceptions, to question if ours and others' words are close to reality.* Once we realize that our words and thoughts are prone to inference—not based on direct experience and coming mostly unchecked from others—we can begin to set ourselves free from the traps of some words and thoughts.

Realizing our thoughts and words are abstractions—conscious of abstracting—is the beginning of critical awareness. Korzybski developed some other tools helpful for critical thinking. He called them extensional devices, critical thinking tools for overcoming the limits of consciousness. The extensional devices include indexing, chain-indexing, dating, et cetera, and hyphens. *Indexing* is the mental practice of noting similarities in differences and differences in similarities. Not all people from another ethnicity, or political party, or religion are alike nor do they think alike. *Chain-indexing* is consciousness of the effects of environment or context. For instance, people from the same culture but who grew up in an urban versus rural setting may have an entirely different base of experience, so we should not assume people from the same culture are the same. *Dating* is an awareness of how time changes realities; that place you visited as a child is not the same place today, and that person you knew at age 18 is not necessarily the same person at age 30. *Et cetera* (etc.) is a reminder that there is always more, always something left out of what we say or think. Our thoughts and descriptions are never complete. *Hyphens* remind us of the interrelationships among phenomena. For instance, many emotions have psycho-physiological implications, where mind is interconnected with body. These extensional devices can be part of your critical thinking repertoire.

Here is another set of standards for critical thinking developed by members of the Foundation for Critical Thinking (Paul and Elder, 2007). They can be used to assess our own and others' reasoning. For instance, if someone is trying to persuade you to give money for a cause or new thing or idea, consider these:

1. Purpose: What is the aim of the persuader, what are they trying to accomplish?
2. Questions: What questions are being answered and do those questions get at the complexities involved?
3. Information: What information are they using to arrive at their conclusions—what evidence, experiences, or facts are presented?
4. Inferences: Is the conclusion not based in actual experience?
5. Assumptions: What is assumed at the foundation of the persuader's reasoning?
6. Points of View: From what point of view are you/they looking at the issue, and is there another point of view that should be considered?
7. Implications: All reasoning, the end of all persuasion, has consequences—what will be the consequences of this persuasion?

Critical thinking will help us to be more mindful and correct for the imperfections of perception, memory, and mind in general. However our memory works, it is full of associations. Some of those associations are based on experiences we've lived through, and some are based on what we've been told by others. Many memories hold value judgments, attitudes, which position us to act favorably or unfavorably toward the object of that attitude. And those memories, schemata, guide our perception as we interact with our environments in the dramas of various social systems.

Creative Moment

Try mapping part of your reality using the structural differential as a model. This could be about any aspect of your life, such as a hobby, a relationship, or things you eat and drink. For instance, that food you ate earlier has been magically converted to different forms of energy by your body at the event level—that's quite a process! Map the various levels: event (process), object (perception), descriptive (words based on direct experience), and inference (words and thoughts not based on direct experience).

Event: The reality is . . .

Object: My perceptions of the reality are . . .

Descriptive: In describing the event, I would say . . .

Inference: Things I think and talk about but have not directly experienced related to the event include . . .

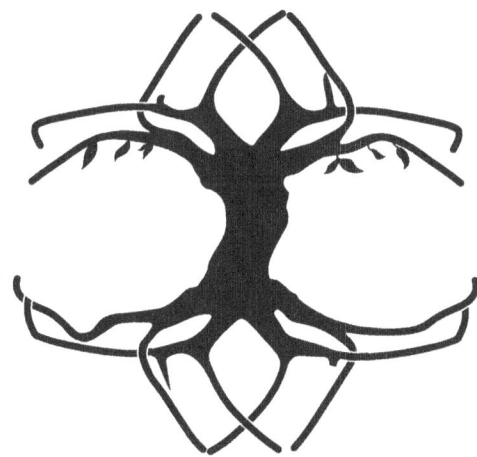

Chapter 5

alphaspirit/iStock/Thinkstock

Making Meaning

**"'Cause we live in a time,
When meaning falls in splinters from our minds.
And that's why I've travelled far,
'Cause I come so together where you are."**
— *Fleetwood Mac, "Sentimental Lady"*

People have searched for meaning on various paths throughout history, from the meaning of a song's lyrics to the meaning of life. Meaning is central to the persuasion process. Persuasion works by identifying motivations, and motivations are built upon sets of interpretations. Meaning moves us.

Put simply, meaning is the interpretation of a message. But it's not so simple. Does that meaning lie within the interpreter, the message, the message sender, or all three? Can meaning exist separate from human interpretation? That is, does a book or a look have meaning without people interpreting? Is meaning the same for different interpreters? If not, do we have a problem when meaning is not consistent between people? The interpretation of meaning itself creates all kinds of philosophical and practical questions.

Brain and mind have something to do with meaning. Your brain is making the associations between symbols and referents, between words and the things to which those words refer. Social systems also play into meaning. *The meaning you derive from experience is somewhat dependent on the company you keep, the actors in your drama.* Meaning is also related to your habitual ways of perceiving the world and your motivations.

In 1923 C. K. Ogden and I. A. Richards published *The Meaning of Meaning*. To understand meaning we look at symbols and referents. Symbols (such as words, gestures, or visual images like logos) stand for the referent, the thing being referred to. Meaning is found in the relationship between symbol, mind, and referent. The triangle in their book (Figure 5.1) shows how a symbol stands for a referent as mediated through thoughts. Further, we can wonder if we have the correct symbol that captures the thought, and if that thought adequately conveys the important aspects of the referent. Words evoke images in mind about the referent; symbols are mediated through mind, triggering neural constellations or a system of associations, to give meaning to things.

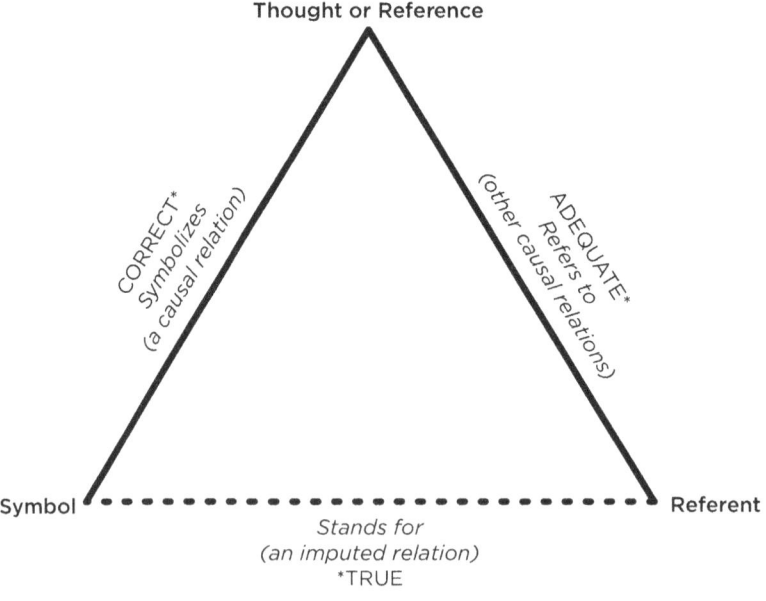

FIGURE 5.1 Ogden & Richards' semantic triangle

Usually symbols are considered to "stand for" referents; words stand for the thought or the thing. Kenneth Burke flips our thinking on this one, leading our thoughts toward the special kind of magic woven into words:

> But, if only as a tour de force, we here ask what might be discovered if we try inverting such a view, and upholding instead the proposition that

"things are the signs for words." That is, might words be found to possess a "spirit" peculiar to their nature as words? . . .

Thus, in mediating between the social realm and the realm of nonverbal nature, words communicate to things the spirit that society imposes upon the words which have come to be the "names" for them. The things are in effect the visible tangible material embodiments of the spirit that infuses them through the medium of words. And in this sense, things become signs of the genius that resides in words. (1966, pp. 361–2)

"Word magic" refers to the many ways in which words can imbue the world with meaning and make things happen.

Philosophers of language distinguish between semantic, semiotic, and pragmatic meaning. *Semantics* is the study of meaning in the interrelationship of words, phrases, and sentences. Where does the meaning of a word come from? To a certain extent, the etymology (the origin and history) of a word matters. Words are created in various ways, with more or less intellectual rigor. Words in the English language come from many roots such as Latin, Greek, Sanskrit, and many earlier languages. Sometimes the new words are consciously crafted from root meanings. For instance, the Latin *sylva* refers to a wooded area, and so that part of the word Penn*sylva*nia is tied to a meaningful root. The roots of words are not always certain. Of course, if we go back far enough, all roots of words were at one time invented, a set of sounds arbitrarily assigned to stand for something. We are, after all, the symbol-making animal.

Semantics is partially concerned with such root meanings, but more with the sense and reference of a word. The reference is *what* is being referred to by a word; the sense is the *way* the word refers to the referent. Referring to a soldier as a "freedom fighter" versus referring to him as a "terrorist" carries very different meanings. The words may refer to the same person, but their sense is quite different, and that sense depends on the side you are on. That is similar to the distinction between denotative and connotative meaning. A word denotes what it is referring to. I can use the word *woman* to denote that female over there. *Connotative meaning is the subjective positive or negative associations we attach to words, or the value-laden baggage that words carry.* Connotatively, the words "woman," "chick," and "babe" carry different baggage, and may stir different emotions in the listener, though they refer to the same person. We should also note that words carry different connotations for different people, so while some might be terribly offended by certain terms, others might use the offensive terms in everyday discussions. A feminist professor may be more offended by "chick" than a chauvinistic meat-packer.

Semiotics is the study of signs and meaning, looking at the signifier, which is the sound made to produce a word, and the signified, the mental constructions associated with that word. Ferdinand de Saussure was the Swiss linguist credited with the early development of semiotics. He was interested in linguistic systems, the interrelationship of sounds with ideas. The systems of sounds are the arbitrary words we assign to represent things, while the systems of ideas are in the mind of each individual. The signifier—the word or sound that stands for something—is a public, communal convention. The signified—the idea, the mental construction—is personal. So meaning is both a *between* and *within* person phenomenon. Or put differently, meaning is in the interactions between symbols and persons, the interactions between language and mind.

Pragmatics is the study of how context affects meaning, both the linguistic context and the situational context. Linguistic context refers to the language surrounding the word, or as Kenneth Burke once noted, words are "defined by the company they keep." In a speech about the medicinal uses of marijuana where the speaker is developing a sympathetic view of pain sufferers, the words *marijuana*, *pot*, or *weed* might be considered in a different light than in a speech about marijuana as a "gateway drug" that leads the user to more hardcore and addictive drugs. In the first case, the company kept by the word grants sympathy; in the second case, the linguistic context casts a less favorable set of associations. Beyond the words surrounding a word, there is also a situational context—the time, place, and action going on in the scene where a word is used. The situational context makes certain words appropriate and others not so appropriate and it can carry connotative freight for words. In the context of the 1960s countercultural movement, Timothy Leary's phrase, "Turn on, tune in, and drop out," seemed to make perfect sense to the pro-hallucinogenic crowd. In the context of a fundamentalist evangelical sermon his phrase might meet more resistance. Or take the case of political misinterpretation. When a popular Democrat says "We're going to help the poor and make the super-rich pay their taxes" at a Democratic convention, the crowd roars in approval. A popular Republican might quote those same words to a chorus of boos at the Republican convention, casting that Democrat as a "tax-and-spend liberal." From a pragmatic perspective *meaning is an interaction of people, words, and contexts*.

Burke mentioned such contextual meanings—the company words keep—in *The Philosophy of Literary Form* (1941). In that early evolutionary step toward his dramatic theory, Burke outlined the ways in which words cluster and interact in making meaning. The three basic forms of word interaction are (1) What equals what? (2) What versus what? and (3) From what through what to what? "What equals what" is the way words get meaning by association to other words, ideas, and things. When you read or listen to people you can get a sense for how they define terms, and perhaps how they think, by looking at the associations drawn in their language. Let's say you're listening to a conservative commentator talking about "those mischievous liberals . . . tax-and-spend types who love to throw money at social projects that don't show any bottom line results . . . and want us to live in their politically correct world of make-believe . . ." You get the picture. The ways the commentator loads the language with connotative choices creates equations for "liberal"—the word defined by what goes with it. And if these connections get hammered into mind through enough repetitions, that sense for the word may gain fashion in certain social circles.

Words also gain meaning in the oppositions that swirl around their usage—the "what versus what." Notice that authors, speakers, and even your friends often imply or name what they stand *against* as they speak *for* such and such. If one stands for world peace, she likely speaks against warfare, bloodshed, bombs, monetary motives, and the like. Contrarily, if one stands for bombing the crap out of our enemies, then he likely speaks against those who don't understand the realities of world conflict. An analysis of "what versus what" in our language choices leads us to how our terms *and lives* gain meaning by what is opposed.

All human action has a progressive form—where we've been, where we are, and where we're going—from what, through what, to what? One sense of this progressive form is found in how our language becomes meaningful by the journey we're on. If you're an old hippy from the sixties (from what) looking for enlightenment (to what), then you might be exploring different means such as good books, adventures, and meditation (through what). Whatever quest you're on, whatever you seek, the language you use takes on certain meanings in the context of your quest. Another sense of the progression is found in the ways people talk about where we should be going based on where we are and where we've been. When people try to persuade us (which happens daily), they often speak of an ideal future state that should follow the past and present. To justify war, for instance, politicians will talk of the necessary and regrettable bombs and bullets (through what) that will take us to the new and better society (to what) and away from the failed system of the past (from what).

Beyond clusters of words, *meaning comes from your identifications*. We get meaning through the social systems we connect with and what those systems stand for. Identification could refer to how you align yourself with other people and organizations—in what social systems do you "hang out"? Identification also comes from what you stand for and against. For instance, you might identify with the peace movement, civil rights, or conservatism. Identification is seen in the life paths you buy into, the progression from the past through now, to the future that gives your life meaning. Each social system has its order, defined good and bad, and "ways of seeing" the world. We will discuss identification more later when we consider persuasion.

Burke also talks of language as action. Language causes things to happen; it has implications. This idea gets developed in John Searle's theory of speech acts. One way to think about speech acts is this: saying is doing. In the present line of pondering we might consider what words *do* as their meaning. Searle classifies five illocutionary speech acts:

1. Assertives: speech acts that commit the speaker to the truth of the expressed proposition. For instance, "I think power corrupts," or "My dog has fleas."
2. Directives: speech acts that cause the hearer to take a particular action, such as requests, commands, and advice. For instance, "Will you help me?" or "Open that door," or "You should really see a doctor about that."
3. Commissives: speech acts that commit a speaker to a future course of action, such as promises and oaths. For instance, "I swear to tell the truth," and "With this ring I thee wed" and "I'll meet you at 7 o'clock."
4. Expressives: speech acts that express the speaker's attitudes and emotions, such as congratulations, gratitude, fear, and hatred. For instance, "I can't thank you enough," and "kill the blasphemer!" and "that bastard!"
5. Declaratives: speech acts that change reality according to the proposition in the declaration, such as baptisms, pronunciations of guilt, and pronouncing a couple husband and wife.

The important point is that language does something, has an impact on reality. Sticks and stones can break your bones, and words can hurt you. Searle's speech acts directly address the social construction of reality, showing us how language causes action.

Searle also talks of indirect speech acts, wherein the speaker communicates to the hearer more than is actually said by relying on their shared background. For instance, let's say you and I have just been talking about Luvvy noting how "she's so stuck on herself; she thinks she's the hottest thing since toasted bread . . ." Later, Luvvy comes into the room and tells us she'll have to pass on our plans to go out because she has a date with Joe. I turn to you and wink, and you nod knowingly, because Luvvy has just confirmed what we said earlier. The wink and nod had meaning from our past communication and shared background. Much of our communication is like that, full of meanings that carry over from prior speech acts within relationships.

Coordinated Management of Meaning

W. Barnett Pearce and Vernon Cronen developed their Coordinated Management of Meaning (CMM) theory around similar ideas. CMM theory looks at the ways in which meaning arises out of social interaction. It also looks at communication as contextualized by several layers of meaningful patterns, including speech act, self, episode, relationship, and cultural patterns. The *speech act*, what we do with our words in an exchange with others, is the basic unit of meaningful utterance. As we engage in that act we have a sense of *self* (and others have their sense of self), which gives meaning to the speech act. If I consider myself a feminist or a postmodernist or a dog lover or a do-gooder, that sense of self infuses meaning into my exchanges. *Episodes* are the recurring things we do that contextualize our patterns of interaction. Episodes might include going to parties, acts of domestic violence, gathering around the hookah, eating dinner, or any number of activities that people do together. The things we do provide context for meaning. *Relationships* give meaning to interactions. Our relationships with others are built with recurring interactions across time in which we develop relational meanings. Different relationships—whether they are romantic, business, family, or friends—develop their own kinds of meanings based on experiences and other factors. Action is also contextualized by *cultural patterns*, which includes subcultures. Your life and speech acts take on different meaning if you are a member of the Fellowship of Christian Athletes as opposed to being a contestant in the Miss Teen America pageant, or any other differences in subcultures. And the wider culture now gives us different layers of meaning than the culture past. Pearce (2002) is quick to point out that this hierarchical picture of contexts is useful, but it makes communication appear too static. Each of those contextualizing influences adds to the texture of meaning, but to depict the meaning arising out of interaction, we need more moving pictures:

> An alternative is to imagine that each moment consists of a field of potentialities constrained by the past but open to the creative force of action

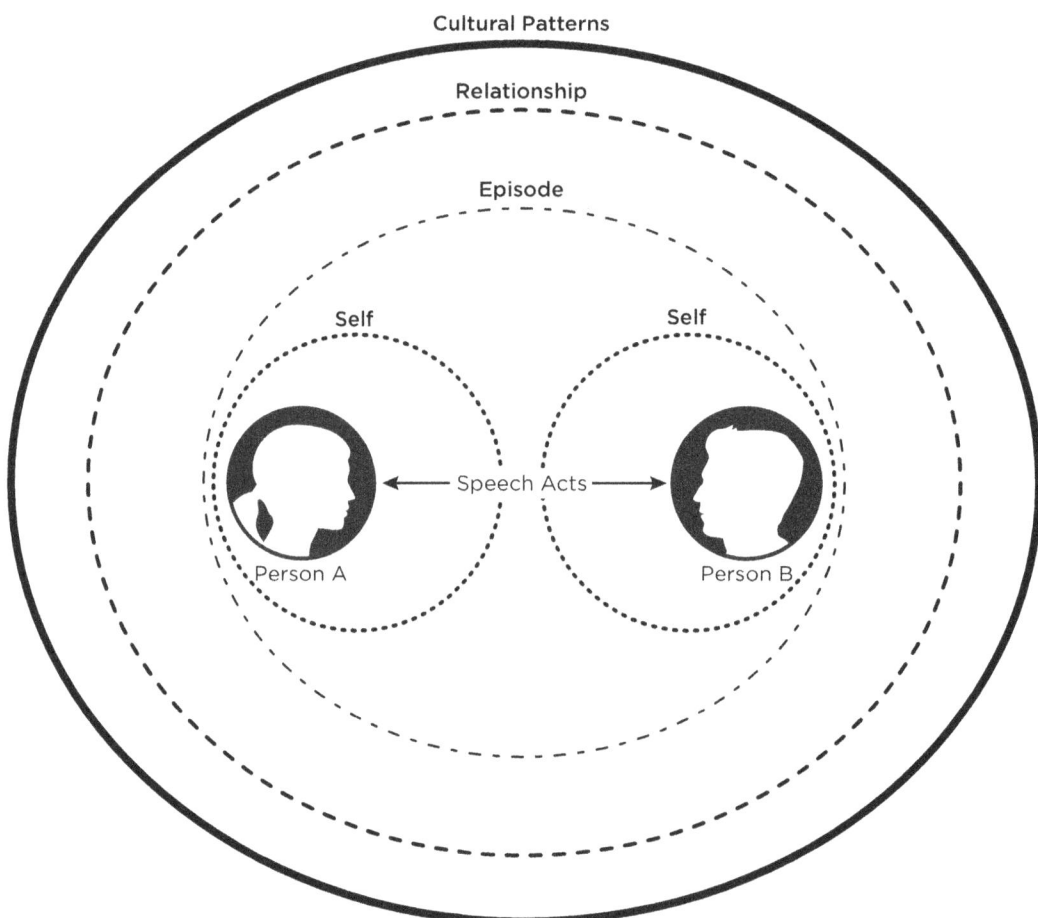

FIGURE 5.2 CMM hierarchy of meaning contexts

in the present moment. This field floats or moves or exists in the magical "now" at the cusp of the past and the future. What we do (whether it is to speak or not to speak; to move toward, away from or against another person; to build or destroy) in each moment "realizes" one (or some) of the nearly infinite possible "presents" and, in so doing, prefigures some of the nearly infinite number of potential futures. (2002, p. 6)

He adds a pinch of existentialism and a sprinkling of chaos theory to a pound of interactional perspective in this revised view of coordinated management of meaning theory.

Essentially, CMM theory shows how we live in separate social worlds where our habits of perception and frames of mind are integrated by patterns of interaction. Those repeated interactions are the essence of relationships, which are the "attractors" of social systems, forming romances, families, organizations, nations and other networks of relations. Our socially constructed worlds have unfolding potential futures that depend on the language choices we make in the present and are constrained somewhat by past choices. Language is fateful, says Pearce, as it sets our course and directs our attention at some things and not others, and brings futures into being.

Here is an extended example of coordinating and managing meaning. Let's say you belong to a group of friends who like to share music, and your preferred music style is a kind of low-key jazz with subtle rock and classical themes. Also assume you live in a large city with lots of cultural options in music, theater, and other amenities. You are somewhat religious and others in your group range from true believers to nonbelievers, and almost everyone is okay with that. Once in a while your interests in music and religion mix. So there's part of the meaning of this motion picture (and it *is* moving): we have the group of low-key, rockish jazzbos living in the city who are a little liberal in their social relations. That subculture contextualizes meaning—gives the group cues on how to interpret, what's a cool interpretation, and so on. Of course, we didn't say what country the city was in, and that makes a difference as all the action would take on a different feel and sense in a "foreign" culture as opposed to the one you are accustomed to. Let's say it's New York City.

Let's assume further that you and your low-key, jazz-loving friends like to sip Scotch whisky and wine and enjoy gourmet meals. Let's say you also like to play music—anything from guitars and fiddles to spoons and congas. A few of the members smoke weed every now and then, but none are addicted, and all veer away from hard drugs. Note that this aspect of your subculture and group gives another layer in the making of meaning. If the group had been into the hardcore drug scene—doing heroin or meth or other soul sappers—it would change the nature of things you all do together and your way of *minding* the world together. And if one member is addicted to something strong and the others disagree with his or her choice, that adds dimension to the drama. Here's where the notion of *episode* comes in. Episodes are what you do together, and doing drugs makes for a whole different kind of ritual dance for the group than, say, watching movies or playing video games. To a certain extent, your culture and subculture and group determine the "dance" you will do. *Episodes are made up of members' meaningful action, the different ways in which what we do together gives meaning.*

Episodes, the things we do together, add meaning to our relationships. JupiterImages/Stockbyte/Thinkstock

So here's your group of wine-sipping, cheese-eating, low-key jazzbos sitting around making music together. As you play a song you are coordinating musical pieces into a meaningful whole. Each individual (self, with accompanying self-concept, what I think others think, and so on) is coming from a different perspective, different mindset, different motives, and yet you play together and enjoy the music. The meanings that emanate from your group's conversations may be different for each member, and yet you coordinate agreements and manage getting through situations together. Coordinating and managing meaning does not mean you all share meaning or think alike, just that you can pull off a show in the social scene.

Remember, this is a moving picture, with group members' different pasts meshing in the here and now and wandering toward different futures. Some of your friends will stay together, some will go, and new actors will enter the stage. Members will tell stories of what was ("Remember that time you . . ."), talk about what is ("Look at this picture"), and wonder about what will be ("So what do you want to do later?"). The whole drama is dynamic and evolving.

Pearce says CMM theory focuses our attention down three paths: coordination, coherence, and mystery. Coordination is a focus on the way our actions mesh to produce patterns, like when we play music together and get meaning from it—perhaps not the same meaning for each, but at least a sense of togetherness. To illustrate this sense of coordination, my mentor Dr. Jim Wilcox once had us imagine an intersection with a four-way stop. One driver approaches from the east, while another approaches from the north. The driver from the east just came from a bar, has had a few drinks, and is thinking about that fun person she just met. The driver from the north is coming from a prayer group meeting and is still thinking about that poor lost soul they were praying for. The two drivers are coming to the intersection from very different mindsets. They both stop. Then the driver from the east proceeds, and the driver from the north proceeds after her. They have successfully coordinated their behaviors and managed to get through the intersections without incident, though they were not thinking in the same way or sharing meanings. Likewise, we can coordinate social interactions and manage communication without sharing meanings.

Coherence directs our attention to the truth in the stories we tell that make our lives meaningful. Sharing stories makes meanings and builds social relations, though, as Pearce also notes, the stories we *tell* are not always consistent with the stories we *live*. It's almost as if two (or more) parallel universes are operating in social dramas—the one with our actions and the one where we talk about our actions—and sometimes the two meet. Coherence is about consistency, the ways in which stories agree, whether it is the internal consistency of one person's story or the external consistency of stories across people. As we coordinate our stories, people might not "be on the same page," as interpretations will vary. Part of the business of social interaction is to get our stories to jibe, to bring meanings and interpretations into closer alignment. Unless, of course, you are trying to emphasize or capitalize on the differences between interpretations, as is often the case in conflicts and par for the course in politics.

Mystery directs our attention to the fact that the universe is far larger and fuller of subtle nuances than our sets of stories can capture. There's always something more to understanding, a way of seeing beyond our current best wisdom. Attention to mystery also teaches us that every utterance is only a part of the whole picture, a fraction of what the speaker is trying to "get at," so there are always secrets left in what goes unsaid, always something dangling at the end of conversation. When all is said and done, mystery still wafts between us, we humans, imperfectly imitating the pure meaning of the original message.

In a nutshell, CMM gives us a communication perspective, a look at human interaction as producing our social *worlds* (not just one reality, like the natural environment, but different social realities across individuals and groups). It focuses on action unfolding as people come together and move apart in the different episodes of various dramas, as past phases into future in the vortex of now. It sees communication as the builder of relationships and the process in which people make their meanings.

Pearce credits prior pioneers for his thinking, including Harry Stack Sullivan and Gregory Bateson, both of whom viewed individuals as gaining meaning and personhood from their network of relationships. While we will come back to Sullivan in Chapter 7, Bateson's ideas can be enlarged here by looking at the work of his mentees, who developed the Interactional View of communication. Watzlawick, Beavin, and Jackson published their groundbreaking book, *Pragmatics of Human Communication,* in 1967. Their book wove the renegade ideas of Bateson into a comprehensive look at the dynamics of relationships and social systems. Five axioms serve to summarize their book: (1) You cannot not communicate; (2) human beings communicate digitally and analogically; (3) communication has content and relationship aspects; (4) relationships depend on how people punctuate sequences of action; and (5) communication is either symmetrical or complementary.

Axiom One: You cannot not communicate. Everything you do, or don't do, communicates something. All nonverbal and verbal action has the potential to mean something to someone, even if you don't intend it. Say you're at a party and you don't feel conversational, so you retreat to a corner where you watch the festivities, not wanting to communicate anything. That action of retreating and *not* communicating communicates a lot to others.

Axiom Two: Human beings communicate digitally and analogically. For Watzlawick and friends, digital communication refers to spoken words, which they assumed corresponded to a digital all–or–nothing firing of neurons in the brain. Analog communication, which includes nonverbal and non-word verbal sounds, corresponds to a different reaction in the human central nervous system. Words are arbitrary sets of sounds applied to a phenomenon—they don't really represent it well—whereas nonverbals such as pictures and gestures can represent the phenomenon well. For instance the word *five* (digital) has little to do with the phenomenon of *fiveness*, but if I hold up five fingers (analog), that gesture represents five things more closely than the word. We can also look at how digital and analog communicate similar or different messages simultaneously. Let's say you are angry with someone, and you tell him, "I am angry with you." The words communicate digitally; but if you are also red in the face and yelling the words, those nonverbal aspects communicate analogically. Now, if you said, "I am angry with you," but you were smiling and looking at the person lovingly, the digital and analogical levels would not be in sync, and may require a more complex interpretation.

Axiom Three: Communication has content and relationship aspects. Basically, content is *what* is said, and relationship is *how* it is said. All interactions between humans carry content and relationship messages. Content refers to the denotative meaning, the relationship between symbols and referents. Relationship refers to the power dimension and the history of prior interactions that give the present interaction meaning. If I say to my son, "Have the car back by eleven," the content is about what time to drive the car home. But there is a relational message implied that I have the right to be telling him when to bring the car home. When a lover says, "Don't go out with your friends; go out with me," there is content, but there is also a relational message in that the lover is attempting to control behavior. Relational (control) issues are at the heart of a lot of persuasion.

Axiom Four: Relationships depend on how people punctuate sequences of interactions. For instance, different people will view "who started the conflict" differently. Our communication unfolds in sequences and people perceive these sequences in different ways, especially the *causality* in the sequence. In an argument, each arguer might blame the cause of the argument on the other—A: "You started it,"

B: "No, you started it." That is, people punctuate the sequence differently. These differences can have serious consequences from interpersonal arguments to international conflicts. For instance, in ongoing hostilities in the Middle East, combatants will often blame their own aggression on the prior aggression of the enemy, often seeing the enemy as the cause for their actions. In interpersonal relations, we tend to be aware of other people causing our behavior, but it is more difficult to see our own actions as causing others' behavior. And of course, the meaning of actions takes on a different flavor depending on how you punctuate the sequence.

Axiom Five: All communication is either symmetrical or complementary. Symmetrical refers to equality in the relationship and complementary refers to inequality. Symmetry implies a sharing of power, and complementary implies that one person is up and the other is down in the power aspect. In a family, if the parents discuss alternatives with children and they decide democratically on courses of action, that shows a more symmetrical relationship. If the parents give orders, and the children defer, that is more complementary. In some cases we find the children giving orders and the parents deferring, which is also complementary.

Summary of Meaning

Where is meaning? *Meaning is partly in people, partly in the interactions between people (as mediated by symbols and mind), and partly context-dependent. Meaning is in relationships.* We cannot say meaning is in words because a word means nothing until mind assigns an association. Though a word can stimulate responses in people, the meaning is born in the interaction of stimulus and response, not just the stimulus, as the same word may evoke different responses across different individuals. Further, meaning is negotiated between people—coordinated and managed between persons within social systems as they phase from past into future. People do not share meanings—hold exactly the same associations in mind—so much as they develop agreements.

There is meaning in the sense of what we are referring to, and there is meaning in the sense of "what is life for?" The search for meaning is a quest that enters many peoples' drama at different times and in different ways. For some it's as simple as trying to figure out what their friend meant by that last comment, while for others it is a deep philosophical search. Viktor Frankl published *Man's Search for Meaning* in 1946 after he was liberated from a Nazi concentration camp in April of 1945. He saw people's search for meaning as the central motivation in the human drama, and credited that search for his and others' survival of the concentration camps. Meaning for Frankl came down to the question: Why go on? Frankl quotes Nietzsche: "He who has a *why* to live for can bear almost any *how*." The meaning we create in life is what ultimately keeps us moving and shapes our motivation.

Creative Moment

Meaning is tied to mindfulness. Frederick Franck (1973) took a journey into meaning in search of "the artist within, who must exist in everyone, for if man is created in God's image, it can only mean that he is created creative." Franck promotes "seeing" by letting go, loosening the grips of our mental maps and flowing with the moment by sketching it. The wonderful thing is you don't have to be an artist. The sketches are spontaneous, fun, and fluid, allowing the fog of preconceptions to lift. Sketching, even doodling, can help clear the mind.

Franck presents his ideas with those of Zen masters through the centuries, his work a living practice of what he is preaching. His creativity is based on a mindset of Zen found in practice. He asks:

What then is Zen?

> Zen is: being in touch with the inner workings of life.
>
> Zen is: life that knows it is living.
>
> Zen is: this moment speaking as time and as eternity.
>
> Zen is: seeing into the nature of things, inside and outside of myself.
>
> Zen is: when all living things of the Earth open their eyes wide

and look me in the eye. (1973, p. 9)

Frederick Franck's *The Zen of Seeing: Seeing/Drawing as Meditation* advocates improving our mindfulness by seeing and sketching. Franck slows us down; calms the chatter of mind; and suggests we take a moment to see the living, thriving, blooming, and buzzing life around us. His book is a story of coming to consciousness, a poem pondering awareness, a map toward "pointed mindfulness."

Exercise

Let's sketch a tree of life, related to the meaning in your life. Draw a line horizontally across a page in your journal, about one quarter of the way up from the bottom of the page. This will be the ground. Draw some squiggly lines going down in various directions, with more squiggly lines coming off of them—the roots. Draw a couple of lines going up from the ground, then some branches off of them, then more branches off those branches. Label some of the roots as elements of nature and nurture that have given your life meaning—perhaps parents, heritage, teachers, preachers—any part of your meaningful nature and nurturance. Label some of the branches with what gives you a sense of purpose in life: What motivates you? What are you striving for? What future goals do you have?

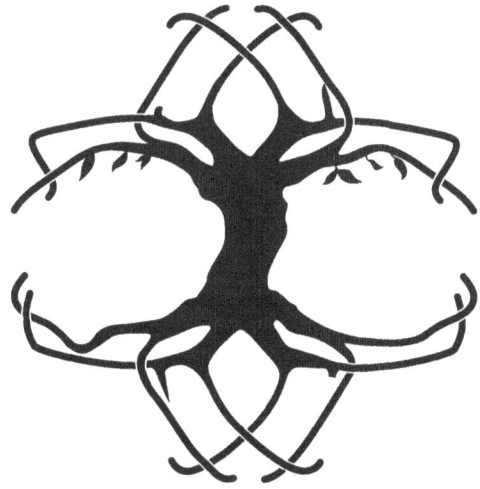

Chapter 6

Dmitriy Shironosov/iStock/Thinkstock

What Moves You?
Motivation

"**He who has a *why* to live for can bear almost any *how*.**"
—*Friedrich Nietzsche*

Why do we do what we do? Is it for love or money or a better lot in life? That is the question when we consider motivation: Why?

We can consider motivation in large and small ways, as we are motivated moment to moment and across a lifetime. Viktor Frankl (2006/1946) pondered motivation in *Man's Search for Meaning*. Frankl survived horrific struggles in a Nazi death camp during World War II where he developed his ideas about "logo therapy" and meaning as the central motivation. The "will to meaning" is tied intimately to purpose in life, and Frankl saw meaning—especially interpretations that help us understand and transcend our situation—as more primary than power and pleasure. Friedrich Nietzsche suggested the "will to power" is humans' most central motive. Sigmund Freud's model suggests the "will to pleasure" is our central motive. Frankl suggested we make meaning, and that is what moves us most.

Many exceptional researchers and teachers and preachers have pondered motivation and provided models of what moves us. You've probably come across the name Abraham Maslow before, but just in case you haven't I'll review his ideas on motivation. We'll also look at William Glasser, Shakti Gawain, and Henry Murray for motivation. Before venturing there, however, let's go back to Burke for a few moments.

Kenneth Burke's central concern was motivation: What is the purpose of actions in the human drama? Recall that he said we are moved by a sense of order. Our ideas about how things should be—of the proper order—cause us to act in particular ways. Order is a motive woven throughout our lives. Burke discussed three key motives: Order, the Secret, and the Kill. Roughly translated, they refer to hierarchy, mystery, and transcendence, and they are motive forces at work in all of our lives.

Order, the Secret, and the Kill

Order is apparent in our language, priorities, hierarchies, and the rules we create. There is order in the way I teach a class and the concepts I deem relevant and important, showing signs of order in my thinking and the order in which I work. That order is constructed by language. The priorities you have—what's most important in your life down to what's least important in your list of things to do today—show order in your thoughts and actions. There's order, or lack of, in your sock drawer, cupboards, garage, and desk. Where do things go? Should your socks be folded in the drawer? On what shelf should the shaving cream go? Should Dick marry Jane? Who's the more capable candidate? All of these are questions related to order, how things should be.

Order is not just ideas in our head, though, because we have to negotiate it with others. Perhaps you live with roommates. You know that the order of your home—cleaning, grocery shopping, paying the bills, and other aspects of living together—gets negotiated. Order is continually being created and recreated, and to depict this, Burke borrowed terms from the realm of religion to discuss social order. He discussed the ever-changing order of human affairs in terms of the "purgative guilt cycle." This circle of terms takes us from the creation of social order, through the breach in that agreement that brings guilt, and the various ways in which people deal with guilt to be redeemed and continue on in the order. Burke's purgative guilt cycle, or "seven interlocking moments," or "pollution-purification" cycle, is shown in Figure 6.1. Burke claimed we are motivated to purge ourselves of guilt because it is like pollution for the soul which must be cleansed. Guilt is created in the recognition that one has disobeyed the rules of the order; one has broken the "covenant." Social systems are built upon pieties, ideas of right, wrong, good, bad,

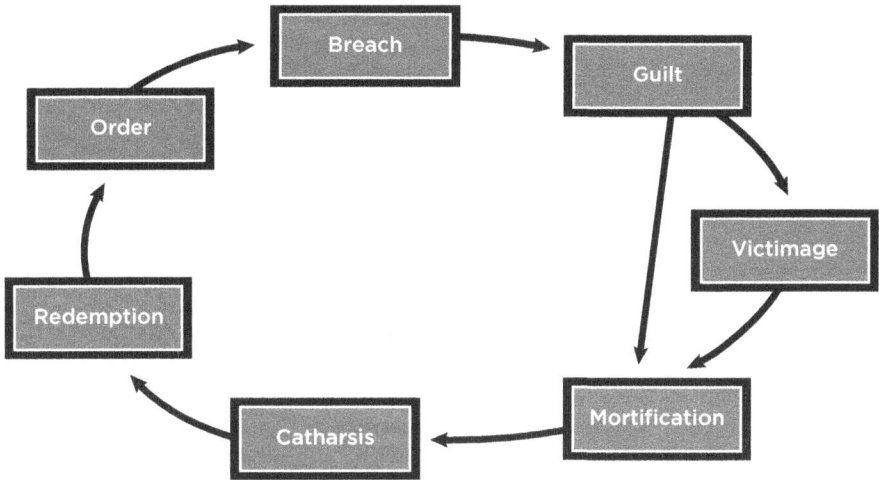

FIGURE 6.1 The purgative guilt cycle

and so on. Groups of people, from a two-person relationship to nations, come to formal and informal agreements about rules for action. And, again, a great portion of those rules are made possible by the negative, our ability to say "do not do this" and "thou shall not."

Order gets established in agreements between people, but there will always be breaches, people breaking the rules or acting contrary to expectations. There will always be guilt arising from breaches in the covenants that make order. Take the example of a new romantic relationship. As the couple goes through phases of development from just meeting, to dating and liking one another, to the magic moment where they say "I love you," they are also establishing formal or informal rules, agreements. For instance, they arrive at agreements about what they will and will not do together, whether or not they will still date others, and a range of other expectations that develop as the relationship develops. One or both are bound to break those agreements at some point, to not fulfill the expectations of the other: "*Wait—you thought we aren't supposed to go out with anyone else? I didn't know that.*" That breach in the contract brings guilt.

As guilt arises we have two basic choices—blame others or blame ourselves. Blaming others is victimage. Blaming oneself is mortification. Now, of course, it is more complicated than that, but those are the basics. Victimage is not only the blaming of others, but any time we use others as a "sacrificial scapegoat" on which we pile our own guilt. Victimage was evident in Hitler's blaming the Jews for the woes of Germany. Victimage was evident when George Bush identified Saddam Hussein as one of the world's great evildoers. And victimage is evident when friends get together to gossip about some target person who's just not with it: "*He's so stuck on himself! Who died and made him Elvis?*" Mortification is more self-blame, seeking atonement for social sins. Mortification is when you say you're sorry for what you said or did. Mortification is when you ask God to forgive you. Mortification is when you say, "I did it," in taking the blame for the group's action. We seem to be motivated to rid ourselves of or redirect guilt through victimage or mortification. Victimage is often the preferred choice in social interaction. There is a tendency to look outward for scapegoats rather than inward.

When we cleanse the guilt through taking the blame or blaming others, there is a catharsis, a venting, and a release of pressure—or, in Burke's terms, a purifying of the pollution of guilt. This leads to redemption, in which the order is confirmed, respect is restored, and on it goes. The cycle continues in our scintillating social dramas.

Think about those you know who might be motivated by guilt—a child who is not living up to a parent's expectations; a lover not living up to his beloved's wishes; a salesperson not meeting her monthly quota; a businessperson who failed in business; a friend who let another friend down in a time of need. And the list goes on. Guilt motivates people. Note that the motivation arising from the need for redemption is a *between-person* phenomenon—the motive force is found in the interactions between people. Also note that guilt is often used in the persuasion process, as guilt often produces dissonance, a state of psychological imbalance, and people are motivated to reduce guilt and restore balance.

Burke's second key motive is the Secret. People are motivated to resolve mysteries of all kinds. Why do people behave the way they do? Why did that celebrity who had so much fame throw it all away through self-destructive behavior? How did that guy make all that money? What's it like to be rich? How can I sell more? How can I get myself elected? What's it like to be a woman? What's it like to be a man? These and so many more are questions that reveal mysteries. There are social mysteries that deal with friendship, love, courtship, conflict, and other relational issues; physical mysteries that present questions of what makes the world and universe tick; natural mysteries, like what makes a plant grow from a seed; supernatural mysteries, such as what happens when we die; economic mysteries, like what will be the next big fad or trend; and so many other mysteries that motivate people to seek answers.

Mystery moves us, and some people seem to have the "secret." Some preachers and teachers and economic prognosticators seem to have the answers to questions. Some celebrities who have made it big seem to have discovered how the game works. Some musicians and poets and authors sell their insights, their secrets, for a better life. Some businesspeople and real estate speculators strike it rich. What's their secret? We are motivated to discover the secrets in many mysteries, and many are attempting to persuade us by offering the secret within some realm of the mystery in which we are wondering and wandering.

Burke's third key motive is the Kill. The "kill" is the motive to transcend, to rise above others' wrongs with our righteousness. He looked at the motive to extinguish others or ourselves, homicide, suicide, and symbolic equivalents. People pave their way "up" by putting others down. That is, people can gain a sense of purpose and satisfaction with their own righteousness by identifying the wickedness of others. So, for instance, when Hitler scapegoated the Jews, some German people received a vicarious lift, a bit of transcendence. To transcend is to go beyond one's limitations, to rise above the limits of nature. We are motivated, said Burke, to justify our own paths by pointing to the misdirected paths of others. He used the term symbolically, but sometimes the kill is literal, as when we go to war and eliminate the enemy over a cause that is named through language. This motive to transcend is also the aim of several persuaders. It is obvious in political persuasion, when a candidate or party seeks our allegiance or vote by excoriating the opponent. And it's obvious when the latest guru shows you how your mind can transcend by correcting that wrongheadedness. But we also see this appeal in everyday persuasion, like when an ad for a cleaning product shows how we can transcend those evil germs.

Motivation à la Maslow

We are motivated by order, mystery, and the need to transcend. That drive to transcend is also seen in Maslow's model of the hierarchy of human needs. Maslow proposed his model as a theory of human motivation in 1943, having studied exceptional and gifted people rather than mentally ill individuals. Maslow's theory saw humans as satisfying lower needs, or "deficiency needs," before moving on to the higher "growth" needs. The hierarchy starts with physiological needs and works up to self-actualization, as presented in Figure 6.2.

We must take care of physiological needs such as eating, drinking, breathing, and procreation for our own survival and the survival of the species. Having met these needs, we can attend to safety concerns: safety for ourselves and loved ones, job security, protection of our belongings, and maintaining a level of wellness that keeps us free from disease and discomfort. Physiological survival and safety motivate us and those motives are the targets for persuasive producers and advertisers. Ads for foods, safe drinking water, and vitamins target our physiology needs, while home security systems and emergency medical alerts take aim at our need for safety.

Having secured the survival and safety needs, we move on to social. We are social animals and demonstrate high degrees of motivation toward social relationships in friendships, family relations, sexual intimacy, and all kinds of social collectives. We need to love and be loved. We seek acceptance and belonging with clubs, religious organizations, teams, gangs, work groups, play groups, therapy groups, and so many other groups. We seem to have a need to interact, and if these needs cannot be met, some will respond with feelings of loneliness, depression, and social anxiety. Many persuasive appeals target our need to belong, from wine and beer ads showing smiling people socializing to ads depicting the happy friends gathered around a social media device.

Esteem needs are the next level in the hierarchy, and they are based on the need to be respected, recognized for one's contribution, and held in high regard. Esteem could come from the outside, as when people seek fame, glory, and adulation from others. Or esteem could be internally generated, based on a person's confidence, competence, and sense of achievement. Some people have a higher need for pats on the back, "ego-stroking" from others, while some are more self-assured and may feel less need for ego strokes. The need for esteem coming from others is considered a lower, less advanced form than the esteem that comes from oneself. The esteem we give ourselves is more akin to self-actualization. Commercials that target our identification with status symbols, such as driving an upscale auto or wearing expensive name-brand clothes, are aimed at esteem needs.

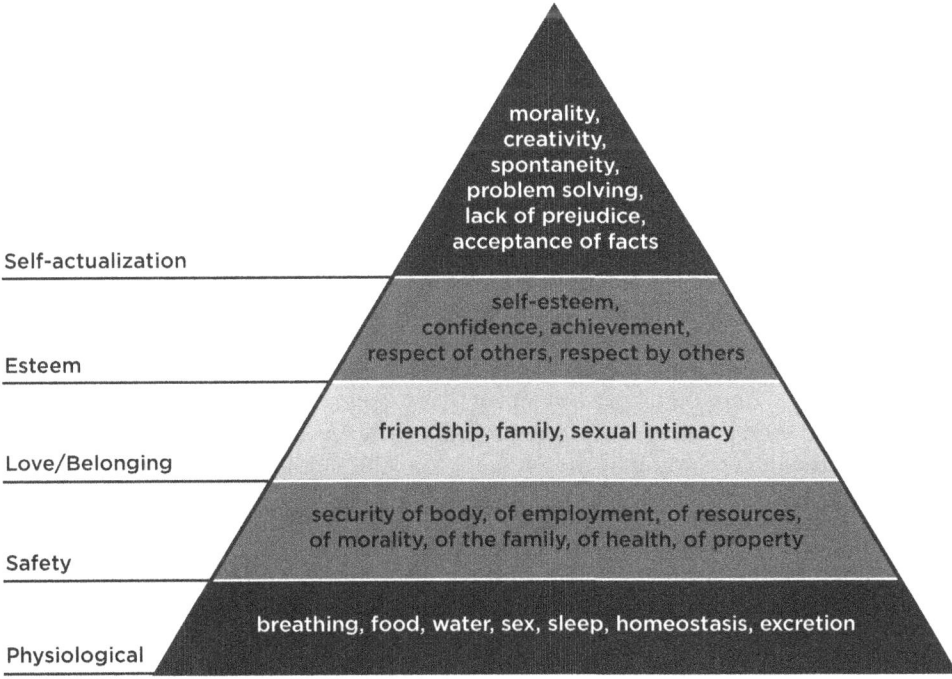

FIGURE 6.2 Maslow's hierarchy of needs

Joseph Campbell said, "Follow your bliss." Discover your motivations.
Digital/Vision Photodisc/Thinkstock

These lower needs, or deficiency needs, usually have to be satisfied in order. You need to eat, drink, and breathe before you can be concerned with safety. You need to be safe from enemies, wild animals, and the elements in order to enjoy the companionship of friends. And much of esteem is based on interactions with others in social circles, so it helps to belong. You can always find the exception to the rule, like the hermit who loves himself, but in general we do find a need to satisfy each need before moving on.

Self-actualization is at the top of Maslow's pyramid, and it is the need to strive toward the best one can be in mind, body, and spirit. The drive toward self-actualization is the push toward becoming what we were meant to be, toward becoming everything we are capable of. Maslow (1954) said, "A musician must make music, an artist must paint, a poet must write, if he is to be ultimately at peace with himself. What a man can be, he must be." He went on to provide descriptions of self-actualizers. They embrace truth, are creative, spontaneous, problem-solvers, and have well-developed powers of discernment. They have a system of morality, appreciate life, and feel a keen kinship with other people. They show tendencies toward awareness, honesty, freedom, and trust. They are working toward their full potential. Self-actualization is not something you accomplish—you reach the top and stay there—but rather it is a quality of living and being that you continue striving toward.

Maslow mentioned the "peak experiences" sometimes achieved by those who are self-actualizing. Peak experiences are moments of transcendence where individuals feel an artistic, intellectual, or spiritual exuberance. These moments sometimes visit at the pinnacle of creativity.

Maslow's hierarchy can be found in just about every introductory book in the social and psychological sciences (I feared being an outcast if I didn't include him). We can complicate this picture of motivation before we simplify it. William Glasser's ideas, stemming from his "choice theory," provide further insight into human motives.

Choice Theory

Glasser (1986, 1998) originally developed "control theory," then later changed and updated his ideas to be called choice theory, as control theory was being confused with another unrelated theory. "Reality therapy" is an application, especially popular in education, which grew out of choice theory. The basic premise behind choice theory is that we choose many of our behaviors. The statement "I do not control the events of the world, but I do control how I respond to them" sums up the spirit of choice theory. There are also ten axioms, or tenets that coincide directly with choice theory. According to choicetheory.com (2008), these axioms are:

1. The only person whose behavior we can control is our own.
2. All we can give another person is information.
3. All long-lasting psychological problems are relationship problems.
4. The problem relationship is always part of our present life.
5. What happened in the past has everything to do with what we are today, but we can only satisfy our basic needs right now and plan to continue satisfying them in the future.

6. We can only satisfy our needs by satisfying the pictures in our Quality World.
7. All we do is behave.
8. All behavior is Total Behavior and is made up of four components: acting, thinking, feeling, and physiology.
9. All Total Behavior is chosen, but we only have direct control over the acting and thinking components. We can only control our feeling and physiology indirectly through how we choose to act and think.
10. All Total Behavior is designated by verbs and named by the part that is the most recognizable.

Glasser claimed we make choices while being driven by five basic needs. Those needs are survival, love and belonging, power, freedom, and fun. Survival is the most primary and physical need of the five. We need food, water, air, shelter, and personal security to survive. We are preprogrammed with automatic responses, instincts, toward survival. Beyond your tendency to jump away from an oncoming bus, your body performs many automatic functions to keep you alive. Survival is genetically programmed, and Glasser made the argument that we are driven by our genes to satisfy the other psychological needs as well.

The need for love and belonging is seen in the formation of human relationships in romance, families, groups, and communities. There are healthy and unhealthy ways to satisfy this need, and reality therapy encourages us to choose healthy alternatives. For instance, it is healthy to satisfy this need by socializing, meeting and greeting people. It is unhealthy to sit on a street corner crying, hoping someone will stop to talk to you.

The need for power is seen in our controlling behaviors and in our personal achievements like learning and winning. Control is at the core of reality therapy and choice theory. People seek control in so many ways: one tries to control with money; another tries controlling through social position in the pecking order; another seeks control of his immediate surroundings by putting things in their proper place; another controls her feelings through psychoactive drugs. People seek control via different routes.

The need for freedom addresses issues of independence, autonomy, and having one's own space. We try to be free in various ways: free from the control of another—be they parent, boss, spouse, or friend; free to roam, not bound by relationships or space; free to travel, the excitement of the open road; free to set our own course, like the empowerment we feel when we design our own destiny. Many reports on job dissatisfaction show that people prefer not having someone else, a boss or manager, dictate their course of action. Freedom is the issue, and we'll discuss it more in later chapters.

Finally, Glasser said we are driven to have fun. We seek pleasure, and different people seek pleasure differently. For one person, pure pleasure would be dancing the night away; for another, pure pleasure would be talking with her best friend forever. People find pleasure in different activities from reading to clubbing to spectator sports, and those needs change over the course of a lifetime. Glasser's five needs share aspects with Maslow's hierarchy. Shakti Gawain presents a slightly different perspective on motivation.

Being, Doing, and Having

Shakti Gawain came onto the self-help scene with a bang in 1979, with the publication of her book *Creative Visualization*. In that book, she discusses the energy that flows through the universe and through each of us. She introduces a number of visualization techniques that lead to a clearer, higher consciousness. Many of her ideas come from Eastern meditation traditions, such as Zen, presented in her book in a fresh, creative way.

Gawain discusses three levels of life: beingness, doingness, and havingness, which we can reconsider as three main motivations. In her words,

> Beingness is the basic experience of being alive and conscious. It is the experience we have in deep meditation, the experience of being totally complete and at rest with oneself.
>
> Doingness is movement and activity, it stems from the natural creative energy that flows through every living thing and is the source of our vitality.
>
> Havingness is the state of being in relationship with other people and things in the universe. It is the ability to allow and accept things and people into our lives; to comfortably occupy the same space with them. (1979, p. 35)

We can consider being, doing, and having as three main motivations. Being is the motivation to develop our self in mind, body, spirit, and relationship to the universe. Doing is the motivation to be active, busy, and productive; it is the driving force behind work and play. Having is the motivation to possess people, money, and things in the world of material goods and ownership.

Gawain notes that *being* should be central and primary, but oftentimes people live their life backward. We might try to *have* more (money and things), so that we can *do* the things we want to do (travel, eat well, do pleasurable activities), so that we can *be* the person we want to be. As if our being depends on having and doing. To a certain extent our being is related to having and doing. There is no doubt that having the money to afford a college education and taking a trip to visit a guru in the Himalayas will influence your being. These motives are woven together. But sometimes people place too much emphasis on having material things and money, and doing pleasurable activities, while snubbing the development of their being. Says Gawain, "You must first be who you really are, then do what you need to do, in order to have what you want" (p. 36). Concerning persuasive appeals, notice many are aimed at having and doing; but the ultimate persuasion, the truest transcendence, may be achieved in the realm of our being. Gawain's ideas add a little dimension to our discussion on motivation. A final author adds more dimension and complexity to our thinking about motivation.

Murray's Motivations

Henry Murray was a Harvard psychologist who published a groundbreaking work on personality and motivation in 1938. *Explorations in Personality* provides a description of what Murray called "psychogenic needs," which we will discuss below. Murray shows us how motivation is complex and contradictory. That is, each of us is moved by any number of different motive forces all the time, and we often have conflicting motives competing to rule our behavior. Perhaps this focus on conflicting needs came from Murray's own drama. When he was thirty years old and had been married for seven years, he met and fell in love with another woman, Christiana Morgan, but was conflicted because he did not want to leave his wife. Morgan was a big fan of Carl Jung's psychology, and after his wife's urging, Murray arranged to meet with Jung in Switzerland. Murray ended up getting analyzed by Jung and began studying Jung's works, which led Murray into a brilliant career in psychology. Murray experienced conflicting needs deeply, and it may have influenced his work.

Murray distinguished between psychogenic (internal psychological) needs and what he called "press" (external, environmental pressures). Oftentimes we are moved by both, and this he termed "thema," a combination of internal needs and external pressures. For example, let's say seventeen-year-old Dave is with his friends who are all drinking Mad Dog wine, and they tell Dave to try it by playfully chiding, "C'mon, you sissy." The peer pressure combines with Dave's internal need for friendships and to be liked, accepted, and such to produce the behavior. That is, motivation is an interaction between internal and external influences, or intrinsic and extrinsic rewards.

Murray's list of psychogenic needs complicates the picture of motivation, adding some necessary complexity to explaining why we do what we do. Murray developed eight different areas with different needs.

Murray's Map of Motivation: Psychogenic Needs

1. Actions associated with inanimate objects
   A. Conservance: the need to collect, repair, and preserve
   B. Order: the need to arrange, organize, classify, tidy, and clean
   C. Retention: the need to remain in possession of objects
   D. Construction: the need to build

2. Actions with respect to ambition, prestige, and accomplishment
   A. Superiority: the need to have power over things and people
   B. Achievement: the need to overcome obstacles
   C. Recognition: the need to excite praise from others
   D. Exhibition: the need to have attention on the self; to thrill

3. Defense of status and avoidance of humiliation
   A. Inviolacy: the need to preserve your good name; avoid criticism
   B. Infavoidance: the need to avoid failure, shame, and ridicule
   C. Defendance: the need to defend the self against blame; justify actions
   D. Counteraction: the need to proudly overcome defeat; defend honor

4. Actions with respect to human power exerted and resisted
   A. Dominance: the need to influence, control, dictate, and persuade
   B. Deference: the need to admire and willingly follow a superior other
   C. Similance: the need to empathize, imitate, and agree
   D. Autonomy: the need to resist influence and authority
   E. Contrariance: the need to act differently, be unique, and oppose

5. Sadomasochistic Dichotomy
   A. Regression: the need to be insulting, injuring, belittling, and blaming
   B. Abasement: the need to surrender, apologize, comply, and atone

6. Inhibition: the need to avoid blame, ostracism, and punishment by inhibiting antisocial and unconventional impulses

7. Affection Actions
   A. Affiliation: the need to form friendships, love, and be loved
   B. Rejection: the need to snub, ignore, exclude, and remain aloof
   C. Succorance: the need to seek aid, protection, and sympathy
   D. Sex: the need to form and enjoy erotic relationships
   E. Play: the need to laugh, amuse, relax, and avoid tension

8. Two complementary needs in all social life
   A. Cognizance: the need to explore, ask questions, look, listen, and inspect
   B. Exposition: the need to teach, demonstrate, relate facts, explain

Murray's map of motivation, or psychogenic needs, is remarkable for many reasons. He points to conflicting motives that each individual has to negotiate.

We may have a need for dominance, to be in control of relationships, but at the same time a need for deference, to relinquish control to others. We have the need for affiliation, to form friendships, but at the same time have a need for rejection, to keep other people away from us. If we think about it, we can see how these needs do get demonstrated in our day-to-day lives. We spend just as much, if not more, time ignoring people around us as we do socializing. Other models of motivation point to the need to belong but don't address these apparently opposite needs.

Murray also hits on some novel motives, those we don't see mentioned in other models. For instance, the need for regression—to be insulting, injuring, belittling, and blaming—shows a somewhat saucier side of people. It points to the darker half of human motivation, but again we need only look around to confirm its existence. We see this type of behavior in friend and foe alike.

Motivation is complex and our needs are often contradictory. Sometimes it's difficult to act because we feel pulled in different directions. We may feel our internal needs in conflict with certain external pressures. For instance, we might wish to make new friends or achieve great things, but the pressures of existing relationships exert a binding influence. Our internal drives and needs are always being negotiated with the demands of relationships as our actions affect and are affected by others.

Motivation refers to the "why" of human behavior. We behave amid many pushes and pulls from various people. Different social systems are competing for our attention, membership, and money while they try to influence us by hitting the magic motivating keys. This brings us to personality and persuasion.

Creative Moment

Julia Cameron, in *The Artist's Way* (1992), looks at some of our habits as creative blocks, including fears, self-limiting beliefs, self-sabotage, jealousy, guilt, addictions, and too much attention to the news and media. We can get so engrossed in day-to-day blips of useless information and images that deeper thought gets sidelined. She also sees loss of faith as a creative block. In fact, faith, the spiritual side of creativity, is the basis of her work.

Cameron chooses to call it God, that primary spiritual force behind all creative endeavors. Shakti Gawain (1998) calls it "a higher intelligence, a fundamental creative power or energy in the universe that is the source and substance of all existence" (pp. 33–34), and she offers a few other names for it, shown in Table 6.1:

TABLE 6.1 Names for the Higher Intelligence

God	Spirit	Inner Guidance
Goddess	Essence	Higher Self
Higher Power	Being	The Universe
Source	Soul	Life Force
The Tao	The Force	Cosmic Intelligence
Buddha Nature	The Light	Christ Consciousness
Great Spirit	I Am	All That Is

No matter what the name, Gawain, Cameron, and many others have noted the ways in which our creative acts tap into and draw inspiration and energy from a grand creative source.

Inspiration is the operative word. From where do we draw creative inspiration? What is the primary mover behind creating and perfecting a project? The motivation could be for a job, for a degree, or for your continuing self-actualization. Whatever the motive force, creative acts spring from some inspirational source and are directed toward meaningful ends. Those ends are often foreseen in the creative process through visualization, and that which is visualized acts as inspiration.

Exercise

Motivation has much to do with goal-directed behavior. Zig Ziglar had a lot of good things to say about setting and reaching goals. Whether you are trying to finish a project, or lose some weight, or change your life, his plan can help. Think of a goal you have, something you wish to achieve, then fill in the following:

1. State the goal.
2. Set a deadline.
3. Identify the obstacles.
4. Identify the people, groups, and organizations that can assist you.
5. List the benefits of achieving the goal.
6. List the skills you will need to acquire to attain the goal.
7. Develop a plan.

Chapter 7

IT Stock/Polka Dot/Thinkstock

Personality

"Know thyself."

—*Socrates*

What is the nature of a person and to what extent does nurturance influence it? Is there a true nature or core personality to a person? These questions and others are part of the mystery of personality.

Everything we've discussed to this point ties to personality. Interaction in social systems, the drama you act in, shapes the self. Mind and brain play into personality, from the ways you make sense to the ways your brain connects constellations of thoughts. Memory, attitude, and perception provide the maps to navigate the thoughts and actions that define you. When we discussed mind with models by Mead, Jung, and Freud, we were also skirting the notion of self. Mead's model gave us the internal conversation between "I" and "me," the unique and idiosyncratic part and the generalized other or social collective inside of mind. The individualized "I" and the self-conscious "me" are integral parts of our sense of self—one the view from the inside and the other our pooled guess at what others think. Freud's structural model of the psyche provides concepts with explanatory value in understanding self and consciousness. Jung's ideas teach us that our conscious self is always influenced by symbolic action simmering in the unconscious. And, of course, people are more or less motivated. Whatever that spark is that makes us conscious is also in the energy that animates self.

The term personality evolved from the Greek *persona*, which means mask. Each of us enters, plays many roles, and then exits. Personality is somewhere amid those roles. This does not mean that one's personality is false or less than real. It just means we do play different roles, and those roles change as we cross social system boundaries.

Your personality is *who you are*. It's the sum total of your person, of how you mind the world and act in it—thinking and doing, cognitions and behaviors. Personality is related to patterns in your thoughts and actions, your typical or habitual ways of thinking and doing, but also related to the *context*, including the current situation and social relations. The social systems you stir in are very much a part of that context.

Personality is cognitive, behavioral, and environmental. It is a product of thinking and doing and mixing in different groups, surrounded by the "scene" in so many ways: the situation and the scene of your friendships, family, work, play, inner life, and outward connections. Our personality happens as we go about the business of living. We can talk of personality from an array of approaches and at differing levels. We can ponder the general factors that comprise personality—the key dimensions or influences that define it. Many before us, from psychologists to musicians, have considered ways to cut it up.

> But at night, when all the world's asleep
>
> The questions run so deep
>
> For such a simple man
>
> Won't you please, please tell me what we've learned
>
> I know it sounds absurd
>
> But please tell me who I am
>
> Who I am . . .
>
> —Supertramp, "The Logical Song"

Factors of Personality

The mid to late twentieth century was marked by an all-out search for factors in the social sciences. Factors are kind of like the essence of phenomena. Perhaps it was a fascination with statistical methods, or maybe it was innovations in computer technology that allowed for quicker computations and manipulations of large data sets. For whatever reasons, social scientists got really excited about finding factors and tried to distill the essence of "personality" and other constructs of interest through various forms of factor analysis. Using "Occam's razor" as a guide—that you should try to find the simplest and most elegant explanation of a phenomenon—researchers attempted to reduce each domain (such as personality) down to as few factors as possible. A "two-factor solution" would be considered elegant, parsimonious, and downright cool.

The search for personality's factors began with Gordon Allport and H. S. Odbert's work in 1936, when they checked dictionaries of the English language for words related to personality characteristics. They found eighteen thousand relevant words, and later reduced the list to forty-five hundred adjectives that describe observable personality traits. Those words were the starting point for Raymond Cattell's work. Cattell was a psychologist who felt right at home with factor analysis. He was, in fact, one of the twentieth century's biggest proponents of factor analytic methods and a highly productive researcher and author. Cattell boiled Allport's list down to its essence, resulting in the following sixteen factors. He called the factors "source traits" because he considered them the underlying source for the surface behaviors that constitute personality. In Table 7.1 the factor is provided in the middle of the two ends of a continuum. Perhaps you can see aspects of yourself and others in the different categories:

Table 7.1 Primary Factors and Descriptors in Cattell's 16 Personality Factor Model

Descriptors of Low Range	Primary Factor	Descriptors of High Range
Impersonal, distant, cool, reserved, detached, formal, aloof (Schizothymia)	**Warmth**	Warm, outgoing, attentive to others, kindly, easy going, participating, likes people (Affectothymia)
Concrete thinking, lower general mental capacity, less intelligent, unable to handle abstract problems (Lower Scholastic Mental Capacity)	**Reasoning**	Abstract thinking, more intelligent, bright, higher general mental capacity, fast learner (Higher Scholastic Mental Capacity)
Reactive emotionally, changeable, affected by feelings, emotionally less stable, easily upset (Lower Ego Strength)	**Emotional Stability**	Emotionally stable, adaptive, mature, faces reality calmly (Higher Ego Strength)
Deferential, cooperative, avoids conflict, submissive, humble, obedient, easily led, docile, accommodating (Submissiveness)	**Dominance**	Dominant, forceful, assertive, aggressive, competitive, stubborn, bossy (Dominance)
Serious, restrained, prudent, taciturn, introspective, silent (Desurgency)	**Liveliness**	Lively, animated, spontaneous, enthusiastic, happy go lucky, cheerful, expressive, impulsive (Surgency)
Expedient, nonconforming, disregards rules, self-indulgent (Low Super Ego Strength)	**Rule-Consciousness**	Rule conscious, dutiful, conscientious, conforming, moralistic, staid, rule bound (High Super Ego Strength)
Shy, threat sensitive, timid, hesitant, intimidated (Threctia)	**Social Boldness**	Socially bold, venturesome, thick skinned, uninhibited (Parmia)
Utilitarian, objective, unsentimental, tough minded, self-reliant, no-nonsense, rough (Harria)	**Sensitivity**	Sensitive, aesthetic, sentimental, tender minded, intuitive, refined (Premsia)

(continued)

Table 7.1 Primary Factors and Descriptors in Cattell's 16 Personality Factor Model *(continued)*

Descriptors of Low Range	Primary Factor	Descriptors of High Range
Trusting, unsuspecting, accepting, unconditional, easy (Alaxia)	**Vigilance**	Vigilant, suspicious, skeptical, distrustful, oppositional (Protension)
Grounded, practical, prosaic, solution oriented, steady, conventional (Praxernia)	**Abstractedness**	Abstract, imaginative, absent minded, impractical, absorbed in ideas (Autia)
Forthright, genuine, artless, open, guileless, I, unpretentious, involved (Artlessness)	**Privateness**	Private, discreet, nondisclosing, shrewd, polished, worldly, astute, diplomatic (Shrewdness)
Self-assured, unworried, complacent, secure, free of guilt, confident, self-satisfied (Untroubled)	**Apprehension**	Apprehensive, self-doubting, worried, guilt prone, insecure, worrying, self-blaming (Guilt Proneness)
Traditional, attached to familiar, conservative, respecting traditional ideas (Conservatism)	**Openness to Change**	Open to change, experimental, liberal, analytical, critical, free thinking, flexibility (Radicalism)
Group-oriented, affiliative, a joiner and follower, dependent (Group Adherence)	**Self-Reliance**	Self-reliant, solitary, resourceful, individualistic, self-sufficient (Self-Sufficiency)
Tolerates disorder, unexacting, flexible, undisciplined, lax, self-conflict, impulsive, careless of social rules, uncontrolled (Low Integration)	**Perfectionism** (psychology)	Perfectionistic, organized, compulsive, self-disciplined, socially precise, exacting will power, control, self-sentimental (High Self-Concept Control)
Relaxed, placid, tranquil, torpid, patient, composed low drive (Low Ergic Tension)	**Tension**	Tense, high energy, impatient, driven, frustrated, over wrought, time driven (High Ergic Tension)

Source: Adapted from Conn & Rieke, 1994.

Meyers Friedman (1974) thought he had an elegant solution in formulating the Type A and Type B personalities. The type A behavior pattern is seen in people who are highly competitive, hostile and aggressive, impatient, time-conscious to a fault, incapable of relaxation, and insecure about status. Type A people are often characterized as workaholics and "stress junkies." Type B personality types are more patient, relaxed, easy-going, and less competitive. There is also a type AB mixed personality profile for people who show a little of both. Friedman and associates theorized that type A personalities were more prone to heart attacks, but research points to only hostility as a risk factor more than the other type A components. This theory of types A/B is sometimes criticized for oversimplifying personality.

The quest for the factor structure ultimately turned up five dimensions of personality that are generally agreed upon, confirmed by Lewis Goldberg (1981). Goldberg collapses the original sixteen into the Big Five factors of personality, and they are openness to experience, conscientiousness, extraversion, agreeableness, and neuroticism. Some use the acronym OCEAN to remember the Big Five. Each factor expands into a number of personality traits, and each can be considered a continuum, so people tend to act within a range from agreeable to disagreeable, conscientious to unconscientious, extravert to introvert, neurotic to emotionally stable, and open versus closed to experience. These only point to general tendencies in a person's patterns of behavior, not to how a person is all the time. Let's look at each a bit closer.

Agreeable people are friendly, helpful, and generous. They value getting along with others and tend to have an optimistic outlook on human nature, believing people are honest, decent, and trustworthy. Agreeable people are easier to like than their counterparts. Disagreeable people are more self-interested and less concerned with getting along. They care less about helping others and hold a more negative view toward human nature. They tend to be unfriendly, uncooperative, and suspicious of others' motives. Agreeable people are more likely to gain success through social networks, but there are situations, careers, and groups better suited to disagreeable personalities. Some people are highly successful, for instance, in playing a curmudgeon on the social scene, so there is hope for those on either end of this continuum.

Conscientious people keep their impulses in check. In Freud's terms, their superego overpowers their id. Conscientious individuals tend to avoid trouble, especially disapproval from others, and often achieve success through planning and persistence. They also tend to have a high need for achievement. When this tendency is carried to compulsive levels they can be perfectionists and workaholics, at times resulting in excessive stress. Unconscientious people tend to be less ambitious, less reliable, and more into short-term pleasures. In Freud's perspective, the id has control of the reins. While such individuals can be difficult to trust, they can also be unpredictable, fun, and colorful.

Extroverts are highly engaged with the external world, seeking stimulation outside of themselves. They often experience positive emotions, have high energy, and enjoy being with people. Extroverts tend to be enthusiastic and are more likely to talk, assert themselves, and draw attention to themselves. Introversion is more of a focus inward, quiet, reflective. Introverts are not as talkative and show less enthusiasm, energy, and social activity. They can come off as thoughtful, reserved, and less dependent on others.

Neuroticism refers to the tendency to experience negative emotions, such as anger, depression, and anxiety. Neurotics are emotionally reactive—they tend to react emotionally to events that might not faze other people—and their reactions can be intense. They are more likely to interpret ordinary situations as threatening, and they are apt to treat minor frustrations as big events. Their emotional states can persist for long periods of time, so they may be perceived as in a bad mood or brooding. That challenge in regulating emotions can hurt a neurotic's ability to think clearly, make decisions, and cope with stress. Individuals at the other end of this continuum tend to be emotionally stable and less easily upset. They are calm, do not dwell on negative feelings, and tend to be more relaxed. On the plus side for neurotics, their negative emotions can be a creative springboard, as some artists, musicians, and performers will attest.

Got to pay your dues if you want to sing the blues.

And you know it don't come easy.

—George Harrison

The final factor of the Big Five is openness to experience, which describes people who are creative, intellectually curious, appreciative of art, and sensitive to beauty. They are cognizant of their environment, aware of opportunities to stimulate the senses. Open individuals tend to be more unconventional and individualistic in their beliefs and have complex interests. People who are closed to experience hold narrow and common interests. They gravitate toward plain, straightforward, and unambiguous experiences, and may regard the arts with suspicion, seeing them as having no practical use. Closed personalities prefer familiarity to novelty and tend to be conservative and resist change. Research has shown that people do tend to change across their lifetime, typically becoming less open and preferring stability with age.

The search for personality's underlying factor structure continues in some quarters, but not with the zeal of early pioneers. The factors are apparent in other views of personality, from Jung to Leary and beyond.

Myers-Briggs Personality Types

One of the most popular personality measures is the Myers-Briggs Type Indicator. It was developed by Isabel Briggs Myers and her mother Katherine Briggs, applying the theory of psychological types described by Carl Jung. The types are based on differences in people's perceptions and judgment, the way you take information in and the way you think about it. Those two are further divided into eight preferences. Myers-Briggs uses the term *preferences* to indicate that our personality is not always on one side of a continuum, but tends to be. The preferences are as follows:

Extraversion (E) or introversion (I): Are you more focused on the outer world or on your own inner world?

Sensing (S) or intuition (N): Do you accept the information you take in as it is or do you prefer to interpret and add meaning?

Thinking (T) or feeling (F): Do you tend to be more logical and consistent or considerate of people and special circumstances?

Judging (J) or perceiving (P): Do you prefer to get things decided or would you rather remain open to new information and options?

Those eight preferences can be arranged in different combinations to make the sixteen personality types. Below are some quick sketches of each of the types found on the Myers & Briggs Foundation website:

Meyers-Briggs Personality Types

ISTJ (Introvert-Sensing-Thinking-Judging)
Quiet, serious, earn success by thoroughness and dependability. Practical, matter-of-fact, and responsible. Decide logically what should be done and work toward it steadily, regardless of distractions. Take pleasure in making everything orderly and organized—their work, their home, their life. Value traditions and loyalty.

ISFJ (Introvert-Sensing-Feeling-Judging)
Quiet, friendly, responsible, and conscientious. Committed and steady in meeting their obligations. Thorough, painstaking, and accurate. Loyal, considerate, notice and remember specifics about people who are important to them, concerned with how others feel. Strive to create an orderly and harmonious environment at work and at home.

INFJ (Introvert-Intuitive-Feeling-Judging)
Seek meaning and connection in ideas, relationships, and material possessions. Want to understand what motivates people and are insightful about others. Conscientious and committed to their firm values. Develop a clear vision about how best to serve the common good. Organized and decisive in implementing their vision.

INTJ (Introvert-Intuitive-Thinking-Judging)
Have original minds and great drive for implementing their ideas and achieving their goals. Quickly see patterns in external events and develop long-range explanatory perspectives. When committed, organize a job and carry it through. Skeptical and independent, have high standards of competence and performance—for themselves and others.

(continued)

Meyers-Briggs Personality Types (continued)

ISTP (Introvert-Sensing-Thinking-Perceiving)
Tolerant and flexible, quiet observers until a problem appears, then act quickly to find workable solutions. Analyze what makes things work and readily get through large amounts of data to isolate the core of practical problems. Interested in cause and effect, organize facts using logical principles, value efficiency.

ISFP (Introvert-Sensing-Feeling-Perceiving)
Quiet, friendly, sensitive, and kind. Enjoy the present moment, what's going on around them. Like to have their own space and to work within their own time frame. Loyal and committed to their values and to people who are important to them. Dislike disagreements and conflicts, do not force their opinions or values on others.

INFP (Introvert-Intuitive-Feeling-Perceiving)
Idealistic, loyal to their values and to people who are important to them. Want an external life that is congruent with their values. Curious, quick to see possibilities, can be catalysts for implementing ideas. Seek to understand people and to help them fulfill their potential. Adaptable, flexible, and accepting unless a value is threatened.

INTP (Introvert-Intuitive-Thinking-Perceiving)
Seek to develop logical explanations for everything that interests them. Theoretical and abstract, interested more in ideas than in social interaction. Quiet, contained, flexible, and adaptable. Have unusual ability to focus in depth to solve problems in their area of interest. Skeptical, sometimes critical, always analytical.

ESTP (Extrovert-Sensing-Thinking-Perceiving)
Flexible and tolerant, they take a pragmatic approach focused on immediate results. Theories and conceptual explanations bore them—they want to act energetically to solve the problem. Focus on the here-and-now, spontaneous, enjoy each moment that they can be active with others. Enjoy material comforts and style. Learn best through doing.

ESFP (Extrovert-Sensing-Feeling-Perceiving)
Outgoing, friendly, and accepting. Exuberant lovers of life, people, and material comforts. Enjoy working with others to make things happen. Bring common sense and a realistic approach to their work, and make work fun. Flexible and spontaneous, adapt readily to new people and environments. Learn best by trying a new skill with other people.

ENFP (Extrovert-Intuitive-Feeling-Perceiving)
Warmly enthusiastic and imaginative. See life as full of possibilities. Make connections between events and information very quickly, and confidently proceed based on the patterns they see. Want a lot of affirmation from others, and readily give appreciation and support. Spontaneous and flexible, often rely on their ability to improvise and their verbal fluency.

ENTP (Extrovert-Intuitive-Thinking-Perceiving)
Quick, ingenious, stimulating, alert, and outspoken. Resourceful in solving new and challenging problems. Adept at generating conceptual possibilities and then analyzing them strategically. Good at reading other people. Bored by routine, will seldom do the same thing the same way, apt to turn to one new interest after another.

ESTJ (Extrovert-Sensing-Thinking-Judging)
Practical, realistic, matter-of-fact. Decisive, quickly move to implement decisions. Organize projects and people to get things done, focus on getting results in the most efficient way possible. Take care of routine details. Have a clear set of logical standards, systematically follow them and want others to also. Forceful in implementing their plans.

(continued)

> **Meyers-Briggs Personality Types** *(continued)*
>
> ### ESFJ *(Extrovert-Sensing-Feeling-Judging)*
> Warmhearted, conscientious, and cooperative. Want harmony in their environment, work with determination to establish it. Like to work with others to complete tasks accurately and on time. Loyal, follow through even in small matters. Notice what others need in their day-by-day lives and try to provide it. Want to be appreciated for who they are and for what they contribute.
>
> ### ENFJ *(Extrovert-Intuitive-Feeling-Judging)*
> Warm, empathetic, responsive, and responsible. Highly attuned to the emotions, needs, and motivations of others. Find potential in everyone, want to help others fulfill their potential. May act as catalyst for individual and group growth. Loyal, responsive to praise and criticism. Sociable, facilitate others in a group, and provide inspiring leadership.
>
> ### ENTJ *(Extrovert-Intuitive-Thinking-Judging)*
> Frank, decisive, assume leadership readily. Quickly see illogical and inefficient procedures and policies, develop and implement comprehensive systems to solve organizational problems. Enjoy long-term planning and goal setting. Usually well informed, well read, enjoy expanding their knowledge and passing it on to others. Forceful in presenting their ideas.

Keep in mind that those characteristics are tendencies that cluster together in personality types. They don't necessarily reflect the way a person always is. You might notice bits of yourself in different types, but there should be a primary and secondary type that defines your typical patterns of thought and behavior.

David Keirsey revised the Myers-Briggs types and developed a personality map of sixteen temperaments. He created the Keirsey Temperament Sorter and then the Keirsey Temperament Sorter II (1998), an instrument that allows people to identify their types. Some people swear by these personality types, while others treat them as something akin to astrology. If finding your type helps you make it through the night, then more power to you.

One problem with the Myers-Briggs Type Indicator and the Keirsey instrument is that they are self-reporting; you fill them out yourself. That may be fine if you know yourself well, but many people don't. There's a good chance that a close friend or loved one might indicate different choices about your temperament or personality preferences. Assessment of our personality might be different coming from our inner view or the external view of our acquaintances. Another problem with naming types (or temperaments or tendencies) is that doing so usually doesn't account for the influence of others on our personality. Is personality something an individual has, or is it more a phenomenon that arises in social interaction? That is, is it more intrapsychic or interpersonal?

Interpersonal Personality

We can consider personality as "interpersonality." From this perspective we see that our self is shaped through various social relationships across a lifetime, and personality unfolds in our current relationships.

Considering human existence as relational, early pioneers like Martin Buber (1937) and Harry Stack Sullivan (1953) were followed by Kenneth Gergen (2009) and many others. Buber (1970, p. 69) said, "In the beginning is the relation," and he based much of his philosophy on the premise that all action plays out with humans inseparably *in relation to* natural, human, and spiritual realms. We are born, socialized, and exist in relation to others. Buber distinguishes between I–Thou and I–It patterns of interaction, where I–Thou respects and encourages the humanness in individual souls while I–It objectifies and demeans the other. Are we in the here and now, truly listening to and caring about that other person? Or is that person just a hindrance in our busy schedule, an object with which we are dealing and attribute no degree of personhood? Buber introduces us to the critical importance of a relational dimension.

Personalities take shape and are expressed in relation to others—interpersonality. Ingram Publishing/Thinkstock

Gergen discusses a relational consciousness, noting that "it is through coordinated action—not individual minds—that meaning originates ... On closer inspection, we find that virtually all faculties traditionally attributed to the internal world of the agent—reason, emotion, motivation, memory, experience, and the like—are essentially performances within relationship (2009, p. 397)." All systems, social and otherwise, are built upon relationship and interaction. As a seed pushes through the soil searching for the sun, the magic is in the relationship; likewise, social networks come to life in the ties that bind.

Harry Stack Sullivan preferred to understand an individual's personality as interpersonal, related to a network of relationships. Relationship is primary to personality, both in the formation of self and in the observable traits that arise in social interaction. Sullivan conceived the self as a system of personality traits developed early that are reinforced in social interactions. A person's social systems, from parents to peers and teachers and preachers, are integral in the development and maintenance of personality. Personality is interdependent with and emerges from the interactions with various others across social systems. You might be a different person at home than you are at work or at school, depending on your interpersonal relationships.

What we do, according to Sullivan, is meant to elicit responses from others—our action is often directed at eliciting a reaction—so our personality is coupled with and dependent on others. These "I–You interlocking behaviors," as Sullivan called them, borrowing from the perspective of Martin Buber, sometimes become interactional habits. Interpersonal and group action-reaction combinations can become habituated. Codependent behaviors, where people become overly enmeshed and needy in relationships, are a good example of such habitual integration. Codependency takes the normal tendency to situate the self in relationships to an extreme, where one becomes overly dependent on another to be complete. Likewise, patterns of conflict between people can become habits. Conflict emerges as an interaction between persons or groups, and if someone changes that interpersonal or group context, brings different actors on stage, the conflict might not arise. For instance, you may know a person you tend to conflict with, but that same person gets along fine with another. The conflict is not so much in the individuals as in the relationship.

Personality is partly dependent on other people in our drama, and again we can see some of those dramatic elements as front stage and back stage. On the front stage we see the person acting in day-to-day contexts, while in the back stage lurks those aspects of a person we don't see. Much like the story of Jekyll and Hyde, we see a duality in human nature, which leads us to wonder about the true nature: As our personalities emerge in interaction, are they the "true self"? Is there a true self?

Gustav Ichheiser (1941) discussed true self, the appearances and realities of personality. He argued we tend to overestimate the unity of personality, assuming a person has a certain central character as opposed to the multiple characters that can be seen across different situations. He claimed behavior is always dependent on personal and situational factors, and the situation includes social opportunities and barriers, relationships to and expectations of others, status, and other variables. He proposed we classify personality characteristics as real, pseudo, or sham. *Real* characteristics belong to the individual independently of the situation and other people; they are inherent qualities like ability, knowledge, and biological givens such as brain function and body type. *Pseudo* characteristics are related to a person's situation, such as money, position, and social status. These characteristics are "borrowed," said Ichheiser. They do not belong to the individual and can be taken away. If one has the luck to be born into a rich family, wears nice clothes, and drives an expensive car, that will affect the image others hold of the person; but those assets are not a part of the real personality. *Sham* characteristics are those that are attributed to the individual by others, but the person does not actually possess them; they are wholly a product of perception. In the movie *Being There*, starring Peter Sellers as Chauncey Gardner, we see how the people surrounding him attribute all kinds of qualities to Chauncey that he does not possess. What's interesting is that these sham and pseudo characteristics can actually play into the real personality, as one's situation and upbringing influences what is learned; and, if people attribute qualities to us, that can affect what and where we *really* get in life.

What Is Personality?

Weaving the above threads together we find personality to be one part cognitive, one part behavioral, one part relational, and one part contextual. Cognitively, it is partly dependent on the constellations of neural circuits that make up our memories and attitudes, and guide perceptions. Behaviorally, personality is partially the learned patterns of action that become habits, regardless of whether they are deterministically conditioned or a product of social learning choices. We sometimes behave in ways that are not cognitively logical and act counter to our professed attitudes, so we can separate cognitive and behavioral facets of personality. Relationally, personality develops through interactions with others and becomes manifest in present interactions. You may be perceived as a different person in the company of different others and you may actually feel like a different person in different company; it depends on the relationships. Finally, personality is contextual, depending on one's scene and situation.

Persuaders, hidden and not-so-hidden, are attempting to "read" your personality and deliver the symbols, associations, and meanings that fit best with who you are. That is a central concern for market researchers who are trying to understand their target audience. They will often develop a profile of their target market's demographics (measurable characteristics like age, gender, education, and income level) and psychographics or lifestyle indicators (attitudes, opinions, aspirations, needs, wants, desires, fears, anxieties, a yearning for learning, and how you spend your time). Personality is part of the psychographic considerations. Understanding how your own personality opens you to certain persuasive appeals will help you understand personality and persuasion in general. Socrates' advice to "know thyself" helps you to understand others.

Creative Moment

Who are you? Let's do a checkup from the neck up. First, go through the Big Five, OCEAN, and consider where you tend to be on the continuums that make up those personality aspects. Are you . . .

Open or Closed to Experience?

Conscientious or Unconscientious?

Extroverted or Introverted?

Agreeable or Disagreeable?

Neurotic or Emotionally Stable?

Next, go online and take a Jung Typology Test. This will give you a 4-letter indicator of your personality type. Do the results fit well with the sketch of your personality from the OCEAN variables above?

Finally, do you think your personality characteristics change at all as you move from one social system to another—from family to friends, or from friends to the workplace, for instance?

Chapter 8

Design Pics/Thinkstock

Who Moves You?
Persuasion

"The most important persuasion tool you have in your entire arsenal is integrity."

—*Zig Ziglar*

Persuasive action is woven throughout our human social systems, from the advertisement inducing you to buy that car to your friends asking you to go out tonight. The process of self-persuasion is likely alive and well within you right now, as you decide about future paths, purchases, and parties with which to affiliate. Let's review a short history of persuasion through the noble practice of rhetoric, and then look at contemporary models like ideas on identification, advertising, and the postmodern condition.

The History of Rhetoric in Five Minutes

The study and practice of persuasion has a long and somewhat glorious past. The history of persuasion is really the history of rhetoric. Though the term *rhetoric* has fallen on hard times these days, usually used to mean "empty words" or people using language to camouflage the truth, the word has a richer history than its current usage would suggest. Essentially, rhetoric refers to the art of persuasion.

The serious study of rhetoric as a discipline was begun about 465 B.C.E. in Syracuse, a Greek colony on the island of Sicily. A tyrannical ruler had been overthrown, a rough form of democracy was established, land was redistributed to the people, and they went to the courts to argue property claims. The Greek legal system required citizens to argue themselves, no lawyers allowed. Corax of Syracuse began teaching people how to speak and argue persuasively. He wrote a treatise, the "Art of Rhetoric," in which he organized persuasive speaking into three domains: introduction, argument of proof, and conclusion. Corax claimed that all arguments deal with probabilities, not certainties or absolute truths.

Meanwhile, up in Abdera, a coastal town in ancient Greece, Protagoras was a philosopher who claimed virtue could be taught. He is credited as having been one of the first Sophists. The root of the word *Sophos* means knowledge or wisdom, and Sophist originally referred to a teacher of wisdom or virtue. Protagoras said, "Man is the measure of all things: of things which are, that they are, and of things which are not, that they are not." This statement seems to say truth is relevant, that it depends on the interpreter. Protagoras was also an early champion of agnosticism, claiming, "Concerning the gods, I have no means of knowing whether they exist or not or of what sort they may be, because of the obscurity of the subject, and the brevity of human life." So here was this godless philosopher saying there is no truth beyond human interpretation. Some Athenians were more than mildly upset by his radical ideas.

Tisias, a student of Corax, brought the Sophistic model of teaching rhetoric to the Greek mainland. When Tisias went to Greece claiming to teach wisdom and the arts of eloquence and argument, he was not met with enthusiasm. Most Greek teachers at the time did not believe wisdom was teachable and thought persuasive speaking, or rhetoric, was less than a true art. The Athenians did not think highly of these foreigners claiming to teach wisdom for a fee.

Plato, one of the world's great philosophers, a wealthy Athenian, student of Socrates, and teacher of Aristotle, got the Academy up and running (or at least walking—they were peripatetic) in Athens. Socrates, Plato, and Aristotle are three philosophers credited with laying much of the foundation for Western thought, so it is very likely that you have "a piece of their minds" operating in your mind. Plato had an ongoing argument with the Sophists about the nature of truth and the role of rhetoric. He equated rhetoric to flattery or cookery, not a true art. Dialectic, the quest for truth by arguing propositions and counterpropositions, was the truer art and pathway to truth according to Plato. Rhetoric was seen as merely a tool for disseminating that truth once discovered. For Plato, the persuasive process is mostly found in dialectic.

Aristotle, a scientific philosopher who loved to categorize and classify things, was the first to systematize the study of rhetoric. His treatise, the *Rhetoric*, was a seminal work that influenced the study of rhetoric through the ages to this day. Aristotle seemed to grant rhetoric more dignity than Plato, saying that it was one of the three key ingredients to philosophy along with logic and dialectic. According to Aristotle, rhetoric is "the ability, in each particular case, to see the available means of persuasion," and those means of persuasion are many. He described three main modes of rhetoric: ethos, pathos, and logos. *Ethos* is a persuasive appeal based on the character or credibility of the speaker. For instance, if you believed Barack Obama's analysis of a political situation because he was president and you trusted him and liked him, then his ethos played into positive persuasiveness. *Pathos* is an appeal to the emotions. When DeBeers, the diamond company, tells you to spend three months' salary on your engagement ring, they depend on pathos and the blindness of your love to drive the decision. *Logos* is a logical appeal. When a scientist attempts to persuade you that global warming is occurring due to greenhouse gasses by presenting numbers and facts, the arguments are based upon logos.

With the decline of Greece and the rise of Rome, many notable Roman rhetoricians, such as Cicero and Marcus Fabius Quintilian, added to the teaching of persuasion. Cicero was a great orator, successful lawyer, and politician remembered for his exquisite letter writing, humanistic philosophy, and popular leadership after the assassination of Julius Caesar in 44 B.C.E. Cicero also taught the canons (or five main areas) of rhetoric: invention, style, arrangement, delivery, and memory. Quintilian wrote *Institutio Oratoria*, which, coupled with Aristotle's *Rhetoric* and Cicero's works, was one of the main rhetorical texts throughout the next millennium. With the decline of Rome around 470 C.E., the study of rhetoric declined as well. Rhetoric rebounded in the middle Ages, when it was taught as one of the seven liberal arts, which included the *trivium* (grammar, rhetoric, and logic) and *quadrivium* (arithmetic, geometry, astronomy, and music). Teaching and learning rhetoric cycled through many different emphases, focusing on human knowledge, beauty, writing, speaking, and scientifically systematizing gestures—all taught along with the writings of Aristotle and others.

The study of argumentation has been an important area of rhetorical theory through the ages. From Aristotle to Stephen Toulmin, scholars have studied the strategies and tactics for debaters. Most of them have focused on the fair uses of rhetorical tools such as syllogisms, enthymemes, and ethical logical reasoning. They teach how to play by the rules. But people don't always play by the rules in argument. In fact, we often see politicians and others resorting to logical fallacies—unfair reasoning that leads to faulty conclusions. Arthur Schopenhauer (1788–1860) presented ways to win in argumentation—stratagems to gain advantage over opponents in arguments. In *The Pessimist's Handbook*, he presented logical fallacies as tools in what he calls "controversial dialectic"—the art of holding your own in a dispute. Most of these are based on logical fallacies, usually considered to be unfair in argument. But you can probably think of many instances when you see or hear them used in debate and conflict. They are provided here for your critical bag of tricks, so that you can recognize them when used in politics, friendly arguments, and other modes of persuasion.

Schopenhauer's Stratagems

1. Diversion: Admit opponent's proposition is true and then show opposing propositions to be also true. "Yes, that's true that hydraulic fracturing has caused some leakage into ground water, but it is also true that the practice has been around for over fifty years and the impact on groundwater has been limited."

2. Instance: Give examples where the opponent's claim does not apply. "If the theory of evolution holds true, why aren't there examples of animals in between apes and humans still around today?"
3. Extension: Exaggerate opponent's position then attack it as absurd. "Your position asks for a redistribution of wealth from the rich to the poor through taxation. That's the same as communists of the past, and just like Stalin's cruel experiment, your ideas won't work now."
4. Overgeneralizing: Make the specific appear general then attack the general issue. "He was caught with a pound of marijuana, which is a gateway drug to heroin and meth, and if we don't put him behind bars for a long time he will be pushing those other drugs on our children."
5. Begging the question: Claiming as true what has yet to be proven. "Ladies and gentlemen of the jury, the prosecution will show that this murderous, scheming, psychopathic individual did indeed kill ten people on the night of November seventh."
6. Anger your opponent: Usually the person who shows negative emotions such as anger in an argument will be perceived less favorably than the person who maintains composure. Oftentimes, debaters will attempt to anger their opponent to throw them off their game.
7. Choose phrases favorable to your position: Some people opposed President Barack Obama's signature health plan. When CNN conducted a poll to measure opposition, the way the health care act was named made a difference. Forty-six percent of those polled opposed "Obamacare" and only thirty-seven percent opposed "The Affordable Care Act," even though they refer to the same thing.
8. *Ex concesis*: Show how opponent's arguments are inconsistent with their own beliefs or claims. "Wait a minute—you say you're a conservative and yet what you are proposing represents a radical change from the status quo—that's not a conservative move."
9. *Mutatio controversiae*: If you observe opponent has an argument that will defeat you, disrupt it or derail to another topic. Changing the topic is always a helpful tactic for those losing an argument.
10. *Ad hominem*: Attack the character of the person, not the issue/argument. "I'd like to believe John's reasoning, but he's been convicted of tax fraud so can he really be trusted?"
11. Appeal to authority rather than reason: "Your argument is based on the ideas of liberal professors; mine comes from God. Who do you think I'm going to believe?"
12. Jargon: If opponent uses technical jargon, declare yourself naïve and infer that he or she is a detached pompous ass. "That's great that you call it *"postmodernity"*—but where I come from in Yazoo City we call it liberal B.S.—and that's what you are feeding us."
13. Categorize opponent's assertions in unfavorable ways: "Okay, if you're arguing for evolution, and the Bible argues for creation, then essentially you are in cahoots with the devil."
14. Claim ideas are OK in theory but not in practice: "Well, yes, that looks good on paper to give the poor food stamps or access cards, but every time we have done that in the past they have abused the system."
15. Puzzle opponent with sheer bombast: This is an especially useful tactic to those who are at a loss for words in an argument. They will begin spewing unrelated facts and fantasy themes until they can get traction with a relevant topic or plan of attack.
16. If opponent is right, but has one faulty proof, refute that proof and claim victory: "You say charter schools are a more economical solution. But charters are draining resources from public education, in fact decimating the economy of our public school systems."

These are just a few of the tactics or stratagems suggested. There are more, just as there are plenty of other logical fallacies that people use often in their arguments and day-to-day reasoning. Schopenhauer notes the *appearance* of victory in argument is important and offers the use of these fallacies in order to manufacture the appearance of victory. Again, if we are to be thinking critically about persuasion, we must be aware that people are using faulty logic in their thinking and their arguments—be aware of the tricks people use in their rhetoric. It is no wonder rhetoric has been given such a bad name.

Please understand that this brief history completely strips the topic to its barest bones, and I only provide it as a context for where we go from here. The history of rhetoric is woven into the history of the field of communication, and that history changed with Kenneth Burke's ideas on identification.

Persuasion and Identification

In the twentieth century Kenneth Burke began redefining and extending our knowledge of persuasion in human interaction. *Identification* is his term for understanding the keys to the persuasion process. Identification is about unifying, said Burke, because people are inherently divided. We are divided biologically (living in different skin), sexually (males are different than females), socially (by status, group, and other strata), and in so many other ways. We use symbols, mainly words, to come together. Interestingly, we also use symbols to separate ourselves, to name differences.

Burke defined rhetoric as "the use of words by human agents to form attitudes or induce actions in other human agents" (1969, p. 41), and considered three types of identification: (1) the process of naming something or someone according to specific properties; (2) the process of associating with or dissociating from others; and 3) the product or end result of identifying, the state of being "consubstantial" (of the same essence) with others. Identification refers to the process and product of feeling psychologically closer to people, and more, as we will soon see.

Identification begins with the assignment of terms to things, applying symbols to referents, naming things. People form agreements in the process of naming. That we both agree that that feline animal over there can be named "cat" is a simple form of identification. We can go on to name properties of the cat like sleek, stealthy, hunter, haunting, and other words, and that too is identification. This aspect of communication, or coming to communion, becomes tricky when we can't agree on how a thing will be identified. For instance, shall we name those guerilla warriors in that third-world country "freedom fighters" or "terrorists"? That depends. And oftentimes it depends on your motives and whose persuasion you buy into. Shall we label that liberal politician as "wise" or "mistaken" or the "antichrist"? It depends on identification.

Identification is the process of associating and dissociating. Sometimes the two are related as we associate with some by dissociating from others, as in "my enemy's enemy is my friend." Burke referred to this as "congregation by segregation," and we see evidence of it all around. Politicians try to move close to you and get your vote by naming common enemies. Capitalists compare their goodness to the sins of

Identification means unifying, associating, minds coming together through symbolic interaction. Purestock/Thinkstock

socialism. Churchmen keep us on the course to good by naming the evil we stand against. Your friend gives you a little buzz of belongingness by gossiping about that other tragically mistaken person. People unify by naming their divisions with others—it's one of the oldest persuasive tricks in the book.

The process of identifying, unifying, coming together through symbolic interaction pervades the human drama. Many of us don't consider the persuasive forces working on our own mind. The process of persuasive identification is obviously at work in religious indoctrination or conversion. As we consider the hereafter and the proper course for the here, we look to identify with religions and people who share a like-mindedness. Persuasive identification is also at work in school as students latch onto theories and concepts and belief systems in which they can believe. There's nothing more dangerous than a student who's just discovered some postmodern truth! Persuasive identification is at work at work, as well, as people try to sell products and ideas, impress the boss, and get coworkers on their side. From the bowling league to salespeople closing the deal, to the coalitions and cliques within every company, the world of work is brimming with identifications.

Identification is the persuasive process as the preacher asks you to pray with her; it's the teacher suggesting you understand the concept *in this way*; it's a teen searching for the magic keys to courtship; it's the salesperson connecting with your wants and needs; it's the girl playing with dolls, pretending to be mama; it's the boy cheering for his favorite football team; it's the feminist inviting you to see the bias in my last statements. *Identification is happening in any case where someone is associating with someone or something, or trying to synthesize minds through symbols.*

Many are trying to better understand the mysteries of identification. Advertisers are at the forefront of attempts to identify and control actions. Market and advertising research continues to work toward influencing consumer behavior. Some people view that negatively, as if advertisers are attempting unethical manipulation. Those critics would likely identify with Adbusters and other organizations critical of advertising. If you identify more with the need for corporate profits and pushing products, you likely view advertising through a friendlier lens. I was watching a television show with my daughter some time ago. The show was about a rich teen who attended an upscale boarding school, and many of her friends were into material things. A commercial came on showing two teen girls enjoying ecstatic friendship through their new cell phone's comparative shopping capabilities, showing them at one point joyfully shopping and trying clothes on. The TV show and the commercial relied on identification with young girls' need for belonging and desire for new things. Their minds came together around cell phones, shopping, and social needs.

Advertising and Identification

Advertising is one of the more visible and most effective forms of persuasion in our age. Ads are omnipresent, in the traditional media and elsewhere, and their influence may be growing. Advertisers want consumers to identify strongly with a product, service, or idea. Advertising was traditionally defined as *paid, one-way communication by a sponsor who controls the message content*. With the advent of the Internet, and later, web-based and social media advertising, much advertising communication is no longer one-way communication.

Advertising is created and placed with the purpose of getting people to behave in a specific manner, usually to buy a product, line of products, or service. Advertising is typically aimed at consumers, an important social system or target audience for marketers. Advertising is distinguished from yet related to public relations, which is two-way communication aimed at many different audiences, or publics, associated with the organization. Advertising, public relations, sales, and marketing now come together in the field of integrated marketing communication (IMC), which uses traditional and emerging marketing channels to build brands and increase sales.

Much advertising still sticks to the traditional formula for persuasive speaking outlined by Alan H. Monroe many years ago. In the 1930s he created the Monroe Motivated Sequence, taking the audience of persuasive messages through steps to try to get them to act. The steps are attention, need, satisfaction, visualization, and action.

1. *Attention*: Get the audience to attend to your message through visual or auditory stimulation, humor, shocking them, involving them in a story, or some novel approach. Stunningly beautiful models, celebrities, computer graphics, cool sound tracks, and other techniques are used to get your attention.
2. *Need*: Show how there is a need for your product or service. This is done by focusing on certain motivations, such as friendship, status, fun, money savings, sex, beauty, youth, and other needs or wants. Advertising often implies the need by showing you something better than what you have now. Sometimes a need is created by producing dissonance, a state of imbalance in the target's mind between the way things are and the way one wishes them to be. A return to psychological balance comes from buying the product or service.
3. *Satisfaction*: Show how the product or service satisfies the need. For instance, show people enjoying the benefits of using your product, such as done by before-and-after comparisons in weight loss ads, or a happy family enthralled by unlimited texting on their cell phones.
4. *Visualization*: The advertiser gets the audience to picture themselves enjoying the positive outcomes of purchasing the product, or picturing the negative outcomes that might occur if they don't. For instance, "if you buy this insurance for your family they will be safe and happy; if you don't buy it they may find themselves on the streets after your untimely death."
5. *Action*: This is where the advertiser provides specific instructions on how to act. "Go to the phone and call 1-800-555-2000"; "Visit our website at www . . ."; "Don't wait—the sale ends Sunday!"

There are many other formulae that apply to advertising, such as AIDA (Attention, Interest, Desire, Action); VIPS (Visibility, Identity, Promise, Simplicity); and FAB (Features, Advantages, Benefits). These may be helpful for putting together persuasive messages, whether you're selling a car, a candidate, or a chocolate bar.

Advertising is pervasive. Each one of us is targeted by thousands of ads per day, with an array of advertisers attempting to position their product in our minds and gain a "share of wallet." Positioning their product or service in our minds is another way of talking about identification. Advertisers want you to identify, to associate, with them. They want their name or image or brand to be the first thing that comes to mind when you consider a purchase within that category. They want to create, maintain, and enhance a personal relationship with you—that is the goal of relationship marketing. It is very much like a courtship, and advertisers want your love (and money).

What makes advertising persuasive? A number of factors play into the identification a consumer feels for anything advertised, including motivation, repetition, humor, and benefits derived from a purchase. The product or service fulfills a need or desire for the consumer. *Motivation is found in wants, needs, desires.* Advertisers key in on certain motivations and visualize their product satisfying those needs. It is easy to see how some products fit with motivations—bottled water does satisfy thirst, a hamburger does alleviate hunger. Ads for such would be closer to real on the ladder of abstraction. But oftentimes advertisers tie abstract motives to the product. So, for instance, self-confidence gets tied to deodorant; social status is found with a cell phone; virility and toughness go hand in hand with a truck; freedom and sociability are gained in a cigarette. Advertising adds meaning to things. These connections are more abstract; they don't necessarily exist in the product until advertising makes that symbolic connection through words, visuals, music, and other means.

Some ads are effective out of sheer repetition. One maxim in political advertising is "if you say it often enough it becomes true." Whether you're selling candidates or crunch-coat candy, your odds of success get better with repetition. Usually it takes a number of repetitions for an ad to crack the surface of our consciousness. We are bombarded by so many messages in our information age that we develop clever ways of ignoring most messages. As we drive down the road, look at a newspaper, or watch TV, we are attending to a few messages and missing most others. Ignoring most messages could be a defense mechanism so that our conscious mind is not overloaded and overwhelmed. So repetitions of messages or ads can help those ads break the threshold of awareness.

Humor is becoming more prevalent in television advertising. The use of humor in ads serves a dual purpose: it gets attention and lowers defenses. Funny ads are more likely to get our attention and to function as an entertaining release—comic relief. Funny ads are also more likely to get people talking about the ad—the "buzz" that is every advertiser's dream to attain. Humor does more than gain our attention and talk. People develop defenses against persuasion. We are persuaded from so many angles—by advertising, family, friends, and more—that we make many ways of saying no to persuasive appeals. But when advertisers use humor, we don't recognize the ad as persuasive as more direct persuasive appeals. Humor lowers our defenses.

Finally, advertisers find greater success by speaking directly to the benefit gained through their product. In the FAB formula for persuading, the marketer reviews the many features of the product, names the advantages, and identifies the benefits. *Features* are the many different aspects of a product or service that build value. For instance, the features in a car might include power windows, power locks, power seats, awesome stereo, super suspension, and so forth. Each feature, each additional aspect, builds value. *Advantages*, in this formula, refer to how the advertised product is better than the competition or better than what the consumer is currently using. "This Kirby vacuum uses soft rotating brushes rather than that hard beater bar like other brands." *Benefits* refer to "what's in it for you," the motivations that will be satisfied by this purchase. Will the product make you feel safer, sexier, or more self-assured? Will it bring you love, friendship, youth, wellness, flexibility, strength, or wisdom? Does it enhance your social status, give you pleasure, or lead to enlightenment? Advertisers associate all kinds of benefits with products to match your motivations. Part of the secret to identification is finding the right motivational key to fit the lock.

Compliance-Gaining Strategies

We can look at the keys to persuasion in the interpersonal context. Gerald Marwell and David Schmitt (1967) named sixteen techniques persuaders use to gain compliance from others. The techniques fall within five general strategies: rewarding activity, punishing activity, positive and negative expertise, activation of internalized commitments, and activation of interpersonal commitments. The sixteen compliance-gaining techniques are developed in Table 8.1.

Table 8.1 Marlow and Schmitt's Compliance-Gaining Techniques

General Strategy	Technique	Explanation	Example
Rewarding	Promise	If you comply with my request, I will reward you.	"If you drive, I will buy the pizza."
Rewarding	Liking	Being friendly so that the other person complies.	"You are about the nicest person I know. Can I borrow your sweatshirt?"
Rewarding	Pre-giving	Giving someone a reward before making a request.	"I bought you this night light at the bookstore. Can you help me study tonight?"
Punishing	Threat	If you do not comply, you will be punished.	"If you don't let me go with you, I'm telling mom you snuck out last night."
Punishing	Aversive Stimulation	Punishing a person until he or she complies.	"You will not get another penny of allowance until you clean that room."
Expertise	Positive Expertise	From an authority: if you comply, good things will happen.	"I've been a counselor for 27 years, and I can tell you if you follow the program you will be successful."
Expertise	Negative Expertise	From an authority: if you do not comply, bad things will happen.	"As your lawyer I must advise you that if you don't take the plea you will go to jail."
Activation of Internalized Commitments	Moral Appeal	You are immoral if you do not comply.	"You said you would help, so now if you say you won't help, you lied."
Activation of Internalized Commitments	Positive Self-Feelings	You will feel better if you comply.	"Imagine how good you'll feel if you volunteer with us."
Activation of Internalized Commitments	Negative Self-Feelings	You will feel bad if you do not comply.	"You're going to fall out of shape if you don't start exercising with us."
Activation of Internalized Commitments	Positive Altercasting	Telling a person that a "good person" would comply.	"If you were a real man you would pay for my dinner."
Activation of Internalized Commitments	Positive Esteem	Other people will think better of you for complying.	"The boss is going to think very highly of you if you can get this done."
Activation of Interpersonal Commitments	Negative Altercasting	Telling a person that a "bad person" would not comply.	"Only bad boys break the rules at school."
Activation of Interpersonal Commitments	Altruism	Telling a person you want to see their better nature.	"Listen to that angel on your shoulder and do the right thing."
Activation of Interpersonal Commitments	Debt	Calling in a past favor to get current compliance.	"You remember that time I loaned you $100? Can I borrow. . .?"
Activation of Interpersonal Commitments	Negative Esteem	Other people will think poorly of you for not complying.	"You know you're going to lose votes if you don't attend our b-b-q dinner."

Source: Adapted from Gerald Marlow and David R. Schmitt (1967, pp. 357–363).

Compliance-gaining strategies are useful as we assert ourselves and ask for what we want in life. Advertising serves a necessary function within society. It provides information and stimulates economic growth for companies and countries alike. More and more, it provides entertainment, social models to be emulated, and comic relief. Moreover, careers in advertising provide opportunities for creativity, the practice of today's rhetoric. There are limits to advertising's benefits, however, and ways in which ads can be seen as dysfunctional; and compliance gaining can even take on a manipulative or even sinister side. A more cynical and suspicious view of advertising sees a world awash in glitzy junk and advertisers pushing people to acquire more. In a postmodern world, consumer culture becomes suspect.

Persuasion and Postmodern Mind

Postmodern perspectives tend to be more critical of traditional persuasive forces found in advertising and the corporate world. Postmodern ideas came into critical conversations throughout the twentieth century, featuring authors like Jaques Derrida, Jean-Francois Lyotard, and Jean Baudrillard. Though the intellectual movement had been fermenting for many years, it burst onto the scene across many disciplines with the translation of Lyotard's *The Postmodern Condition* (1979). The ideas had been brewing long before that, with streams of postmodern thinking evident in architecture, art, music, literature, philosophy, and elsewhere long before Lyotard. But that book and others, and perhaps that moment in the cultural milieu, brought about a more widespread critique of the problems posed by modern society. "Postmodern" has many potential meanings for different people. *Essentially, postmodern is a reaction to modern society and its ideals.*

Derrida was a philosopher who distinguished himself through his method of *deconstruction,* a form of philosophical and literary analysis. He enjoyed studying life and language and especially the ways language shapes life. Deconstruction assumes meaning is not stable and truth is not absolute. From this perspective, meaning, as we saw earlier, shifts across time and varies from person to person and system to system, and truth is constructed within the shifting sands of our linguistic systems. Essentially, social systems get into habits of interpretation and whole constructions of social reality, and deconstruction seeks to break those habits. Our social reality has been constructed by several institutions—government, religion, education, corporate, and others—and Derrida shows us how to deconstruct those realities, to look for different meanings. Derrida uses a critical tool of *decentering* or questioning traditional definitions and interpretations established by those of power and influence, past and present. Take the contemporary celebration of Christmas in America, for example. Christmas has been socially constructed over the years, evolving into the gift-giving, carol-singing, Santa-coming holiday it is today. These activities and rituals are part of the mythology of Christmas that has slowly taken shape over time, and accelerated with the advent of mass production, mass advertising, and mass consumption. Moreover, many corporate interests coalesce around making Christmas sales a success, as many businesses have a stake in keeping the myth alive and thriving. The holiday has been constructed, and to deconstruct it a good postmodernist could reveal how each aspect was added by different cultures and subcultures along a historic timeline, how each of those aspects might not fit with the original intent and teachings of Jesus, and how alternative meanings are available. This oversimplifies the ideas of Derrida, but we see that postmodernity takes a critical stance toward the persuasive forces of socially constructed culture.

Lyotard also looked at the ways we are persuaded by the very structures in society we have created, especially the stories we tell and how those stories define and limit our lives. Not stories like "Once upon a time . . . ," though that could be part of it all. He uses story in a wider sense of the repeated themes in the ways a culture talks about itself. Those stories are evident in the popular culture. For instance, on television these days we see a plethora of advertisements about tough guys driving tough trucks on roads in the American West. Those images tie into the past push westward, rugged pioneering spirit, and the freedom of the wide-open range. The story of the American West defines part of the past and is used in the present to give meaning and encourage people to identify with products. Or we see images and commercials of people enjoying the thrill of shopping, stories that define us as a consumer culture. We see stories of sports, business, love, and other themes that define who we are and what we might care about. Stories persuade us—they are an invitation to identification.

Those stories are told within the confines of a wider story of what's going on right now with humanity, an overarching "grand narrative" or "metanarrative" that defines what can properly be said and done in cultures. *The grand narrative structures our understanding; it is the larger story that gives meaning to our day-to-day dramas.* Lyotard viewed "science" as the grand narrative that defines our drama today. Science and the scientific method (which tells us not to believe anything unless we can verify it with our senses in repeated trials) have brought about big changes in the way life is lived. Science, especially the technological innovations derived from its applications, has radically changed the world and humankind. Science—the world of nanotechnology, biogenetics, smart phones and smart bombs—is now tightly enmeshed and dominant within the human drama. And it is not just science, but the *language of and the language that supports* science that interests us here.

Going back to the Enlightenment of the late 1700s, we find the pushes for democracy and enhanced knowledge of the liberal philosophers, coupled with utilitarianism and the rapid dissemination of ideas through technologies, giving birth to modern methods of production. Based on Adam Smith's 1776 *Wealth of Nations* and so many other ideas, the industrial revolution booms, and the industrialized nations begin going to the far corners of the globe for the resources they need to keep the machine fed. We find Europeans, Western civilization, colonizing people and places around the world. Great chunks of Africa, Asia, and South America are forced into the service of the industrial order, controlled by corporations and governments in the United States and Europe. The story themes that support such conquest include science is right; innovation is good; production is good; making more money is good; it is our right to colonize other people and control their resources for the purpose of profitable production. This story persuades people, with many participating in its plot lines to greater or lesser degrees.

Lyotard saw the collapse of the grand narrative based in the Enlightenment as the rise of postmodernity. People are playing "language games," a borrowed phrase he used to differentiate a multiplicity of *communities of meaning*. We see many different social systems, communities of meaning, vying for their interpretation to be the accepted or controlling interpretation. Take, for example, the protests that often surround meetings of the G8. The G8, or Group of Eight, is eight countries that control much of the world's production, money, and military might. Finance ministers from the G8 meet annually in one member's country, and the meetings are protested by various groups focused on such topics as poverty, global warming, and globalization. Leaders of the G8 are playing in a different language game than the protest groups. While one group's motives are guided by a language that justifies the productive order and the need to continue making and moving goods, the protest groups use a different language that doesn't talk so fondly of the corporate world. Each group is vying for its interpretation to gain favor with select groups and the general public. They are playing language games.

As each of us believe in and buy into language games, we are persuaded and perhaps even join or give money to the cause. Some believe in the language of peace, some support war. Some guide their lives by a language that promotes freedom and liberal ideals, while others are more guided by conservative discipline. Some focus on pleasure, some focus on work, and a few even get pleasure from work. Some love the language of music, some the language of math. Look around you and you'll see evidence of people buying into different language games, different words and beliefs and ways of life; different definitions of what *is* and *should be*.

The school of postmodern thinkers is full of questions. Jean Baudrillard (Bo-dree-ar) was a French social critic who eventually found an interest in media and technology. He updated the meaning of the *simulacrum*, mentioned by Plato, Nietzsche, and others before him. Plato used the term to refer to intentionally distorted reproductions of reality. Nietzsche used it to refer to the distorted copy of reality philosophers get when they rely on language and reason rather than their senses. Baudrillard used simulacrum to refer to the simulated reality we live as the real and symbolic get converted into signs that trigger images. Our thoughts and experiences of reality are re-presentations, said he, and based more on distilled symbols than on the actual event. Our ideas about products and people on TV, for instance, are based on mediated images more than rooted in reality. We deal only with surfaces and images, and live a life full of reproductions and media-manufactured experiences: *hyper-reality*. Baudrillard had a deep interest in consumerism and its connections to mass media, and hyper-reality is very much a product of that relationship.

We needn't go far for evidence of Baudrillard's hyper-reality. Consider two people texting each other on their cell phones, moved by not only the words they thumb in but also hooked by the allure of secrecy and fun offered by the medium. The worth of the cell phone and the value of the fun they are having by texting each other has been built up in the imagery and language of ads put out by cell phone sellers. There is also social value and power to having a cell phone, and having texting and other smartphone capabilities now plays into belongingness; we might be left "out of the loop" without it. The pleasure of such an activity is derived from playing with symbols (word play), but there are so many other layers of meaning and motivation attached to that play, and a big part of the meaning comes from images skimmed from the surface of media representations (ads). Whether you believe that our reality is hyper-real, you must admit the media likely have something to do with making our mind.

The postmodern perspective takes us to a more critical stance on persuasive practices, beyond the salesman to the persuasion that is built into our institutions and social interactions. Power, identification, and social influence are operating in all of our social systems, from interpersonal to mass media.

Creative Moment

How are you being persuaded? Make a mind map of the many persuasive influences operating in your mind. Start with your beliefs, values, and interests in the middle, and network outward to the various people and ideas that make your mind. Is the foundation for your ideas found in parents, teachers, or preachers? Is it in the music or the movies? Maybe your mind is made from key quotes, or notes, or experiences. Can you identify any socially constructed realities that persuade you? What persuades you—what are the sources of your identifications?

Chapter 9

Purestock/Thinkstock

Media and Mind

**"Invisible airwaves crackle with life
Bright antennae bristle with the energy"**

—*Rush, "The Spirit of Radio"*

The Medium and the Message

Watch this, shop for that,

Watch this, shop for that,

Watch this, shop for that . . .

    They say the medium's the message,

    And the media's messages say:

    Watch more on the media,

    And patronize those who pay . . .

Watch this, shop for that,

Watch this, shop for that,

Watch this, shop for that . . .

    That Madison Avenue magic

    Has me in its spell,

    That old black magic,

    Lead'n me straight to . . .

Watch this, shop for that,

Watch this, shop for that,

Watch this, shop for that . . .

    I used to have the capacity,

    To think a thought or two,

    But now haven't the audacity,

    To question Big Brother Tube . . .

Watch this, shop for that,

Watch this, shop for that,

Watch this, shop for that . . .

    I'm always into what's new,

    A media-fried mall creature, you know,

    My life is worth lots too,

    With all these goodies to show . . .

Watch this, shop for that,

Watch this, shop for that,

Watch this, shop for that . . .

    And if there comes a new fashion,

    You bet I'll join the crowd dash'n,

    Straight from the screen to the store,

    Anxious hunger always needs more.

    At the time I wrote that I was just learning the postmodern scene—a latecomer to that game—and feeling a bit down on material, corporate, capitalistic society. I've since revised my view but still wouldn't be considered a good shopper.

    The media are often considered within the purview of postmodern thought and are certainly a part of persuasion theory. Some postmodern media critics argue that the media are linked with corporate and political interests in a new form of colonization: the mass colonizing of minds. Do you think the media have power in your mind? Authors have pondered the persuasiveness of the media for a long time now, and though we have fascinating theories about how media affect us, there is not complete agreement on how it works.

The information age is saturated with media. We should keep two things in mind about the media before considering their influence: (1) they are plural, and (2) they are a business.

Media is plural for medium, usually referring to the electronic, print, and broadcast media, such as television, radio, newspapers, magazines, music, Internet, outdoor; and now refers more and more to the social media (like Facebook, Twitter, Hulu, and others) as conveyed by smartphones, tablets, and other devices. So, when someone says, "the liberal media," referring to it as if it is singular and single-minded, that is a mistake. "Media" encompasses all kinds of different organizations, large and small, across the political spectrum, and oriented toward news, information, entertainment, and more. You can find multinational liberal newspapers, local conservative talk-radio programs, and websites with Internet campaigns for every brand of political persuasion.

The media are a business, and many decisions are driven by financial considerations. Media managers and executives are always concerned about numbers: numbers of people watching, listening, and reading; numbers of advertisers and advertising revenues; their numbers in the ratings and share of market. The "bottom line" is the difference between how much money is coming in and how much is going out, and many decisions about programs and production quality are based on the bottom line. The relationship between a medium, target audience/consumers, and advertisers is the crucial relationship that keeps the media going and keeps markets hopping. Media need advertising revenues; advertisers need consumers to buy goods; consumers seek information and entertainment from the media and then, it is hoped, buy goods from the advertisers. Walter Lippmann (1922) discussed this relationship in detail in his brilliant book *Public Opinion*.

The Media and the Message

Marshall McLuhan was one of the most prominent and interesting media theorists of the twentieth century. He was one of the first to ponder publicly how the electronic media were radically altering life in the new Age. And what was that Age? McLuhan traced the history of media developing through four historic epochs: tribal age, literate age, print age, and electronic age. Humans entered each new epoch as new communication technologies were developed. During the tribal age, which had people organizing into community units, the spoken word in face-to-face communication was predominant. That was, and is, the *oral tradition*, when teaching, learning, and passing knowledge from one generation to the next was done by word of mouth.

With the invention of phonetic alphabets between 3500 and 2500 B.C.E., human civilization began phasing into the early days of literacy, so the literary age lasts roughly from then until Gutenberg's Bible. The educated elite began sharing knowledge by writing and reading, alongside the face-to-face communication of the oral tradition. Words began to proliferate, as they could be created by coupling sounds that were assigned root meanings. We should note that even though McLuhan calls it the literate age, most of the world remained illiterate.

When Johannes Gutenberg used movable metal type to print a Bible around 1450, the print age was born. Printing at that time was relatively slow because letters and words needed to be loaded by hand into cylindrical rollers before inking and printing. Slowly, over the next three hundred years, publications like books and pamphlets became more prevalent. By the time of the Enlightenment in the late 1700s, the printing press and publications played a key role in the revolutionary political and philosophical thinking that drove many changes. For instance, Thomas Paine's prerevolutionary war pamphlet, *Common Sense*, served to stir emotions against the king of England among colonists. Note again, however, that even with the faster printing and more rapid dissemination of knowledge, literacy rates still remained low. In the late nineteenth and throughout the twentieth centuries concerted efforts were made to raise literacy rates, but a 1998 United Nations estimate still found 20 percent of the world's adult population illiterate.

The invention of the telegraph, and especially the laying of the transcontinental telegraph line, according to McLuhan, was the technological leap that ushered in the electronic age. With the invention and use of electronic media through the rest of the nineteenth century, the pace of change picked up, leading to the twentieth century, where the pace accelerated tenfold. The time between technological innovations became compressed as more rapid information-sharing proceeded. We coexisted with just spoken words for tens of thousands of years. After alphabets, the innovations came faster, and with printing faster still. With electronic media the innovation curve shot upward. Now, with computers and Internet and cell phones and so many technologies for rapid-image diffusion, innovation occurs at a breakneck pace. The rate of change is accelerating.

McLuhan addressed how technological change leads to cultural change. Our way of life coevolves with changes in communication technologies. This is *technological determinism*, which means our lives are structured by technologies. McLuhan also claimed that each technology serves as an extension of human senses and faculties. Books are an extension of the eye, wheels are an extension of the foot, and electronic circuitry is an extension of the human nervous system. Thus the world seems to get smaller as our senses get connected through media, as we get wired into the "global village."

One of McLuhan's more playful quips was "The medium is the message." He later added, "The medium is the massage" and "The medium is the mass-age," which brought about all kinds of interpretive debate and fun. Scholars and people on the street were trying to figure out what McLuhan meant, granting him mystical status. The humor of it all was caught in Woody Allen's film *Annie Hall*. In the movie, Allen and Diane Keaton are waiting in line for a movie when a pompous professor starts pontificating about what McLuhan means; Allen interrupts to disagree with the interpretation; the professor claims credibility with his credentials—he teaches TV, Media, and Culture at Columbia; then Marshall McLuhan himself steps in to tell the professor he is mistaken. The moment in film caught the confusion and playful persuasion of the times. McLuhan might've meant that the technologies themselves, let alone the content that comes across them, affects the way we live. For instance, television has changed peoples' habits within their houses and socialization patterns outside of the home. It is notable that people sit and watch and can be engaged with their television sets for sometimes long periods of time. Television and other media structure behavioral habits, and in this way they are persuasive.

Media Effects

Many theories exist for how the media influence or persuade people. We will look at a few here to get a sense of the media's potential influence in our mind. Theories about media influence vary from *direct effects* to *selective exposure* and others. Direct-effect theories depict the media as having a strong influence on human behavior, while selective-exposure theories see that influence of media as more limited and affected by human interaction and choice.

Two events from the twentieth century gave credence to the direct-and-powerful-effects theorists. On the eve of Halloween in 1938, Orson Welles broadcast on CBS Radio an adaptation of H. G. Wells' *The War of the Worlds*, making it sound like a radio news broadcast. A large number of listeners panicked, and some actually packed belongings in cars and headed for the hills, believing the earth was being attacked by Martians. In 1954, Dr. Frederick Wertham, a psychiatrist, published *Seduction of the Innocent*, a work about the evils of comic books and how they led to the delinquency and sexual perversion of minors. Public outrage stemming from the book was followed by U.S. Senate subcommittee investigations, and eventually led to stronger self-regulation by the comic book industry. This episode in media history is sometimes called the "comic book scare." Taken together, the *War of the Worlds* broadcast and the comic book scare are testaments to powerful media effects. Those "hypodermic needle" theories (implying the audience is defenseless against the media's intravenously injected messages) have not gained many believers among media critics and academics. But many people in the public still buy into the hypnotizing powers of the media, as do some politicians, especially when bashing the media can gain votes.

Most media critics agree that people choose different media, and those media have different effects on different individuals. That is, *people are selectively exposed to various media with varying effects*. One popular selective exposure theory is *uses and gratifications*. Uses-and-gratifications media theory was developed by Dennis McQuail, Jay Blumler, Elihu Katz, and others in the 1970s. The central tenet is that people *choose media to fulfill needs*. The media are not some single-minded monster that influences all people or even many people in the same way. Rather, we seek the media that gratify certain motivations. Those motives, or gratifications, originally identified include diversion, personal relationships, personal identity, and surveillance (McQuail, Blumler, and Brown, 1972). McQuail later added more dimensions to the four general categories of media usage: information, personal identity, integration and social interaction, and entertainment. Here are the uses that find gratifications through media fare:

Information
- finding out about relevant events and conditions in immediate surroundings, society, and the world
- seeking advice on practical matters or opinion and decision choices
- satisfying curiosity and general interest
- learning; self-education
- gaining a sense of security through knowledge

Personal Identity
- finding reinforcement for personal values
- finding models of behavior
- identifying with valued others (in the media)
- gaining insight into oneself

Integration and Social Interaction
- gaining insight into the circumstances of others; social empathy
- identifying with others and gaining a sense of belonging
- finding a basis for conversation and social interaction
- having a substitute for real-life companionship
- helping to carry out social roles
- enabling one to connect with family, friends, and society

Entertainment
- escaping, or being diverted, from problems
- relaxing

- getting intrinsic cultural or aesthetic enjoyment
- filling time
- emotional release
- sexual arousal (McQuail, 1983, p. 73)

The media provide several uses and gratifications, from relaxation and information to identification. Allan Danahar/Digital Vision/Thinkstock

People actively seek and use those media that provide gratification of an array of needs, and different people use those media differently. For instance, one person might use the Internet more for news, another uses the Internet to visit chat rooms and maintain cyber relationships, while still another uses the Internet to do research. This uses-and-gratifications model depicts media consumers as free choice-makers more than mindless sheep obediently following mass orders. Another helpful model of media influence is social-learning theory.

Bobo Dolls and Beyond

Albert Bandura developed his brand of social-learning theory in the 1970s following his now-famous Bobo doll experiment. In his experiment, young children watched a video of an adult woman aggressively attacking a plastic clown, the "Bobo doll" that bounces back up when you knock it down. In the researcher's words, " . . . the model pummels it on the head with a mallet, hurls it down, sits on it and punches it on the nose repeatedly, kicks it across the room, flings it in the air, and bombards it with balls . . ." (1973, p. 72). After witnessing the beating of Bobo, the children were placed in a room with attractive toys, but they were not allowed to touch them. In theory, this built frustration and anger. Then the children were brought to another room that had identical toys as in the Bobo video and they were allowed to touch the toys. Bandura and company found that most children exhibited the aggressive behaviors seen on the video. In other words they kicked the crap out of Bobo, and it was theorized that the media made them do it.

That experiment demonstrates the process of social learning, which includes modeling, observation, and imitation. The children observed a model beating Bobo. Then they imitated the behavior. Likewise, much of our learning has resulted from observing and imitating others. This takes us back to Mead's play-and-game stages, where we develop our "self" by imitating and identifying with others. Or think of learning skills. All the skills you've learned—from cooking a meal to performing an athletic move, or writing and reading—have been learned by observing others.

Here is how social learning works, in a nutshell: (1) We witness a behavior, either in person or through the media; (2) we imitate that behavior; (3) we determine that the behavior has value, such as social value (helps win friends) or instrumental value (helps accomplish goals); and (4) in some cases, the behavior becomes part of our ongoing behavioral repertoire—it gets retained, becomes a part of who we are. Here's an example: I see a comic tell a joke on TV; I tell the joke next time I'm with friends; they laugh, so I assume my imitation of the modeled behavior has social value. Maybe I'll tell that joke over and over again in the future—it gets retained in memory. I doubt it, though. I can't remember jokes.

Social learning theory is useful in viewing many mind/media relationships. Much of advertising includes modeled behavior that we imitate in buying and using the product. Or think about young teens struggling to find an identity and "trying on" different personalities they see in the media and in their circles of friends and acquaintances. A lot of self-development occurs through social learning. Some media critics decry the social learning that has negative consequences, like when boys see a bowling ball dropped off a highway bridge on a *Beavis and Butthead* cartoon and then try it themselves. There are plenty of dysfunctional models in media to catch our concern.

Please keep in mind that Bandura's and others' theories are quite a bit more complicated than this. His social-learning theory explains human behavior as a continuous reciprocal interaction between cognitive, behavioral, and environmental influences. We think and act amid the influences of media, friends, and other social systems. And in those systems, someone is setting the agenda.

Who Sets the Agenda?

Agenda-setting theory is based upon Bernard Cohen's statement in 1963 that "The press may not be successful much of the time in telling people what to think, but it is stunningly successful in telling its readers what to think about." The media may not control minds, but they are very good at establishing the agenda for what will be on people's minds. McCombs and Shaw (1972) studied media and audiences during election campaigns and purported to find a relationship between the media's agenda and voters' agenda. The question then becomes, did the media cause the voters to think about certain issues, or did the media just reflect what voters were already thinking? Two assumptions guide agenda-setting theory: (1) The press and the media do not reflect reality, but rather filter and shape it; and (2) media concentration on a few issues and subjects leads the public to perceive those issues as more important than other issues.

You can probably see evidence of how the media sets the agenda in your own life. The music you listen to on the radio is likely from a play list chosen by media executives based on popularity that has been pushed by recording industry executives. In conversations with your friends about sports, fashion, or interesting new discoveries, it is likely that your information comes from media sources. Again, many of these decisions about what you watch, hear, and read are based on the bottom line—what sells?

McCombs later altered the original agenda-setting model, claiming the media do indeed influence the way we think, especially in the ways stories are shaped to influence interpretations: how a story is *framed*. Framing is accomplished through selection, emphasis, exclusion, and elaboration. News organizations, for instance, in producing a story (1) select certain elements and ignore others; (2) emphasize or highlight certain aspects of the selected story lines; (3) exclude elements that don't fit well with the angle or preferred interpretation; and (4) elaborate on, fill in details, and ponder potential spins on the selected story. Saying it another way, they are presenting us with an abstract version of the event that is produced and packaged with a certain angle in mind. Often that angle includes conflict or contention. It is said of news programming, "if it bleeds it leads," meaning news decision-makers tend to choose stories of murder and mayhem over granny baking cookies. Conflict sells more papers and gets more viewers than peacefulness.

Cultivating Minds

All the conflict and murder and violence we witness on TV and in other media may impact the way we see the world. George Gerbner, et al. (1994) suggested ways in which the media warp our views of reality. They developed the "cultivation perspective" around the idea that people who are heavy viewers of television will perceive reality differently than light or non-viewers. Heavy viewers were defined as those who watch four or more hours of television per day. Those who watched two hours or less of television per day were in the light-user category. Heavy viewers perceived the world as more violent, had more fear, and were more suspicious of other people's motives than light viewers. Heavy viewers are also likely to think the police are more active than they really are. On TV, police jobs are full of action-packed excitement, confronting intriguing criminal characters. The actual job is not usually that exciting, though it has its moments. TV viewing cultivates perceptions of reality.

Another theory of interest, especially in the way it depicts the media-human interaction, is Elisabeth Noelle-Neumann's (1974) "spiral of silence" theory. People are less likely to express a political opinion when they perceive they are in the minority, for fear of reprisal and social isolation. When people start to express an unpopular or non-majority viewpoint, they tend to look to the mass media for confirmation, to see if interest in the viewpoint begins to diffuse. If they do not see evidence of the opinion diffusing they will tend to be less and less vocal with time. This theory may help to explain the apparent silencing of war protestors during the early years of the Bush administration, as his vice president and secretary of defense labeled such protestors unpatriotic, aiding the enemy, and dangerous. Later in the Bush presidency, as stories of torture and mistaken assumptions that led to war began to surface, protest spiraled back into the forefront of media attention.

Beyond the influence of television content and viewer profiles, some media analysts look at the wider picture of influence. Neil Postman looked at the ways in which the media are pleasuring us into submission. Stuart Hall views the media more from a Marxist point of view.

How do the media influence your ways of minding the world? In his classic book *Amusing Ourselves to Death* (1985), Postman looked at the ways we're hooked into the media via the pleasure principle. He opened by comparing the media-mind relationship from George Orwell's *1984* to Aldous Huxley's *Brave New World*. Orwell's image is of a central government, Big Brother, controlling minds by controlling information and motivating behaviors through mass-mediated words and images. Huxley's image is more about media and technology titillating consumers to the stimulus-saturation point where they can no longer care. Postman finished his foreword thus: "In *1984*, Huxley added, people are controlled by inflicting pain. In *Brave New World*, they are controlled by inflicting pleasure. In short, Orwell feared that what we hate will ruin us. Huxley feared that what we love will ruin us" (1985, p. viii). Postman went on to show how the age of show business has infiltrated all aspects of our lives. From entertainment to church, from the forms that have us laugh and cry to the forms of prayer and what we think it's all about, mass-mediated images and the social structures that deliver them are in our mind, and we love it!

Postman described our culture's "technopoly," where our thought worlds are monopolized and manipulated by entertainment. The media are a central player in the culture's business and political games of conquest and financial gain. Technology is pervasive, and the entertainment technologies are intimately coupled with the way we live. Postman said, "The culture seeks its authorization in technology, finds its satisfaction in technology, and takes its orders from technology" (1992, p. 28). Take, for example, the business of war. Government and corporate officials are authorizing transactions involving billions of dollars to pay for the weapons of warfare. Technology drives decisions. Postman wondered the extent to which we tool users are now used by our tools. Do computers, televisions, IPads, and the like use us? Persuade us? Control us?

Stuart Hall takes a slightly different tack. The sociologist from England uses a variation on Marxist criticism to analyze power relationships among media and social systems. Hall looks at how the media serve political and economic interests and help dominant people stay dominant. People use media as a tool to get power, maintain power, and gain position in the hierarchies of our many social games. For instance, in recent wars in the Middle East, media executives made decisions about what and what not to show in their news stories. Hall maintains that those stories lean toward a corporate-friendly slant and that U.S.-based media dominate the news industry. He says we usually don't realize the extent to which media saturate our lives. We may unknowingly participate as pawns in the culture wars, oppressed by powerful people pulling levers from behind the media production curtain. Cultural critics like Hall seek to get our necks out from under the boot of the media-corporate oppressor, if indeed that's where our necks are.

Hall's ideas share similarities to Michel Foucault's, a postmodernist who discussed secrets in the mysteries of communication and social power. Mass media, for Foucault, serve to carry the dominant (and dominating) *discourse* of the day. Like Lyotard's "metanarrative," Foucault used "discourse" in referring to the grander story in which we participate, and the preferred interpretations that give meaning to the story. Certain powerful people—the "power elite" of the political-media-corporate world—control the discourse. That dominant discourse then gives us a framework of interpretation in which we make meaning. For instance, for many people the holiday hoopla that surrounds Christmas may seem innocent fun. From Foucault's perspective, the consumer-crazed mania engineered by corporate marketing and advertising may not be seen as so innocent. The dominant discourse favors buying, selling, shopping, acquiring new things, exchanging money, and many other acts defined as good within the confines of consummate consumerism. That dominating discourse that shows how to be a "good shopper" has many people going into debt over their heads, chasing the good life as depicted in advertising. The discourse guides, and in many cases controls, human thought and action.

Other concerns about media, especially the rapid adoption of social media, are growing as we jump into hyper-mediated culture. *Digital stress* is a malady affecting increasing numbers, a combination of information overload, anxiety from constant contact, and a feeling of falling out of human touch as our technologies for being in touch proliferate. Smartphones, tablets, and emerging innovations like Google Glass have seen a sharp rise in sales and consumer demand. People want them and grow to need them—but at what price?

Whether you see the media as powerful or limited, modelers of ideal behaviors or as mass mind control, a brave new world or the watchful eye of big brother depends on your perspective. Any way you look at it, we need to gain perspective on the media, reflecting on these invisible airwaves that crackle with life.

Creative Moment

Do the media help or hurt your creativity? How have your media habits potentially encroached on or enhanced your life experience? Let's do a photo shoot of your media habits. Collect pictures of you interacting with media: playing video games, watching TV, on the phone, listening to music, reading, at the computer—wherever your media take you. Take photos of your media reality. Now, for each medium, create a caption about its impact in your life, especially how it might limit or free your mind. Do the media bring freedom, oppression, or both?

Another Moment

Name these times in which we now live. Beyond the "Information Age," what else can be said about this Age?

Chapter 10

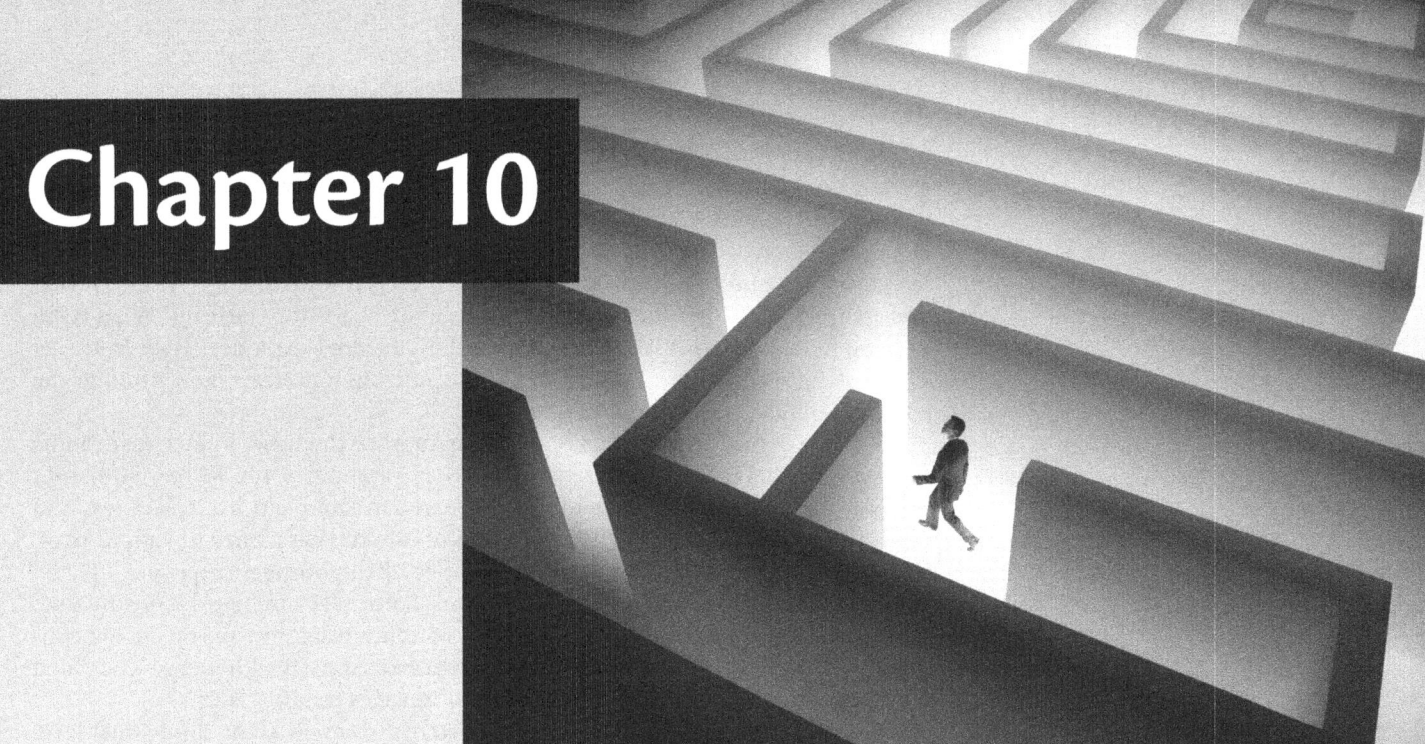

Stewart Sutton/Digital Vision/Thinkstock

Getting Past Fear
Communication Apprehension

"Expose yourself to your deepest fear; after that, fear has no power, and the fear of freedom shrinks and vanishes. You are free."

—*Jim Morrison*

Fear can be funny. In the movie *What About Bob?*, Bob Wiley (Bill Murray) is a guy with a multi-phobic personality who overcomes his fears through a vacation therapy that drives his therapist crazy. Early on, the psychiatrist (Richard Dreyfuss) asks him, "So the real question is: what is the crisis, Bob? What is it that you are truly afraid of?" Bob answers, "What if my heart stops beating? What if I'm looking for a bathroom, I can't find it, and my bladder explodes? Have you ever heard of Tourette Syndrome? . . ." Bob has some big-time fears, and through the course of the film he overcomes them.

We don't consider our fears to be funny most of the time. In fact, fear can be annoying, destabilizing, and destructive. Fear paralyzes some people and stops many from realizing their potential. Our fears can stunt our persuasiveness and make us more vulnerable to the persuasion of others. Fear comes in various sizes, from slight worries to major panic, and varies in the number of people affected from one person to mass hysteria in millions. Some fears are natural, instinctual. Some fears are learned. We are conscious of some fears, but many are subconscious, lurking below our threshold of awareness. First we'll address fear associated with communication, and later we'll look at linkages to other fears.

James McCroskey defined *communication apprehension* as an "individual level of fear or anxiety associated with either real or anticipated communication with another person or persons" (1984, p. 41). It is a fear of social interaction, doing it or just thinking about it. Researchers have distinguished between communication apprehension, reticence, shyness, and unwillingness to communicate. Reticence is more about being reserved, uncommunicative, but not necessarily afraid. Apprehension is about fear and anxiety with communication, and it comes in many forms. Let's look at different categories of communication apprehension, then visit causes, implications, and strategies for dealing with it.

Categories of Communication Apprehension

McCroskey and Virginia Richmond (1988) named four distinct types of communication apprehension (CA): (1) Traitlike CA, (2) Context-based CA, (3) Audience-based CA, and (4) Situational CA.

Traitlike communication apprehension is "a relatively enduring personality type . . . across a wide variety of contexts" (McCroskey, 1984, p. 16). This is where a person experiences fear or anxiety when communicating in most situations. If you have fear of communicating in a face-to-face setting, in small groups, and when speaking in public, that fear would qualify for traitlike CA. Most people feel a little anxious in communication situations. That is completely normal. When the anxiety becomes debilitating or gets in the way of achieving goals, the problem may need to be addressed.

Context-based communication apprehension is anxiety experienced by people in a particular communicative context. The basic communication contexts are (1) intrapersonal—communication with oneself; (2) interpersonal—"dyadic" communication between two people; (3) small group communication—typically between three to seven people, give or take a few; (4) public speaking—one person speaking to many; (5) organizational communication—various forms of talk, writing, and presentation in company, corporate, or nonprofit settings; (6) intercultural communication—exchanges with people from different countries, ethnicities, and subcultures; and (7) mass communication—traditionally considered to be the broadcast media, but now includes computer-mediated forms. Most people experience anxiety in public-speaking situations. I have little problem with public speaking, but do notice more anxiety in certain small group settings. Some others have extreme misgivings about the dyadic context but are relaxed in groups. We will upgrade this description of context later, but for now these basic skeletons will do.

Audience-based communication apprehension is an anxiety or fear felt in exchanges with a particular person or group of people. Perhaps you are fine when chatting with friends or family, but feel great trepidation when talking with the boss. Or talk with one parent flows well, but talk with the other parent makes you a little or very nervous. A student might be able to talk easily and naturally in conversation with friends but then become flushed with frustration when answering a question in the classroom. Each case shows an anxiety produced by interactions with a certain audience.

Situational communication apprehension is experienced with a particular person or group, but only in certain situations. For instance, maybe you feel fine talking with police officers in social settings, but when you are being stopped for a traffic violation and the cop bellies up to your car window, you stutter with fear. When communicating with co-workers, many people feel at ease. But in situations where those same co-workers are evaluating you, perhaps with the chance of better pay or advancement tied to the evaluation, you may experience heightened nervousness in their presence. Situational CA is a combination of audience-based and context-based.

Each of us has likely felt one or more of these forms of fear at some point in our lives: the sweating and stumbling in a public-speaking assignment; extreme embarrassment in a group where your competence is questioned; the fear of facing an audience who will be judging you; or the pacing, practice, and pain of calling that first date. We experience apprehensiveness differently, just as there are different causes for how we "catch" it.

Where Is Fear From?

What causes fear and anxiety with communication? What causes any fear? Fear is often defined as an emotional response to real or imagined danger. It is emotional, so it is not only tied into our higher brain functions but also the early-evolved reptilian brain and midbrain. It is a response occurring as triggered by some stimulus or stimuli. And the danger that triggers it may be real or a figment of imagination. If I believe there is a boogey man waiting to get me around that dark corner, I will feel fear whether he's there or not. If he is not there, my fear will have been based on something not real. Either way, the fear is a construction of the mind.

Our lives are full of fear, some we've constructed and some more natural. We may fear death, illness, pain, or eternal damnation. We may fear people, places, or whatever lurks at the bottom of bad dreams. We fear the unknown, such as the dark mystery of the deep sea at night, or if that person we ask will say yes. We fear loneliness but might also fear intimacy. We fear failure and success. We fear others might suspect us of being something we are not and fear being revealed for who we really are, whatever that is. We have all kinds of fears, and much of their power lies in the social constructions that make up our minds.

Fear of communication and fear in general come from a variety of sources, including heredity (nature), conditioning (nurture), personal cognitive creations, and the context or situation.

Communication apprehension may be inherited as a trait of ethnicity, family, or even a chemical predisposition in the brain. People from some ethnic backgrounds do seem more predisposed to talk than others. Some families seem more likely to communicate than others. The movie *My Big Fat Greek Wedding* is a fun example where one family (the bride's) is much more talkative and argumentative than the other stoic family (the groom's). Some people's genetic coding predisposes them toward talk more than others.

Fear may also be found in the way our brains process stimuli. Think of talking to a person of high status that you've been wishing to meet. Would you be excited or terrified? One person's brain might take that anxiety-producing stimulus and translate it into excitement, whereas another person would translate it into terror. Excitement and terror are, in fact, very close to each other as chemical action in the brain. It's only a small jump in interpretation to think of stage fright before a speech as energizing as opposed to scary. But try to tell that to the person giving the speech!

Fear of communication can also be conditioned, the result of prior interactions that did not go so well. Operant conditioning refers to changing behavior through positive consequences (reinforcement) or negative consequences (punishment) that follow action. It can occur as (1) positive reinforcement, receiving a favorable or pleasant reward (stimulus) following the behavior; (2) negative reinforcement, withholding an averse, unpleasant stimulus; (3) positive punishment, receiving an averse stimulus after behavior, such as a shock or other pain; and (4) negative punishment, where a favorable reward is withheld. In one scenario, we might find a child who attempted to speak in public at a young age, was laughed at by peers, and thereafter associated the speaking situation with that painful positive punishment. Of course, it's more complicated than that. A different child might treat being laughed at as positive reinforcement, and in that interaction we may find the early developmental days of a class clown. McCroskey and company also looked at parent and child interactions for keys to understanding reinforcement's role in developing communication apprehension. Children who engage in communication with parents and receive praise for their efforts are much less likely to develop apprehensiveness than those who are punished for communication, like kids who get yelled at because "children should be seen and not heard."

Communication apprehension can also result from a person's unique meanings assigned to the social situation. Throughout our lives we build associations in mind for people, situations, and meanings thereof. Should we fear that a person will say no to our request? Should we feel anxious among people we don't know? Somewhere along the trajectory of your life you have plugged in meanings, symbol-laden responses for these situations. The way you think about a social situation, the meanings you assign, impacts the effectiveness of your communication.

Finally, fear might be caused by the relationship of persons and context. Context is everything. What's the difference between walking through a carnival house of horrors and your house? The context is very different (you might hope). The surroundings, the sensations, the place, the time, the frame of mind, and the people you're with all are part of the context. The context is also very much defined by your relationship to the people you're with. So the context of talking to your parents in your childhood home about something important is very different than talking with friends at the pub about the same topic. Even if we talk with parents at home and friends at home, the relationships give a different context to the conversations. In a way, each of us is a different person depending on with whom we are communicating, as we discussed in the chapter on personality. You, in relation to your parents, are a somewhat different person than in relation to your friends—sharing different histories, different expectations, different frames of together-mind, and more. And those relationships and contexts can be the source of fears.

Our fears may be products of heredity, social interaction, meanings we develop, and relational contexts. Fears have implications.

The Impact of Apprehensiveness

Fear of communication affects our lives. Communication can be a pathway and product of living life with a general feeling of wellness. If our fears get out of control they can impact self-esteem, social status, career choices, and emotional and physical health.

Communication apprehension can have a negative impact on self-esteem. Our image of self is constructed through social dynamics, from the development described in Mead's stages to everyday interactions where we get clues about how others perceive us. As we communicate we're aware of how we're doing, a continuous feedback loop of self-reflection sometimes called self-monitoring. Some people are high self-monitors, keenly aware of their behaviors and how the self might be seen by others. Some are low self-monitors, not reflecting a lot on their own behavior and thinking. This self-monitoring has value, allowing us to consider our impact on others and how we're being perceived. (After all, people do not always perceive us as we think they are or wish they would.) Self-monitoring can also have negative attitudes attached, so a person might be aware and critical of self. It's fine to be self-critical, but there's a line where self-critique can shade into self-defeating.

In situations where we feel fear in communication, that self-critical loop can attack our esteem. Like that time you said something you immediately wish had not passed your lips ("Oh, *why* did I say *that*!?"). We can engage in self-criticism to try to avoid the mistake in the future. But we need not let that incident, that regrettable comment, become a spiraling loop of self-loathing. The superego in attack mode can encroach on our mind's freedom to explore and learn. Pounding your ego over and over again based on some fear is something you do to yourself (with the help of other actors in your drama), and it is something you can change. We will discuss ways to relax and change your mind later.

People who suffer from an extreme level of communication apprehension tend to have more difficulty advancing on career and other paths. Students are less likely to get involved in activities and less likely to talk to peers, professors, and others who can offer social support. They are also less likely to go into careers that call for communication skills. In career organizations and many social systems, success is tied to your ability to communicate, especially asserting yourself and asking for what you want. My friend was up for promotion to a high-level executive position in his company. His pre-promotion review found that he wasn't assertive enough with key clients, so the company hired a coach to teach him to be more assertive. He got the promotion and is asserting himself happily ever after. His success includes financial gain, but "success" can be found in richer friendships, more rewarding conversations, and lifelong learning in enhanced social interactions.

Another implication of fear in communication is emotional discomfort. According to Maslow, Murray, and other motivational theorists, we need friendships, need to belong. McCroskey and others showed that people with high communication apprehensiveness (high CA) report feelings of inhibition and inadequacy, and may be perceived as less popular and desirable than low CAs. These social concerns can create an array of emotional responses. We can also work on emotions in communication, dealing with anger, frustration, spite, and fright through discussion, conversation. Talking to a friend can be the best way to beat mild depression, feelings of inadequacy, or any feeling that tells us we're no good.

Communication apprehension can have physical effects as well. Perhaps you've felt some or all of these symptoms in getting up to give a speech: rapid heartbeat, sweating, blotchy cheeks, shaking, need to urinate, dry throat, restless legs, and other psychophysiological reactions. *Thoughts have physical manifestations.* Not only do thoughts have physical appearances outside of mind, but those fear associations can become physical repeating patterns in the neural networks of our brains. If you associate fear with a certain stimulus long enough it becomes habituated, a part of the way your brain does business. So the physical aspects of fear are happening at a number of different levels.

Fear is a part of life and natural in the communication process. It can be helpful, having survival value, and it can be dysfunctional. Whether you sweat excessively at the podium, sweat asking mom for cash, fear asking the boss for a raise, or fear the fear itself—there are paths to comfortable communication.

Letting Go of Fear

Have you ever heard this advice? "Let it go." Let go of fear. Let go of that worrisome thought. "Consider the lilies in the field . . ." Let go of dysfunctional and destructive self-talk. That is good advice, but often easier said than done.

Once in a while we do get a chance to analyze our fears, recognize them and see they may not be so gripping, and change the course of our thoughts and actions. Some people even make it a part of their adventure, their quest, to face their fears in life. The other day I saw a video clip of an eighty-year-old grandma. She was bungee jumping. That was a bit extreme, but she certainly faced her fears. I'm thinking more along the lines of getting up the gumption to make that call we've been hesitating about, or finding the will to ask for what we want, and whether we can change from fearing to free. We can change our orientation toward fear through *motivation, relaxation,* and *visualization.*

Getting yourself motivated to stop fearing is a good first step. It helps to set our minds on a goal, to have a purpose, to be doing something we consider meaningful. Letting go of fears is meaningful because doing so will free us to enjoy a wider realm of activity and awareness. Going beyond communication barriers to talk with people, listen, and understand some of the stories surrounding us can have a positive impact in several areas of life. More than simply saying we'll stop fearing, however, we've got to want it. Motivation is a must. It sounds like I'm channeling coaches now, but it's true. Truly wanting to change helps us change. It also helps to practice. To become a better speaker, practice speaking; a better listener, practice listening. Anything we wish to do better: practice. Once we get the motivation fire lit, practice may flow more easily.

Yoga, tai chi, meditation, and visualization can enhance relaxation and help let go of fear.
Acnakelsy/iStock/Thinkstock

Relaxation can also help overcome fear and change communication habits. Relaxation is both a means and an end to better communication. Fears are often built upon anxieties, and anxiety is born between stressed variables. It could be stress in our minds from conflicting thoughts, dissonance, guilt, or any number of mental stressors. It could be stress stemming from social relations; conflict, competition, and codependency can produce anger, hate, helplessness, and other negative emotional states. Stress feeds fear, and relaxation is an important part of letting go. Several relaxation techniques are available, including progressive muscle relaxation, yoga, and visualization techniques.

Progressive muscle relaxation (PMR), developed by Edmund Jacobson in the early twentieth century, is an easy technique to learn and very helpful for physical relaxation that leads to mental calm. PMR works by tensing and relaxing muscle groups up and down your body. We often don't realize how much stress is being carried in our muscles. With practice, you get better at controlling the muscle relaxation and can get to the point where you can relax the muscles by simply thinking about it.

Before beginning PMR, consider the following recommendations: If you have problems with muscles or health concerns, consult a physician before trying these techniques. Try to practice in a quiet place without distractions. Wear loose clothing and remove your shoes if possible. Avoid eating a lot right beforehand, as the digestive process may interfere with relaxation. Try the procedure sitting comfortably in a chair. Do the procedure for about ten minutes each day.

Take a deep breath; let it out slowly. Repeat. Now work your way through the various muscles listed below, tensing for ten seconds then relaxing. As you relax, imagine stress flowing out of the muscles. Concentrate on how the muscles feel, specifically the contrast between tension and relaxation. After practicing this for a while, you'll be able to recognize tension being held in specific muscle groups. Try to tense only the muscles in focus. At first this may be difficult, but with practice it will become easier. Try not to hold your breath, grit your teeth, or squint. Breathe slowly and evenly, and think only about the tension relaxation. Work your way through the following muscles, tensing for ten seconds, relaxing for fifteen; repeat, and move on.

1. *Hands*: Tense your fists; relax. Extend your fingers; relax.
2. *Biceps and triceps*: Tense your biceps (make a muscle—but shake your hands to make sure you're not tensing them into a fist); relax (drop your arm to the chair). Tense your triceps (try to bend your arms the wrong way); relax (drop them).
3. *Shoulders*: Pull them back (careful with this one); relax them. Push your shoulders forward (hunch); relax.
4. *Neck* (lateral): With your shoulders straight and relaxed, turn your head slowly to the right as far as you can; relax. Turn to the left; relax.
5. *Neck* (forward): Dig your chin into your chest; relax. (Bringing your head back is not recommended—you could break your neck.)
6. *Mouth*: Open your mouth as far as possible; relax. Bring your lips together or purse them as tightly as possible; relax.
7. *Tongue* (extended and retracted): With your mouth open, extend your tongue as far as possible; relax (let it sit in the bottom of your mouth). Bring it back in your throat as far as possible; relax.
8. *Tongue* (roof and floor): Dig your tongue into the roof of your mouth; relax. Dig it into the bottom of your mouth; relax.
9. *Eyes*. Open your eyes as wide as possible (furrow your brow); relax. Close them tightly (squint); relax. Make sure you completely relax your eyes, forehead, and nose after each tensing.

10. *Breathing*: Take as deep a breath as possible—and then take a little more; let it out and breathe normally for fifteen seconds. Let all the breath in your lungs out—and then a little more; inhale and breathe normally for fifteen seconds.
11. *Back*: With your shoulders resting on the back of the chair, push your body forward so your back is arched; relax. Be very careful with this one, or don't do it at all.
12. *Butt*: Tense your butt tightly and raise your pelvis slightly off the chair; relax. Dig your buttocks into the chair; relax.
13. *Thighs*: Extend your legs and raise them about six inches off the floor or the footrest, but don't tense your stomach; relax. Dig your feet (heels) into the floor or footrest; relax.
14. *Stomach*: Pull in your stomach as far as possible; relax completely. Push out your stomach or tense it as if you were preparing for a punch in the gut; relax.
15. *Calves and feet*: Point your toes (without raising your legs); relax. Point your feet up as far as possible (beware of cramps—if you get them or feel them coming on, shake them loose); relax.
16. *Toes*: With legs relaxed, dig your toes into the floor; relax. Bend your toes up as far as possible; relax.

Yoga is another wonderful way to relax. Many different kinds of yoga are available to you through various means, from local instructors to international gurus. Classical yoga is separated into eight *limbs*, each a part of the complete system for mental, physical, and spiritual well-being. Four of the limbs deal with mental and physical exercises designed to bring the mind in tune with the body. The other four deal with different stages of meditation. There are many types of yoga, all with the same goals of health and harmony but with varying techniques. Hatha yoga, probably the most commonly practiced in America, is a highly developed system of nearly two hundred physical postures, movements, and breathing techniques designed to tune the body to its optimal health. Yoga philosophy believes the breath to be an important facet of health, as the breath is the largest source of *prana*, or life force. Hatha yoga utilizes *pranayama*, which means control of breathing. Hatha yoga works practitioners toward strength and flexibility, mental awareness, and spiritual enlightenment. Regular practice will promote gracefulness, balance, agility, flexibility, strength, and an overall feeling of wellness, along with a reduction in stress and anxiety.

Many of the yogic postures and meditations begin with breathing. That simple act of inhaling and exhaling—oxygen in and carbon dioxide out—is crucial to energy at every level. Little do we realize the magical interactions occurring in our cells throughout our bodies as they gain energy from respiration. Breath is cleansing and is the foundation for relaxed, meditative states of mind. For many of us breathing has become short and incomplete through disuse. As babies we screamed and worked our lungs well. Through life, we tend to stop breathing so fully unless we are athletes, singers, wind musicians, or others who depend on lung power. We can reclaim some of that lost lung range and relax while we're at it.

Creative Moment

Visualization techniques are a form of meditation in which thought is focused and purposeful. There are many forms of visualization with all kinds of goals, from peace to prosperity. From athletes and businesspeople to those seeking a better game and those seeking God, visualization is being used across many life paths. Shakti Gawain (1978) offers techniques in *Creative Visualization*, which takes a new path to an old school with thinkers like Dale Carnegie, Norman Vincent Peale, Claude Bristol, and others. In essence, she says what has been obvious to positive thinkers over the years—if you want something to occur, start thinking about it occurring, and keep thinking about it. That is, visualize it and persist in that visualization as your actions move toward the goal. You want to create an outstanding portfolio? Start visualizing it—imagine yourself presenting it; imagine the contents—actually see the polished and professional pieces you wish to create. It's like making a wish. And sometimes wishes do come true.

Visualization techniques vary. Images to keep in mind include white light, total darkness, flowing water, relaxing natural scenes, your workshop, the color spectrum, 3D shapes, and other mental exercises. Most teachers suggest relaxation, "getting quiet," before imaging. Gawain (1978, 1998) outlines many varieties of things to think, much of it based on a technique she learned in a Silva Mind Control course. "The most important technique I learned in that course was the basic technique of creative visualization—relaxing deeply and then picturing a desired goal in your mind exactly the way you want it to be. I started to practice the technique and found that it was amazingly effective" (1998, p. 13). These imaging/visualizing techniques are used across disciplines, from sports and business to psychological, medical, and spiritual healing treatments.

Here is a simple visualization, a combination of images used by many practitioners. The steps are as follows:

1. Relax with three complete breaths. Keep breathing slowly and relaxing throughout the exercise.
2. Imagine the color spectrum (red, orange, yellow, green, blue, indigo, violet) slowly, one color every 15 seconds or so.
3. Imagine pure darkness.
4. Imagine pure, shimmering, white, healing light flowing into your head and through your body.
5. Imagine yourself flowing as a drop of water in a stream.
6. Imagine yourself in a relaxing natural scene.
7. Imagine yourself doing something you wish to do.

Some people have difficulty seeing colors in their imagination, and if you do, you can imagine three-dimensional objects—apples, oranges, trees—with the colors. The color spectrum lulls your thoughts away from moment-to-moment concerns. Imagining darkness encourages "no mind," emptying your thoughts. Imagining white light energy that radiates from the sun can have therapeutic effects. White, shimmering light imagery is often used in healing therapies. Water imagery can help loosen you up and connect to life-giving flows. Natural scenes can be in a field, in the woods, at the beach, in the water or air—whatever surrounding you find soothing. The final step is to visualize something you wish to happen. Perhaps it's a performance you are anticipating, a presentation, or something you need to write. Maybe you need to talk to someone, there's a chore that needs to be completed, or you're trying to get past a fear. Picture yourself doing it. The lesson here is that the mind is very powerful and we can often think ourselves into a more relaxed state.

Many meditation exercises entail breathing in certain ways. Try a "complete breath." Begin by sitting comfortably in a chair or on the ground. Take a deep breath and exhale completely. Begin breathing in slowly through your nose, pushing out on the belly as you do so, for five counts. This allows the diaphragm to drop, letting air into the lower lungs. Continue inhaling while allowing the chest to expand for five counts. For the final five counts, raise your shoulders as you inhale to your maximum. Hold your breath in for a few counts. As you exhale slowly, imagine all stress and tension flowing out of your body. Doing these complete breaths will increase your lung power, stamina, and relaxation, as well as prepare you for other moves and meditations.

A number of meditation and visualization techniques are available to help you relax and let go of fear. Beyond relaxation and forgetting fear, meditation can enhance the quality of your awareness in social action and actualization of mind. For peak performance in communication, it helps to be in the present moment. Many meditation techniques help us make contact with the present, getting in touch with the here and now, awakening the "mind's eye." Our thinking often wanders to the past or future with regrets or worries or any assortment of anxieties. The aim of many meditations is to come into the present without judgment (those sneaky attitudes) and to downplay the chatter of chaotic and limiting thoughts. Meditation is intrapersonal communication at its best, communicating with your self in ways that unlock the powers and mysteries of mind.

Again, meditation begins with breathing. One simple meditation is entirely focused on breathing. Sit comfortably. Inhale slowly, exhale slowly, thinking about your breath. Try to think nothing; just breathe. If a thought, worry, plan, or anxiety-producing idea comes to mind, just let it slide out with your breath. Breathe.

Some meditations couple breathing with sound. When the Tibetan Buddhist monks of Gaden Shartse Monastery visited our town, they shared a six-syllable mantra—*om mani peme hung*—where each sound unfolds into meanings about the right goals of mind and life as well as negative aspects to be purified. Chanting the mantra can have a soothing effect on the soul. If nothing else, repeating the sounds allows the mind to wander from worries, fears, and other psychobabble to a more relaxed state. But that state is not a stagnant thing, just as the still water of a pond is not still; though the surface is calm and better reflects nature.

The goal of many meditation practices, as mentioned by Jon Kabat-Zinn in his *Wherever You Go, There You Are*, is mindfulness. Mindfulness is being in the present moment, letting go of fear and worry and other hindering mental constructs. It is an awakening of wonder and putting in check the tendency toward constant judgment. Mindfulness is, paradoxically, achieved by letting thoughts go. Let go. Be here now.

Chapter 11

Frizzantine/iStock/Thinkstock

Communication Competence

"Ask, and it shall be given you;
Seek, and you shall find;
Knock and it shall be opened unto you."

—Matthew 7:7

When employers are surveyed on what they wish to see in new hires they often answer, "Communication skills." Communication is central to an employee's ability to train, learn, and get along with co-workers. Reading, writing, listening, and speaking are found at the core of personal development, in the organization and otherwise. In fact, your ability to get what you want in life is intricately woven into your ability to communicate well, and it can always be improved. In this chapter we will look at communication competence and the steps to asserting yourself.

Communication competence is the degree to which your goals are achieved through effective and appropriate interactions. Communication is goal-directed in many ways and at a number of different levels. One basic goal of communication is to share meaning. Whether we are in conversation, writing a letter or texting a friend, we usually hope others will understand us, will get our meaning. Other goals of communication include (1) self-presentation goals, (2) relational goals, and (3) instrumental goals. Self-presentation goals have to do with how you want to be perceived. If you are presenting a speech on some hot issue you will likely want people to think you know what you're talking about. Relational goals have to do with developing, maintaining, and terminating relationships. Perhaps you want to meet that likable person across the room from you; or maybe you're considering strategies for breaking up with your current intimate other; or maybe you merely want to change the relationship. Those are relational goals. Instrumental goals have to do with manipulating people or situations to achieve desired ends. If you are using communication skills to sell somebody something, manage conflict between people, or gain compliance, then you are working on instrumental goals.

Not all communication is consciously goal-directed. Phatic communication, for instance—communicating for the sheer enjoyment derived from communicating—may not be aimed at a specific goal. As you sit chatting with friends you may not have any ulterior motive other than the pleasure derived from being with them. But even such purposeless communication could be viewed as having goals to relay information and enhance friendships. So while you may not be trying to consciously persuade or manipulate, there are usually goals to your communication.

Clarity—the ability to clearly express yourself as a communicator—used to be considered a measure of competence, and it still is to some extent. In many situations, it is helpful to be clear. But clarity is not always necessary or appropriate for social situations. Eric Eisenberg (1984) borrowed a phrase from Kenneth Burke, "strategic ambiguity," to comment on the benefits of being unclear. Indeed, due to the equivocal nature of language itself—different people will interpret words differently—it is difficult if not impossible to be completely clear anyway. And there are times when we will want to be strategically ambiguous. Political situations, where a candidate fears committing wholly to one position so as not to upset other constituents, call for strategic ambiguity. Or when your friend has just come home with the most hideous tattoo you've ever seen and asks how you like it, you might answer, "It's interesting," to protect feelings. Clarity is okay, but it is not always necessary to be a competent communicator.

Effectiveness is a measure of communication competence. Effectiveness is the extent to which communication helps you achieve desired outcomes or goals. If you are trying to sell Girl Scout cookies door to door and that nice lady at the house across the street buys some, then you were effective—you achieved your desired outcome. If you are asking a teacher to change a grade she gave you on a research paper and she changes it, then you achieved your goal. If you confront your roommate to stop leaving crumbs all over the couch cushion and he agrees to change his behavior, then you were effective. Communication can help you reach goals.

Appropriateness refers to using the right communication for the context. As mentioned under pragmatics and the coordinated management of meaning, what is "right" for the context depends on social expectations and rules. What makes our social dramas interesting is that different people hold different ideas for what is appropriate. One child might get praised for performing the same act that another child gets spanked for ("You won that fight in school—good boy, Johnny!"), depending on the expectations of the family system. A speaker might tell a joke with one group that gets uproarious laughter, while that same joke might be met with cold stares by a different group. Or consider the dramas of different funerals. At one funeral—possibly most—it might be considered rude to be laughing near the casket; while at another funeral friends tell funny stories and laugh about their friend in the casket. Appropriateness depends on the context, social system expectations, and the nature of relationships.

Spitzberg and Cupach (1984) claim communication competence depends on motivation, knowledge, and skills. Motivation has to do with one's tendency to approach or avoid social situations, as well as the desire to improve one's communication. Knowledge refers to both topical and procedural awareness. Knowing the topic being discussed enhances one's competence. For instance, if you find yourself in a group of people who are discussing gardening techniques, a discussion of herbal remedies or the past of a political party, knowledge of those topics will help in the discussion. Procedural knowledge deals with how to act in the social situation, or how to proceed given the circumstances. If you need to give a speech, knowing how to introduce a topic, develop some variations on a theme, tell stories, and conclude will add to your credibility and competence. Communication skills are about the ability to perform social behaviors such as public speaking, listening, dyadic interaction, storytelling, and other forms of self-expression. If you have the desire to improve your communication (motivation), commit yourself to learn about various topics (knowledge), and practice communicating in different contexts (skills), your competence will grow.

Other determinants of communication competence include adaptability, conversational involvement, conversational management, and empathy (Canary and Cody, 2000). *Adaptability* refers to flexibility and your ability to change behaviors and goals to meet needs. Mental and social flexibility play into this area of competence, and they describe adaptability through six factors: experience, composure, confirmation, disclosure, articulation, and wit. *Social experience* comes from participating in various social interactions with different groups, which helps you develop a range of behaviors. The wider your range of experience, the easier it is to adapt to different social situations. *Social composure* refers to keeping calm even in trying circumstances. Remaining socially relaxed, whether in a conversation or a public presentation, is one of the most telling signs of communication competence. *Social confirmation* means you acknowledge others' participation and goals. Skill at including others in conversation is a valued quality as a communicator. *Appropriate disclosure* refers to the amount and type of information you share. Knowing when to reveal or conceal information about yourself and others is critical to practicing tactfulness, a crucial part of competence. *Articulation* is your ability to express ideas through language. Becoming more articulate often comes with learning and practice in social situations. *Wit* refers to your ability to use humor in social situations. It enhances the flexibility in social interactions by easing tensions. A little wit is as helpful as a little wine to free the fluidity of conversation.

Conversational involvement refers to being *with* your conversational partner or group both in mind and action, cognitively and behaviorally. Canary and Cody mention responsiveness, perceptiveness, and attentiveness as marks of involvement. Responsiveness is knowing what to say and when to say it in conversation. Perceptiveness is your awareness of how others perceive you, and being aware of contextual cues and other unspoken but meaningful communication. Sometimes there's more meaning in the empty spaces than the words themselves. Attentiveness is about listening, not being preoccupied with your own thoughts while others are speaking. Getting involved in conversation requires that we let go of some worries and calm the chatter that sometimes buzzes in our minds.

Conversational management refers to the way communicators regulate their interactions, keeping them going by managing who speaks, changing speakers, and changing topics. Groups have assorted and sometimes funny ways of controlling participation of members in conversation. I have a nephew and niece who are always good for a lot of laughs at parties, weddings, and other gatherings. They're both very witty, saying things off the cuff that would take me about three days to think of. They both are also expressive, gregarious, and can each easily command the attention in a room. What's funny is when they are both part of the same group in conversation, and she's talking a lot, he will say something like, "Yep, that's her, always got to dominate the conversation." His move is a light poke and an attempt to shift the conversation. We can also manage conversations by asking quiet members for their thoughts, or artfully segueing from one topic to the next—and it can be done as simply as saying, "That reminds me of . . ."

Empathy is our ability to understand the viewpoint of others and share emotional experiences, to "walk in another's shoes," so to speak. To empathize is to identify with others' feelings and thoughts, to understand where they're coming from and going to, to laugh and cry and otherwise match our emotions to theirs. Sometimes all it takes to empathize is motivation—wanting to feel the world from another's perspective. That's part of the beauty of good theater, good books, and good conversation—to let us live the world through another's eyes and to dive more deeply to the depths of our and their emotions. *Empathy gets us outside our self-contained world and is one of the strongest ingredients in forming relationships and loving bonds.* Empathy requires that we slow down a bit. It's tough to feel others' feelings if we're in a hurry to get on to the next important place, the next critical time. To empathize is to lose yourself in the perspective of others, to drop your own worries to address theirs, and it works wonders for relationships.

Learning to Listen

To empathize is to listen. The answers to just about anything we want to know are out there if we can take a few moments to tune in—if we can listen. All of us have questions, like how do I get that job, or how can I ace that test, or how can I sell this set of steak knives, or how will I know when it's love? At times the answers are right there in front of us, right in our own backyard, or even right in our own head; and all it takes is asking a question and listening.

Listening is not easy. We should know that, but most of us don't. Most of us assume listening is easy—you said something; I heard it. But of course, listening is much more difficult than that. Listening is different from hearing. Hearing involves registering sound, but listening involves connecting to meaning. Hearing is physiological, with physical sound waves vibrating in a physical audio apparatus then sending an electrochemical impulse to the brain. Listening is more social/psychological and connected to the physical, where the words and gestures interpreted between people produce meaning and meaningful responses. Hearing is more the reception of sound, whereas listening is more the social construction of meaning. Hearing is sensing; listening is thinking.

Why is listening so difficult? For one, we have not been trained to listen. One report I saw years ago said that listening is the communication activity we perform the most yet receive the least amount of training in. In our total of time communicating, we typically spend 14 percent writing, 16 percent speaking, 17 percent reading, and 53 percent listening (or at least in situations where we could be listening). Those averages will vary for people because some talk more, some read more, and so on. Our schooling includes lessons in reading, writing, and speaking; but it's a rare person who's had listening training. So listening is the communication activity we do the most but in which we are least trained.

Listening is also difficult because our own thoughts get in the way. We have psychological barriers, such as mental chatter, fears, and the tendency to think about other things while others are speaking. Some say it's because our minds have so much free time to wander during listening, due to the difference between the rate of speech and our capacity to comprehend. Studies have shown that people can comprehend speech even at the rate of 500 to 600 words per minute; but the average rate of speech is only about 150 to 200 words per minute. Because we can comprehend faster than words come in, our brains have time to dance around other thoughts, and often do. So the process of listening is often a tuning in to the speaker, then tuning out to think a little, then tuning in, and so on. Seldom do we stay completely focused on the speaker. This difference in the ratio of speech rate to comprehension is a major barrier to listening.

Another barrier to listening is found in the many varieties of noise. Environmental sounds like traffic, horns, wind, voices, music, and more can interfere with listening. Visual noise can also distract attention, like people walking by or things moving around. Distracting speaker characteristics, from annoying vocal qualities to an unzipped zipper, can also function as noise.

Yet another barrier to listening might be our motivation—perhaps we simply don't want to listen. There are plenty of reasons not to listen. We've determined that the content of what's being said is not important; we don't care for the person doing the talking; we believe what's being said has been said before; the words and the speaker have no value for us; and so on. We should note that not listening can have survival value, saving us time or protecting our minds from worthless chatter. But often we don't listen even when we do care about the person, the content has value, and an answer may be waiting in the words. Listening is difficult for many reasons.

Listening opportunities abound, in conversations and beyond. We listen for many reasons—to comprehend, to evaluate, to empathize, and to enjoy. Listening to comprehend is what we do in learning situations, in trying to obtain knowledge and understand the world around us. Listening to evaluate is what we do in critical and discriminating situations, as when we're evaluating a speech or choosing between people's ideas or listening to political candidates. Listening to empathize is trying to feel the other's emotions and see the world from their point of view. Listening for enjoyment—sometimes called aesthetic or appreciative listening—can be done for relaxation, artful awareness, and so much more. We can enjoy music, lyrics, a lecture, sounds of nature, or any moment where we stop long enough to listen. I remember listening to my ten-year-old daughter read me a story, and it was a pleasure.

Better listening comes from these habits:

1. Caring, motivating yourself to listen
2. Suspending judgment, turning off criticism for a few moments
3. Concentrating, avoiding distractions
4. Optimistically opening your mind to others' perspectives
5. Getting excited about ideas and the power of information

We can get better at listening, and it will likely lead to rewards. Not only will listening lead you to answers that help in your quest, in whatever it is you strive toward, and not only will it bring you to profitable gains, but it will also connect you to others in a more pleasing fashion. When we begin to care more about what others have to say we get connected in more satisfying relationships. And that, I think, leads to a richer life.

Becoming a More Competent Communicator

When we begin to listen we begin to more fully communicate. And when we begin asking for what we want, we are on the road to more competent communication. There are so many opportunities to improve our lives by asking. Ask for better treatment from others; ask for a better deal in the marketplace; ask that teacher to grade you more fairly; ask your friend to carry his load; ask a roommate to clean up after herself; ask a parent for money! Many good things might happen if only we ask. Let's explore the art of asking for what we want, but first a short journey into why we don't. Much of the following material comes from a course I took on assertiveness with Ray Tucker years ago at Bowling Green State University. Tucker once said *it's better to deal with the anxiety of asserting ourselves than the frustration of not*. We should add this caveat: sometimes it is better not to act, not to confront, not to argue, not to assert; but most of the time it is preferable to assert yourself and only you can decide. Choose your battles wisely, as they say.

Keep in mind that self-assertion is happening within context and in relation to various people. So what might be right in one context, with a certain person or people, may not fit in another context. Engaging in argument or voicing your opinion can be the fitting response to one situation and not another. Tactfulness is found in discernment, knowing when to act and when to be patient.

Why do we not ask for what we want? Albert Ellis, who developed his own brand of assertiveness therapy, provided answers to that. Ellis created Rational Emotive Behavior Therapy (REBT) in 1955 and continued to teach it, preach it, and revise it until his death in July 2007. The Albert Ellis Institute in New York City continues to promote REBT, which their website said "is an action-oriented psychotherapy that teaches individuals to examine their own thoughts, beliefs and actions and replace those that are self-defeating with more life-enhancing alternatives."

In his *Guide to Rational Living* (1970) Ellis outlined the irrational ideas that circulate in our thoughts and stop us from asking for what we want. He revised those ideas throughout the years and they were eventually offered online on the REBT Network.

Twelve Irrational Ideas That Stop Us from Asserting Ourselves

1. I must be loved and approved by everyone. The idea that it is a dire necessity for adults to be loved by others for almost everything they do—instead of their concentrating on their own self-respect, on winning approval for practical purposes, and on loving rather than on being loved.
2. If you commit an act against me, you must be punished. The idea that certain acts are awful or wicked, and that people who perform such acts should be severely damned—instead of the idea that certain acts are self-defeating or antisocial, and that people who perform such acts are behaving stupidly, ignorantly, or neurotically and would be better helped to change. People's poor behaviors do not make them rotten individuals.
3. If things don't go my way it is catastrophic. The idea that it is horrible when things are not the way we like them to be—instead of the idea that it is too bad, that we would better try to change or control bad conditions so that they become more satisfactory, and, if that is not possible, we had better temporarily accept and gracefully lump their existence.

(continued)

(continued)

4. Misery is external, caused by someone else, and I am not in control of it. The idea that human misery is invariably externally caused and is forced on us by outside people and events—instead of the idea that neurosis is largely caused by the view that we take of unfortunate conditions.
5. I must obsess about my fears. The idea that if something is or may be dangerous or fearsome we should be terribly upset and endlessly obsess about it—instead of the idea that one would better frankly face it and render it non-dangerous and, when that is not possible, accept the inevitable.
6. Difficulties and responsibility should be avoided. The idea that it is easier to avoid than to face life difficulties and self-responsibilities—instead of the idea that the so-called easy way is usually much harder in the long run.
7. I am completely dependent on others. The idea that we absolutely need something other or stronger or greater than our self on which to rely—instead of the idea that it is better to take the risks of thinking and acting less dependently.
8. I must always prove myself competent. The idea that we should be thoroughly competent, intelligent, and achieving in all possible respects—instead of the idea that we would better do rather than always need to do well and accept our self as a quite imperfect creature, who has general human limitations and specific fallibilities.
9. I am a victim of my past. The idea that because something once strongly affected our life, it should indefinitely affect it—instead of the idea that we can learn from our past experiences but not be overly attached to or prejudiced by them.
10. I must always be in control. The idea that we must have certain and perfect control over things—instead of the idea that the world is full of probability and chance and that we can still enjoy life despite this.
11. Happiness is found in complete relaxation. The idea that human happiness can be achieved by inertia and inaction—instead of the idea that we tend to be happiest when we are vitally absorbed in creative pursuits, or when we are devoting ourselves to people or projects outside ourselves.
12. I am not in control of my emotions. The idea that we have virtually no control over our emotions and that we cannot help feeling disturbed about things—instead of the idea that we have real control over our destructive emotions if we choose to change the narcissistic ideas we often employ to create them.

We can use those ideas from Ellis as a springboard to self-expression. Tucker defined assertiveness as "maximizing self-expression while optimizing outcomes for self and others." Expressing yourself while working to enhance relationships—that's assertiveness; as opposed to aggressiveness, which manifests as hostility that deteriorates relationships. Asserting yourself does require a bit of courage, a willingness to see yourself as a work in progress, and a readiness to rethink certain behaviors. No longer can we allow ourselves to say, "Well, that's just the way I am," and no longer can we blame our emotional state on someone else—once we're aware of the choices we make in creating our frame of mind. And we don't have to fret that we're not the best we can be, that we make mistakes, and that things are not going our way, because we know that we are changing; and *we can change*.

Asserting yourself, expressing yourself, asking for what you want, is at the core of communication competence. There are classes, workshops, and other training programs available to you, but it begins with a decision you make. That decision sounds something like this: "I'm not going to back down anymore," or "From now on, I will not be afraid to ask for what I want." As with other changes in your life, motivation plays a key role.

Training programs usually focus on stock issues such as the ability to say no and disagree, replacing aggression with more gently assertive strategies, psychophysiological coping skills, conversation management, and optimizing negotiation skills. So many aspects of our lives are negotiated—our careers, interpersonal relations, and everyday lives—developing these skills in making better deals will pay off many times. Tucker presented an "Assertive Bill of Rights," which he cobbled together from Ellis and other sources. That bill of rights has gone through much iteration through the years, with many people adding and changing items. Here is the basic list with explanations to follow.

Assertiveness means maximizing self-expression and asking for what you want. Purestock/Thinkstock

The Assertive Bill of Rights

You have the right to

1. ask for what you want;
2. change your mind;
3. say "I don't know";
4. not be liked and approved by everybody;
5. make illogical decisions;
6. say "I don't understand";
7. say no and not feel guilty;
8. say "I don't care";
9. do less than is humanly possible;
10. not justify your life to everyone;
11. judge whether other people's problems are your problems;
12. take time, slow down, and think.

Let's look at each right and consider how it might apply to our own situations.

You have the right to ask for what you want. This is one area where many people seem reluctant, whether it is asking a friend for help, asking a roommate to clean up after himself, or asking for a promotion or better job. Many fear rejection or that the person they ask might say no. But when we think about it, that's not such a bad thing. In fact, a little rejection can build character—"whatever doesn't kill you makes you stronger" and all that. When I sold vacuums as a summer job, my boss had a practiced spiel about how "'no' makes us stronger." The more you face rejection, he said, the more people tell you no, but if you keep persevering, the stronger you become. So when you seek that first job, ask for that date, or ask that publisher to publish your book, remember rejection is part of the game—keep asking.

You have the right to change your mind. Some people want to force you into always staying consistent with the past. While it is honorable to be a person of your word and to meet commitments, it is also true that things change, people change, relationships change, and your mind can change. So if you're in a relationship that is going nowhere fast, and you decide you want to pursue different friendships, and the person throws you "but you said you love me!" you can politely say, "I'm sorry; I changed my mind." If a wonderful new opportunity has come up for you, but a co-worker says, "But you agreed to do this," you can tell him you've changed your mind. This doesn't mean we should just bounce willy-nilly through life, changing our minds at a whim each day. But we can change—our mind and our course through life.

You have the right to say "I don't know." We do not have to appear competent all the time. That fear that "I must always appear competent" (see Albert Ellis's irrational idea #8) can prevent us from learning a lot in life. In some learning situations—from learning to use a new computer program to learning a new game to pursuing a new hobby—we are going to benefit from asking others for help. Some shy away from asking because they don't want to appear incompetent. If we are going to thrive on lifelong learning, then we'll have to admit there's a lot we don't know. And it's okay to say so.

You have the right to not *be liked and approved by everybody*. It is normal to seek approval from others. We do it from childhood ("Mama, mama, look at what I did!") through adulthood. But we should not need everyone's approval, and in fact, we cannot get everyone's approval. There are people out there who do not like you just because of who you are, because you're a woman, a man, black, white, too tall, too short, too American, too un-American—and the list goes on. We can give up the effort to be approved by everyone because it can never be fully achieved. If we are overly hooked into approval seeking, it will hamper assertiveness, stopping us from saying no and disagreeing when we need to.

You have the right to make illogical decisions. We are human, and one of the wonderful aspects that separates us from machines is our capacity for emotions. Some decisions in love and war and elsewhere are driven by emotion. When I was selling vacuums, an important part of the demonstration was to surround customers with piles of dirt on white pads; the dirt that their current vacuum was not picking up. I wanted to create a situation where it would be totally illogical for them to refuse to buy. "If the Kirby leaves, the dirt stays—and do you know what's in that dirt?!" Many people want you to act right now because it's the logical thing to do to save money, save time, or save the whales. Sometimes, though, you have to go with your gut instincts, and logic will just have to wait.

You have the right to say "I don't understand." Again, in learning situations, we need not fear looking stupid. I've seen situations where whole classrooms full of people didn't understand a concept, but no one was brave enough to ask for clarification. Don't worry that you "might be a bother" to the teacher or boss or friend who is explaining something. Most people feel good about explaining, and most would rather have you get it right than to pretend and go away and mess up later because you didn't fully understand. Once in a while you might run into a person who seems upset by a request for further explanation, treating the requestor like he's mildly impaired or worse. Those are likely the types who also assume that communication is a simple act and most people should get it because I said it. But in fact communication is not simple, much does need further explanation, and you should not be afraid to say "I don't understand."

You have the right to say no and not feel guilty. Some people have no problem saying no. I am not one of those people. I used to say yes to more requests than I could handle, which got me in trouble, overcommitted, and unable to do everything I had agreed to do. I've learned over the years that I can say no to requests—to be on committees, to give money, to help with some cause—and it is okay. This might go back to the need to be approved, and feeling like people won't think highly of you if you deny a request. But most people will respect you for thoughtfully considering what you will and will not agree to. It's wonderful to help people, give your time and money to worthy causes, and be a giving person—but you can say no.

You have the right to say "I don't care." Tucker used to say, "I care, but not too much." Many people want you to buy into their cause: global warming, feed the hungry, end war, help the homeless, cure a disease, save the children, end pollution, go green, give money, and buy a magnetic ribbon. It's great for you to care, but you can't care for every cause. Choose your charities, where you'll put your money and effort; and to the others you can say, "I care, but . . ."

You have the right to do less than is humanly possible. Perfecting things is a noble course of action, but you needn't get upset if you can't get everything perfect. We are typically involved in many activities at once, at home, at work, at school, and so on. Rarely do we have the time to complete everything in perfect fashion. If we consider most projects a work in progress and don't set our expectations too high, that will save us a lot of anxiety. In this area, Tucker gave us his "90/10" formula. He said you can get 90 percent of the best possible job done in 10 percent of the time it takes to do a job to perfection, and it takes 90 percent of the time to work at that final 10 percent of perfection. For example, you can probably write a pretty good ten-page paper in two hours; but if you want to work toward perfecting that paper for publication, it may take twenty hours or more. When we were in grad school, rushed to do too much work in too little time, after Tucker's course many of us would say, "90/10 it!" when in a time crunch.

You have the right to not justify your life to everyone. "Why did you do that?" is a question we will hear often. You can choose whether or not you wish to explain. Asking for an explanation is a power move, of sorts, similar to when parents demand a child's justification for behavior. It is often a social move that comes just prior to pointing out why you were wrong. But you don't need to explain your motives. Motivation, as we saw earlier, is complex and you might not even know why you behave the way you do. Also, there are often more explanations than one for why you do as you do. Of course there are times when you should try to explain yourself, such as court proceedings or when you're asking forgiveness, but very often we can respond to "why?" with "because I felt like it."

You have the right to judge whether or not other people's problems are your problems. People like to involve us in their stories. Sometimes friends or family or co-workers might try to involve you in their dramas. For instance, they might tell you a story about how they were wronged by person X or what a wicked jerk person X is, to get your sympathy or to identify with you in opposition to that person. Before you know it, you might be entangled in their battles. Or your friend might ask your advice on a personal problem and later grow to expect that advice. Or two friends who are fighting might ask you to determine who is right. You may wish to give your advice or pass judgment, but you can determine if the problem is yours or if the decision should stay in others' hands. You have the right to say, "That's not my drama."

You have the right to take time, slow down, and think. In so many situations people will try to rush your decision. It may be a lover who wants you to decide *now*, or it may be the salesperson telling you the deal is only good today, or maybe it's a child screaming, "Give me that now!" Sometimes you do need to decide now, but more often than not you can take time to think about your decisions. When I was asking my customers to buy a vacuum, I wanted them to decide and put a down payment on it right then, because I knew if I walked out their door without the order, chances were 99.9 percent that they were not going to buy. But if they called me the next day and said, "I'll take it," I would gladly go with the price offered the night before. Try to put time on your side in your various negotiations.

The assertive bill of rights can help you when dealing with social situations, but again, motivation is the key ingredient. *Asserting yourself is a decision you make.* It may be a decision you make because you're tired of letting other people manipulate your life, you're fed up with accepting bad deals, you're being treated unfairly, some other evil is operating and you wish to make it stop, or you've simply decided to ask for what you want.

Ray Tucker had one more helpful bit of advice. He had a sign on his desk that read "Do it now." When it comes time to be assertive, many will procrastinate. The reasons are many: I don't feel like calling him right now; I don't need the hassle; maybe tomorrow; if I don't do it, maybe it will go away; I don't have time; this is not the place; I'll wait till it feels right; and so on. It's never the right time to ask a teacher to change a grade, to ask that person out on a date, or to ask the waiter to take your steak back to the chef and cook it as you ordered it. We can always think of a reason not to do what needs to be done, but sometimes we just have to go ahead and jump in. Do it now.

We can find many opportunities to work on social skills and on becoming more assertive. Competent communication can be developed throughout a lifetime, always working to improve our listening, speaking, and social relaxation.

Creative Moment

Think of a few opportunities in your life where asking for what you want will help. Perhaps it's a job you'd like to get, a relationship to be improved, a grade to be changed, or help you'd like to receive. Consider situations where asserting yourself will enhance your life, then list them.

For each item on your list, consider if there are one or more irrational ideas holding you back. What's stopping you?

Chapter 12

Creating Your Social Reality

" . . . Nothing you can do, but you can learn
how to be you in time. It's easy.
All you need is love . . ."

—The Beatles, "All You Need Is Love"

Your mind is a weave of social influences, so many symbolic interactions, in relation to many others. You have grown up and continue to live amid many persuasive influences, each providing symbols, ideas, and attitudes that help you on your merry way. The words of others have provided equipment for living, strategies for handling situations. I hope this book has provided you with some helpful strategies for peace and freedom of mind.

Summarizing the Story So Far

This book begins with the assumption that we create our social realities in various social systems. Those social systems are our drama, and there are dramatically different dramas playing out right now across humankind. While one person's quest is for power, another's is for peace, and another is just fighting to survive (and still another is searching for that perfect Gucci purse!). My drama—the reality I live of social systems and relationships woven together—is not the same as yours. We live in different skins and different stories. There may be one earth, one physical reality, but many social realities play at the same time.

In the dramas of our social systems, our minds are influenced by and connected within a grander Mind. We are connected with ages past through ideas that transcend time. We are connected to each other and interdependent with a wider consciousness. Call this consciousness God, Nature, the Gaia principle, the Way, Grand Wisdom, or whatever widest term you choose, we are woven together in the All—and it is mind and communication that connect us. We exist within a grand matrix of information that is always moving, always interacting.

As we grow through interaction with people in different contexts, our individual minds develop within that grander pattern. Bateson once called mind "the pattern which connects," that somewhat mysterious tie that binds. On the path of our nurturance we acquire assorted ways of thinking and being from others, but also begin to mesh into that web of human relationships in which we will act and become our selves. In those interactions with others we pick up attitudes and ways of thinking that equip our minds for surviving the various trials and tribulations of life. For instance, maybe a past coach gave you words or attitudes that help you persevere when the going gets tough; or a friend gave you words that help you relax in uptight situations; or a preacher provided terms that grant insight on the path to God or love or peace. You've picked up language that acts as "equipment for living," in Burke's terms, as you weave your meanings in the mazes of social games.

You've also picked up patterns of memories, attitudes, and habits of perceiving your world. Created in communication with others, these MAPs are central to your social constructions—your social reality. That "reality" depends a lot on how your memories and attitudes get linked to experience as you perceive. And your perceptions are abstractions, a reproduction of the world out there brought to you by thoughts made by language, interaction, and patterns of mind. Your ideas of reality are *not* the reality. As Korzybski taught, "the map is not the territory." Awareness of our own abstracting is the beginning of critical thinking. We are an abstracting animal, perceiving and talking and thinking about only fragments of the total reality as we make and seek our meaning together.

What is meaning? That depends on your drama. Some will seek deep wisdom, while others are after the next good time; and both have their place. But that meaning is not so much in you as it is in the relationship of you to the world and others. Meaning arises in contexts and builds through interactions between people. As such, meanings are constructed, and as Pearce pointed out, coordinated and managed between actors. The words on this page that may inspire meaning for you will mean little to a person who can't decode the English language, and they have no meaning to a child more interested in a magical toy land. Meaning happens *between* and *within people*, and is part of that pattern which connects you to all else, part of the grander pattern of Mind that pervades all.

The meaning you get, the way you abstract your world and what inspires you, is central to motivation. The way you name your world is tied to motives, said Burke. The language we internalize moves us, causing us to act in certain ways. If I name a person or group as "evil" and deserving of annihilation, then I will act toward them quite differently than had I named them as "mistaken" and in need of help. The way you label orients you toward the labeled and motivates you to act in ways consistent with the label. Language guides thought and motivation. The perspective of this book leans toward Viktor Frankl's synopsis: the main motivation is meaning. The way we make meaning is the way we make our mind, and that is the way we are motivated.

What motivates you is very much a part of your personality. Your actions, beliefs, and the "why?" for which you live are all central to your being. Again, there is no one single "why," no one motive, that moves you, but rather an array of motives and several dimensions of personality that define you. Who are you? That depends on who you're with and who you've interacted with before. It depends on current circumstances, your frame of mind, and the relationships. As you read these words and quietly contemplate how communication creates your mind and being, you may feel like a different person than the last time you were in a heated argument with someone. Personality arises in interaction. Some people and situations help bring out the best in you, and some the worst.

"Who you are" got shaped in past interactions and is influenced by present relationships with many others, as the whole drama unfolds into futures. All of those relationships are persuasive in some way, from parents trying to set you on the right course, to friends appealing with you to play with them, to teachers wishing you to think in certain ways, to preachers praying for your salvation. You are surrounded and enmeshed in persuasive linkages with every relationship having a dimension of influence. From mama to preachers to teachers to the media—all work their magic to influence you.

The media play a prominent role in our persuasive network of relations. Remember "the media" are plural—they are an array of organizations—so when people try to characterize the media as a single-minded entity they are wrong. Those who control the media have learned a few things about social control, especially in the ways your network of peers can be used persuasively. The media have crept into our mind and action in many ways, though in different dosages for a public with very different media habits. Some are media-fried, hardwired to news and entertainment to the point of high anxiety. For others, media are background noise that adds to a rushed, consumer-driven existence. Still others use the media for access to valuable information. For some, the media are an oppressive force, the very chains that hold them to the family room easy chair or keep them wanting the next terrific technology. For some, media are the pathway to freedom, relaying news of the world and possibilities for growth and change. The media are the opiate and elixir of mind and masses. They are big business, big brother, big adventure, and big-time persuasion. Their images and ideas are woven into our mind and dramas, a different act depending on what you're tuned in to. Again, what the media are depends on your relationship to them—good, bad, and all points in between. They are a force to be cherished and criticized.

Face your fears about communication. Whether you're apprehensive about speaking in public or sharing secrets in private, working in groups or crossing borders, asking questions or being asked, you can work to lessen the grip of those fears on your social life. I can't say it works all the time—and some fears are debilitating enough to seek counseling and medicine—but sometimes just facing your fears and slowly acting to do those things you fear is therapy enough. Fears are relational as well—becoming manifest in the interactions between you, others, and situations. A few of your fears are found in the ways you've defined situations, where you've learned to associate pain or threat with certain people and scenes. Those fears have been learned and they can be unlearned—you can redefine situations. So much of what holds us back from becoming who we wish to be is rooted in one fear or another. Dealing with them is a lifelong project, so we needn't worry if change comes slowly. Just knowing that we are changing gives motivation.

Practice competent communication. As we make our way through the tangle of persuasive influences, it will help to be mindful, critically aware, and to ask for what we want. Keep going. Let the road go on and on, never quite arriving "there" but picking up bits of wisdom along the way, as you meet and grow with other adventurers on your way to Ithaka.

Ithaka

As you set out for Ithaka
hope your road is a long one,
full of adventure, full of discovery.
Laistrygonians, Cyclops,
angry Poseidon—don't be afraid of them:
you'll never find things like that on your way
as long as you keep your thoughts raised high,
as long as a rare excitement
stirs your spirit and your body.
Laistrygonians, Cyclops,
wild Poseidon—you won't encounter them
unless you bring them along inside your soul,
unless your soul sets them up in front of you.

Hope your road is a long one.
May there be many summer mornings when,
with what pleasure, what joy,
you enter harbors you're seeing for the first time;
may you stop at Phoenician trading stations
to buy fine things,
mother of pearl and coral, amber and ebony,
sensual perfume of every kind—
as many sensual perfumes as you can;
and may you visit many Egyptian cities
to learn and go on learning from their scholars.
Keep Ithaka always in your mind.
Arriving there is what you're destined for.
But don't hurry the journey at all.
Better if it lasts for years,
so you're old by the time you reach the island,

wealthy with all you've gained on the way,

not expecting Ithaka to make you rich.

Ithaka gave you the marvelous journey.

Without her you wouldn't have set out.

She has nothing left to give you now.

And if you find her poor, Ithaka won't have fooled you.

Wise as you will have become, so full of experience,

you'll have understood by then what these Ithakas mean.

—C. P. Cavafy

Part of my quest is to come to terms with a relational perspective—to understand how our meanings are socially constructed and how those constructions work their magic among us.

Thoughts on a Relational Perspective

1. *The path to understanding human action leads to relationships, not just individuals.* Everything exists *in relation to*. Concepts like personality, power, and persuasion are understood as between-people phenomena as much as within person.
2. *Interdependence and independence are eternally at work in relationships.* As Burke noted, we are *a part of* and *apart from*. Both are crucial. Relationships are a mutual need, reciprocity and interaction between entities—interdependence—whether we're talking about people, or cells, or nations. But independence is important too, especially independence of mind. Maintain your independent mind.
3. *Love is the tie that binds in social relationships.* There's a hymn that begins "Blest be the tie that binds," and that tie may be love. Love—as an emotion, an attitude, a frame of mind, and a way of life—lays a foundation for the interactive bonds between us. I'm not talking about love as only an intimate or friendly term, but as openness to understanding and wanting to participate in the grander pattern—the pattern of wisdom that pervades all.
4. *A relational ethic recognizes the interconnectedness of all, united by Mind, the pattern that connects.* Call it the Gaia principle or cosmic energy or Holy Spirit: there is an interlacing network of symbol, mind, and action that connects us in the fabric of the universe. This isn't just hokum about something unseen—we see the connection in a seed sending out a sprout searching for the sunshine. A relational perspective is within that grand connectedness. Relationships are built by interacting information. In fact, some are now suggesting the whole universe, or multiverse, is a web of vibrant changing information. Our human relationships are just fractal parts in the grand information matrix.
5. *Compassion should guide action.* Accompanying terms like *empathy*, *tolerance*, and *understanding* guide our attitudes and action, integrating and synthesizing to counter the inherent separation and disintegration in the human drama (inherent, in fact, in all systems). Conflict is inevitable in the social games we play, but we can enter the playing field with friendly or nasty intentions, and I believe it's better for all when it's friendly. Blessed be the peacemakers.
6. *Critical thinking can aim at synthesis, not just separateness.* You can be critically aware from a stance that identifies with others, not necessarily separating from what you critique. People are apt to think a critical frame of mind must be hard, tough, divisive, or cynical. Phrases like "tough love" and "compassionate conservatism" approach the attitude I'm suggesting, but those phrases carry baggage in certain circles. We can seek a critical openness.
7. *A relational perspective is an appreciation for communication in all of its many forms.* That is a directive to keep dialogue open, to continue the conversation. We may not have the answers to all our problems, or resolution in the many conflicts, but should be willing, in the interest of that ultimate identification, to keep the discussion open. Give peace a chance.

You construct your social reality with the symbols, meanings, and choices you make together.
kzenon/iStock/Thinkstock

Look around; you'll see the unity happening, hopefully just as much or more than you can see the battle lines being drawn. Many are working on the project to enhance human relationships and practice nonviolent action and communication.

Of course that relational ethic may sound weak to some, especially those taking a hard line in conflicts. I realize conflict happens, but I encourage you to choose an integrative orientation over disintegrative. The problem is there's so much money and so many friends to be made by disintegrative orientations, from the cash generated by bombs to the unity gained by spreading fear and hate. I'm not blind to all this. I just believe that working toward nurturing love makes more positive energy than the mistrust and vengefulness that grows from protracted conflicts—even if they are profitable.

That relational ethic also breeds awareness of relationships in all aspects of the universe, not just human bonds but all things.

Connecting Patterns

Ultimately, we each are trying to connect in one way or another. In *Mind and Nature: A Necessary Unity* (1979) Gregory Bateson explained the pattern that connects—the interconnectedness of *all* as recurring interactions and much more. All of nature has a kind of intelligence woven throughout that is communicated by patterns at many levels, and the big one—the pattern of patterns. *Just as we talk to each other through cycles of information given and received, so too do our nerves and cells and other aspects of nature communicate.* It's all happening at once, and most of it is difficult or impossible to see. It even seems that germs and viruses have means of communicating as they "think" of ways to outsmart our defenses. Germs may not think in the way we think, but at some level they are conscious of their situation and able to adapt, seeking a better way to survive. Perhaps, like us, they even seek to survive in style. I can't imagine a germ wanting to drive a Cadillac, though.

We are just beginning to understand mind and communication. Many are seeking that pattern that connects, what Burke called *ultimate identification*. Just as there is so much unused neural capacity in the brain, there is so much of this pattern of patterns that we have not yet seen or described. Once we begin to seek it, though, we begin to find it in its many manifestations.

The ideal would be for this book to enhance your mind, sense of self, interactions, and relationships; and that begins with a kind of critical awareness. Critical thinking begins with the realization that we are abstracting animals. Go back to Korzybski's point that our tendency is to believe our maps are the reality. More often than not, our abstractions only capture bits of the total picture, and so we should question them and always strive toward more and better information. Such an awareness of abstracting encourages us to check our own and others' information, always on the lookout for differences between what is and what we say and think. This becomes more difficult now as technology allows people to deceive in so many ways, where audio and video creations can misrepresent reality and take us down problematic paths. The presentation of photos that led the United States into the Iraq War, showing proof of mobile weapons labs and weapons of mass destruction turned out to be mistaken. Many lives were lost for the mistake. We need to be forever on the alert of people misrepresenting reality because there are implications.

We need to doubt. But we also need to believe. If we are always doubting people's information, always critical or cynical or attacking the source's credibility, we will never be able to act. The art of discerning comes down to a balance between doubting and believing, not being fooled by the follies of abstraction and yet capturing that information necessary to social and physical survival. Karl Weick (1979) called it an *ambivalent attitude*, and we should cultivate it in our critical awareness. I can believe the event I see on the evening news happened yet also doubt that the way they framed it includes all or most of the important details. I can believe what the president says about an enemy and still not agree with his or her recommended course of action. I can believe what you tell me, while still being aware that your and my abstractions capture only part of the whole reality. Awareness has elements of doubt and belief.

Awareness comes as much from *letting go* as it does from acquiring information. Some see taking in information and obtaining knowledge as the royal road to awareness. While it's good to love learning in life, you also need to be cleaning house, letting go of thoughts and actions that constitute clutter. Sometimes we get caught in cycles of memory and perception that are dysfunctional and destructive; sometimes our attitudes spew hatred and vindictiveness where we would prefer love; and sometimes our act is motivated by fear, seen and unseen. We have emotional baggage—you, me, and everyone. Part of the trick to getting in the moment, being right here right now and aware, is identifying and letting go of the attitudinal baggage that bogs us down.

Learn to let go. If I were to write a poem right now I would begin, Learn to let go. Let go of stress, anger, fear, and stale thinking. Some thoughts are stale—and some stink. How does your mind smell?

Are we after some kind of ultimate understanding or clarity of vision? Is that what it comes down to for those who seek transcendence and enlightenment? Perhaps—but how to get it right is probably very different from behind each other's eyes. That's how I would characterize the goal of awareness—being right with the world. We'd like to get to a point where our attitudes and actions are adjusted to our situation.

Kenneth Burke seemed to be seeking such awareness as he considered comic frames of acceptance and tragic frames of rejection in *Attitudes Toward History* (1937). Beginning with the attitudes of William James, Walt Whitman, and Ralph Waldo Emerson, Burke built his case for the charity created by a comic frame. Let me try to take his volume and reduce it to a few sentences (talk about abstracting!). We continually make choices about whether to accept the universe or protest against it, according to James. In our language we adopt attitudes (incipient acts) and adapt ourselves to situations and other people. If our language comes from a comic frame of acceptance—a frame of mind that guides our actions—it is more charitable, forgiving, and open to understanding. Contrarily, if our language leads us to a tragic frame of rejection, we tend toward seeing people as mad or bad and seek to eliminate or isolate them so that their evil will not flourish. A comic frame is not so much seeing humor in the human drama as it is openness to a diversity of actors and motives. A tragic frame closes one off to possibilities and tends to give birth to pugnacious cycles of action. Burke ultimately equated a tragedy with war and comedy with peace.

A comic frame can potentially loosen uptight social relationships. A comic frame says, "That drug addict is mistaken, but perhaps he can change." A tragic frame says, "Throw the bum in jail before he infects my children." A comic frame says, "I don't agree with her, but her argument has some validity." A tragic frame says, "I don't agree with her and need to hurt her before her opinion hurts me." *A comic frame is compassionate. A tragic frame mistrusts and misunderstands. The comic frame builds bridges and lets the waters of social awareness flow. The tragic frame builds walls and dams.*

The comic frame is found on the road to awareness and understanding. Ironically, we'll need to wander off the path to find it. If we're going to continue toward a fuller understanding—to become wise and all that—we can't get too comfortable with what we know now or too adapted to the present social scene. What works as a survival strategy in one situation may be harmful in another. For instance, while drinking wine in social situations can enhance relaxed interactions, if you carry the pattern too far you may become a pickled drunk. What constitutes a clear understanding at this point in our lives might not cut it as top-shelf thinking later. The people who used to talk tough, for example, about those mealy-mouthed environmentalists a few years ago might now see error in their past attitudes. Life's like that, steps into new doorways, dives into deeper waves, and in each new dimension we may need to get lost in order to find the way.

We can acquire attitudes, pick up tricks to soothe our thoughts and smooth our actions along the way—in a song, a poem, or a conversation with a friend; in exercise, in contemplation, in prayer; in our pleasure and through our pain we can go on learning. Enrichment and enlightenment may be found on the paths of interactions and relationships with others.

We need to learn to sit still for a moment. This is a hyperactive age, in which often we feel on our way anxiously to some goal, no time to stop. My old neighbor Joe—the wise botanist who made gardens grow and thrive—used to say, "Go slow." He understood.

Be still. That's the lesson of mindfulness and being with nature. Stop. Take a moment to think, to not think, to talk to a friend, or maybe even talk to an enemy. You have your goals and places to get to, but they'll still be waiting after you've taken some time to be with someone, to interact in the moment, to join in the pattern that connects.

Half my life ago we were camping at the Red River gorge in Kentucky, atop Eagle's Peak, looking at the stars and in awe with the universe. I began to say something that sounded like worry about the future and my brother's friend said, "Be here now."

Be Here Now

Years later my friend D.P. quoted from the same eternal wisdom: "Yesterday is history and tomorrow is a mystery, but today is a gift; that's why we call it the present." That quote has been attributed to Eleanor Roosevelt, Babatunde Olatunji, and Joan Rivers, but I still remember it from D.P. It's funny how wisdom and words transcend time, providing motivation for first ladies, world drummers, comedians, and professors. Interactions that give insight have instilled in me words for the way to be, reminding me often—as often I forget—to take time, slow down, and think.

Be here now. That's the existential ideal. It's not bad to remember the past, to think happy childhood thoughts, to sigh with nostalgia, or even drum up old fears once in a while, unless such memories consume you. It's okay to look toward the future, to have a plan, to set your goals, and work to achieve them. But if you become so over-planned and goal-driven that you miss opportunities now—you get so hooked on the future that you're missing the present—then you may want to mix it up a bit and create some moments that enrich your life and the lives of others. Being in the moment is the focus of a helpful book by Eckhart Tolle (1999), *The Power of Now*. To interact, form relationships, and evolve mind, we need to be here now.

Not only are you *being* in the here and now, but you are *becoming* as the present flows into the future. Awareness that we are becoming wiser can help us adjust to some of the pains and embarrassments of the present. We don't have to feel inadequate that we are not now the person we wish to be. Rather, we can rejoice in the knowledge that we are working toward it. This attitude of becoming is openness to your potential and ever wider realms of experience, and those realms are realized through relationships with others—preachers, teachers, parents, and friends—those you've known, now know, and have yet to meet.

As our life paths branch into so many choices, our drama unfolds; and all the while the larger drama unfolds on world and universal stages. Your individual life follows a winding road into the grand mystery. Others are on their roads. Sometimes we bump into each other, and sometimes it leads to good things. We don't choose everything in this life—sometimes our lot is dumped in our lap. But we do choose frames of mind. From moment to moment, how will you mind your world?

Ultimately there is a kind of mindfulness to be attained in communication, identification—oneness that places us in the here and now, listening and talking to one another. This reminds me of a line from the song "Tin Man" by America: "Sometimes late, when things are real, and people share the gift of gab between themselves . . ." Sometimes we get closer to that ultimate identification, that communion of minds within Mind, and it brings us closer to our being.

Tree of Being

Tree of being

Roots of been

Branches of to be

Mindful now

Learn from then

Toward visions we can see

We weave the present

From ancestors past

Toward children's future free

Tree of being

Roots of been

Branches of to be

References

Allport, G. W., & Odbert, H. S. (1936). Trait names: A psycholexical study. *Psychological Monographs, 47*, 211.

Austin, J. H. (1999). *Zen and the brain*. Cambridge, MA: The MIT Press.

Bales, R. (1970). *Personality and interpersonal behavior*. New York, NY: Holt, Rinehart and Winston.

Bandura, A. (1973). *Aggression: A social learning analysis*. Englewood Cliffs, NJ: Prentice-Hall.

Bandura, A. (1977). *Social learning theory*. New York, NY: General Learning Press.

Bateson, G. (1972). *Steps to an ecology of mind*. San Francisco, CA: Chandler Publishing Co.

Bateson, G. (1979). *Mind & nature: A necessary unity*. New York, NY: Dutton.

Baudrillard, J. (1994). *Simulacra and simulation*. Ann Arbor, MI: University of Michigan Press.

Bennington, G. (1993). *Jacques Derrida*. Chicago, IL: University of Chicago Press.

Blumler, J., & Katz, E. (1974). *The uses of mass communications*. Beverly Hills, CA: Sage Publications.

Bormann, E. G. (1972). Fantasy and rhetorical vision: The rhetorical criticism of social reality. *Quarterly Journal of Speech, 58*, 396–407.

Burke, K. (1937/1984). *Attitudes toward history* (3d ed.). Berkeley, CA: University of California Press.

Burke, K. (1941/1973). *The philosophy of literary form: Studies in symbolic action* (3d ed.). Berkeley, CA: University of California Press.

Burke, K. (1966). *Language as symbolic action: Essays on life, literature, and method*. Berkeley, CA: University of California Press.

Burke, K. (1968). *Collected poems*. Berkeley, CA: University of California Press.

Burke, K. (1984). *Permanence & change: An anatomy of purpose* (3d ed.). Berkeley, CA: University of California Press.

Cameron, J. (1992). *The artist's way: A spiritual path to higher creativity*. New York, NY: Penguin Putnam.

Canary, D. J., & Cody, M. J. (1994). *Interpersonal communication: A goals-based approach*. New York, NY: St. Martin's Press.

Cohen, B. C. (1963). *The press and foreign policy*. Princeton, NJ: Princeton University Press.

Conn, S. R., & Rieke, M. L. (1994). *The 16PF fifth edition technical manual*. Champaign, IL: Institute for Personality and Ability Testing, Inc.

Derrida, J. (1992). *Acts of literature*. New York, NY: Routledge.

Edwards, B. (1999). *The new drawing on the right side of the brain*. New York, NY: Penguin Putnam.

Eisenberg, E. (1984). Ambiguity as strategy in organizational communication. *Communication Monographs, 51*(3), 227–242.

Ellis, A., & Harper, R. A. (1970). *A guide to rational living*. Englewood Cliffs, NJ: Prentice-Hall.

Fishbein, M., & Ajzen, I. (1975). *Beliefs, attitude, intention, and behavior: An introduction to theory and research*. Reading, MA: Addison-Wesley.

Franck, F. (1973). *The Zen of seeing: Seeing/drawing as meditation*. New York, NY: Vintage Books.

Freud, A. (1937). *The ego and mechanisms of defense*. London, UK: Hogarth Press.

Freud, S. (1949). *The ego and the id*. London, UK: Hogarth Press.

Friedman, M., & Rosenman, R. H. (1974). *Type A behavior and your heart*. New York, NY: Knopf.

Gardner, H. (1973). *The quest for Mind: Jean Piaget, Claude Levi-Strauss, and the Structuralist movement*. New York, NY: Knopf.

Gardner, H. (1993). *Multiple intelligences: The theory in practice*. New York, NY: Basic Books.

Gardner, H. (1999). *Intelligence reframed: Multiple intelligences for the 21st century*. New York, NY: Basic Books.

Gawain, S. (1979). *Creative visualization*. Novato, CA: New World Library.

Gawain, S. (1998). *Living in the light*. Novato, CA: New World Library.

Gerbner, G., Gross, L., Morgan, M., & Signorielli, N. (1994). Growing up with television: The cultivation perspective. In Jennings Bryant & Dolf Zillman (Eds.), *Media effects: Advances in theory and research* (pp. 17–41). Hillsdale, NJ: Lawrence Erlbaum Associates.

Gergen, K. J. (2009). *Relational being: Beyond self and community*. New York, NY: Oxford University Press.

Glasser, W. (1986). *Control theory in the classroom*. New York, NY: Perennial Library/Harper & Row Publishers.

Glasser, W. (1998). *Choice theory: A new psychology of personal freedom*. New York, NY: HarperCollins.

Gleick, J. (2011). *The information: A history, a theory, a flood*. New York, NY: Pantheon Books.

Goffman, E. (1967). *Interaction ritual: Essays on face-to-face behavior.* New York, NY: Doubleday.

Hayakawa, S. I. (1949). *Language and thought in action.* San Diego, CA: Harcourt, Brace, Jovanovich.

Ichheiser, G. (1941). Real, pseudo, and sham qualities of personality: An attempt at a new classification. *Journal of Personality, 9*(3), 218–226.

Jacobson, E. (1938). *Progressive relaxation.* Chicago, IL: University of Chicago Press.

Jung, C. G. (1947). *On the nature of the psyche.* London, UK: Ark Paperbacks.

Jung, C. G. (1966). The practice of psychotherapy: Essays on the psychology of transference and other subjects. *Collected Works,* Vol. 16. Princeton, NJ: Princeton University Press.

Jung, C. G. (1981). The archetypes and the collective unconscious. *Collected Works,* Vol. 9 (2d ed.). Princeton, NJ: Bollingen.

Kabat-Zinn, J. (1994/2005). *Wherever you go there you are: Mindfulness meditation in everyday life.* New York, NY: Hyperion.

Kandel, E. R. (2006). *In search of memory: The emergence of a new science of mind.* New York, NY: W.W. Norton & Company.

Keirsey, D. (1998). *Please understand me II: Temperament, character, intelligence.* Del Mar, CA: Prometheus Nemesis Book Company.

Korzybski, A. (1994/1933). *Science and sanity: An introduction to non-Aristotelian systems and general semantics* (5th ed.). New York, NY: Institute of General Semantics.

Leary, T. (1957). *Interpersonal diagnosis of personality.* New York, NY: Ronald.

Lippmann, W. (1922). *Public opinion.* New York, NY: The Free Press.

Lyotard, J-F. (1979). *The postmodern condition: A report on knowledge.* Manchester, UK: University of Manchester Press.

Maslow, A. H. (1954). *Motivation and personality.* New York, NY: Harper.

McCombs, M., & Shaw, D. (1972, Summer). The agenda-setting function of mass media. *The Public Opinion Quarterly, 36*(2), 176–187.

McCroskey, J. C. (1976a). The effects of communication apprehension on nonverbal behavior. *Communication Quarterly, 24,* 39–44.

McCroskey, J. C. (1976b). The problems of communication apprehension in the classroom. *Florida Speech Communication Journal, 4,* 1–12.

McCroskey, J. C. (1977a). Classroom consequences of communication apprehension. *Communication Education, 26,* 27–33.

McCroskey, J. C. (1977b). Oral communication apprehension: A summary of recent theory and research. *Human Communication Research, 4,* 78–96.

McCroskey, J. C. (1982). Oral communication apprehension: A reconceptualization. *Communication Yearbook, 6,* 136–170.

McCroskey, J. C. (1984). The communication apprehension perspective. In J. C. McCroskey & J. A. Daly (Eds.), *Avoiding communication: Shyness, reticence, and communication apprehension* (pp. 13–38). London, UK: Sage Publications Inc.

McCroskey, J. C., & Richmond, V. P. (1988). Communication apprehension and small group communication. In Robert S. Cathcart & Larry A. Samovar (Eds.), *Small group communication: A reader* (5th ed., pp. 405–420). Dubuque, IA: Wm. C. Brown.

McQuail, D. (1983). *Mass communication theory.* London, UK: Sage.

McQuail, D., Blumler, J. G., & Brown, J. (1972). The television audience: A revised perspective. In D. McQuail (Ed.), *Sociology of mass communication* (pp. 135–165). Middlesex, UK: Penguin.

Mead, G. H. (1934). *Mind, self and society.* Chicago, IL: University of Chicago Press.

Mitchell, M. (1936). *Gone with the wind.* New York, NY: Macmillan.

Murray, H. A. (1938). *Explorations in personality.* New York, NY: Oxford Press.

Neisser, U. (1976). *Cognition and reality: Principles and implications of cognitive psychology.* New York, NY: Freeman.

Noelle-Neumann, E. (1974). The spiral of silence: A theory of public opinion. *Journal of Communication, 24,* 43–51.

Noelle-Neumann, E. (1993). *The spiral of silence: Public opinion—our social skin.* Chicago, IL: University of Chicago Press.

Ogden, C. K., & Richards, I. A. (1923). *The meaning of meaning: A study of the influence of language upon thought and of the science of symbolism.* London, UK: Routledge & Kegan Paul.

Paul, R., & Elder, L. (2007). *The miniature guide to critical thinking.* Dillon Beach, CA: Foundation for Critical Thinking Press.

Pearce, W. B. (2001). A brief introduction to "the coordinated management of meaning" (CMM). *Sistemas Familiares, 17,* 5–16. Retrieved from http://www.russcomm.ru/eng/rca_biblio/p/pearce.shtml

Pearce, W. B. (2007). *Making social worlds: A communication perspective.* Malden, MA: Blackwell Publishing.

Postman, N. (1985). *Amusing ourselves to death: Public discourse in the age of show business.* New York, NY: Penguin Books.

Postman, N. (1992). *Technopoly: The surrender of culture to technology.* New York, NY: Alfred A. Knopf.

Rosenberg, M. B. (2005). *Nonviolent communication: A language of life.* Encinitas, CA: PuddleDancer Press.

Searle, J. (1969). *Speech acts.* Cambridge, UK: Cambridge University Press.

Sullivan, H. S. (1953). *The interpersonal theory of psychiatry.* New York, NY: Norton.

Tolle, E. (1999). *The power of now: A guide to spiritual enlightenment.* Vancouver, Canada: Namaste Publishing.

Watzlawick, P., Beavin, J. H., & Jackson, D. D. (1967). *Pragmatics of human communication: A study of interactional patterns, pathologies, and paradoxes.* New York, NY: W.W. Norton.

Weick, K. (1979). *The social psychology of organizing.* Reading, MA: Addison-Wesley.

Weick, K. (1995). *Sensemaking in organizations.* Newbury Park, CA: Sage.

Weiner, N. (1948). *Cybernetics or control and communication in the animal and the machine.* New York, NY: Wiley.

Wilder-Mott, C., & Weakland, J. H. (1981). *Rigor and imagination: Essays from the legacy of Gregory Bateson.* New York, NY: Praeger.

Index

1984 (Orwell), 110

A
Abstraction, 46–50, 140
Act, in dramatic pentad, 22
Adaptability, communication competence and, 125
Ad hominem, 92
Advertising, 94–96
Agency, in dramatic pentad, 22
Agenda-setting theory, 109–10
Agent, in dramatic pentad, 22
Agreeable personality type, 81
AIDA formula for persuasion, 95
Allen, Woody, 106
Allport, Gordon, 79
Altruism, 32
Ambivalent attitude, 141
Amusing Ourselves to Death (Postman), 110
Anima/animus, 33
Annie Hall (film), 106
Apprehension, communication. *See* Communication apprehension
Appropriate disclosure, 125
Appropriateness, communication competence and, 125
Aquinas, St. Thomas, 29
Archetypes, 33–34
Argumentation, study of, 91
Arguments, in relationships, 9
Aristotle, 12, 90, 91
Articulation, 125
The Artist's Way (Cameron), 74
Assertive Bill of Rights, 130–33
Assertiveness, communication competence and, 128–33
Assertives (speech act), 57
Attitude, 41–42
Attitude-behavior discrepancy, 42
Audience-based communication apprehension, 115

B
Back-stage elements in social situations, 23
Bales, Robert, 23
Bandura, Albert, 108–9
Bateson, Gregory, 6, 10, 11, 28, 30, 46, 140
Baudrillard, Jean, 98, 100
Begging the question, 92
Being here now, 142–43
Beingness, 72
Being There (film), 86
Beliefs, attitude formation and, 42
Bergland, Richard, 37
Bergson, Henri, 17
Bessie the cow, 48–49
Blaming, 67
Blumler, Jay, 107
Bobo doll experiment, 108
Bodily-kinesthetic intelligence, 36
Bormann, Ernest, 23
Boundaries of social systems, 5–6
Brain
 left and right, 37
 meaning and, 54
 mind vs., 28–29
 thinking-feeling distinction and, 42
Brave New World (Huxley), 110
Bristol, Claude, 121
Buber, Martin, 84–85
Burke, Kenneth
 on attitude, 41
 on comic frames of acceptance, 141–42
 definition of humans, 16, 20
 on hierarchies, 18–19
 on language, 21–22, 29
 on meaning making, 54
 on meaning of words, 54–55, 56
 on motivation, 66–68
 on the negative, 17, 30
 on persuasion, 93
 on symbols, 17
 on technology, 18

C
Caesar, Julius, 91
Cameron, Julia, 72
Campbell, Joseph, 36, 70
Carnegie, Dale, 121
Cattell, Raymond, 79–80
Cavafy, C.P., 138–39
Chain-indexing, 50
Chapin, Harry, 19
Choice theory, 70–71
Cicero, 91
Clarity, communication competence and, 124
Classical yoga, 120
Cliques, 5
Closed personality type, 81
Codependency, 85
Cognition, emotion vs., 42
Cognitive schemata, 43, 44
Cohen, Bernard, 109
Collective unconscious, 33–34, 37
Comic books, 107
"Comic book scare," 107
Comic frames of acceptance, 141–42
Commissives (speech act), 57
Common Sense (Paine), 106
Communication
 Coordinated Management of Meaning theory on, 60–61, 62
 of germs and viruses, 140
 as goal-directed, 124
 group, 23
 interactive model of, 2
 linear model of, 2
 Mead's model of mind and, 34, 35
 mindfulness attained in, 143
 models of, 2–3
 relational perspective and, 139
 report-and-command aspect of, 6
 social systems perspective of, 3–4
 transactional model of, 3
Communication apprehension, 114–22
 audience-based, 115
 categories of, 114–15
 causes of, 115–16
 context-based, 114–15
 defined, 114
 facing, 137–38
 impact of, 116–18
 letting go of, 118–20
 overview, 114
 situational, 115
 sources of, 115–16
 traitlike, 114
 visualization and meditation techniques for, 120–22
Communication competence, 124–33
 appropriateness and, 125

Communication competence (*continued*)
  assertiveness and, 128–33
  clarity and, 124
  defined, 124
  determinants of, 125–26
  effectiveness and, 124
  listening and, 126–27
  practicing, 138
  Rational Emotive Behavior Therapy (REBT) and, 128–29
Compassion, 139
Competence, communication. *See* Communication competence
Compliance-gaining persuasive strategies, 96–98
Connotative meaning of words, 55
Conscientiousness, 81
Consciousness
  connection with a wider, 136
  Freud on, 30, 31
  Jung's model of mind and, 32, 33, 34
  nature of, 29–30
Context-based communication apprehension, 114–15
Contextual meanings, 56
Control theory, 70
Conversational involvement, 125–26
Conversational management, 126
Coordinated Management of Meaning (CMM) theory, 57–62
Creative moment, 11–13
  asserting oneself exercise, 133
  mindfulness and meaning, 62–63
  personality analysis, 87
  persuasion exercise, 100–101
  photo shoot of media habits, 112
  right brain exercises, 38
  story of life video, 25
  structural differential exercise, 50–51
  visualization techniques for communication apprehension, 120–22
Creative process, 11–13
  dialectic in, 12–13
  as evolutionary, 11–12
  forces inhibiting and enhancing, 13
  relaxation and, 13
  yin-yang dialectic and, 12, 13
Creative Visualization (Gawain), 71, 121
Creativity
  inspiration for, 74
  multiple intelligences and, 36
  primary spiritual force and, 74–75
Critical thinking, 49–50, 139, 140–41
Critical thinking tools, 50
Cronen, Vernon, 57
Cultivation perspective on media, 110

D

Darwin, Charles, 29
Dating (critical thinking tool), 50
Death, foreknowledge of, 19–20
Decision tree, 10–11
Declaratives (speech act), 57
Deconstruction, 98

Defense mechanisms (Freudian theory), 31–32
Denial, 32
Derrida, Jaques, 98
De Saussure, Ferdinand, 55
Descartes, René, 29
Descriptive level, in structural differentiation, 47–48
Digital stress, 111
Directives (speech act), 57
Disagreeable personality type, 81
Doingness, 72
Drama
  creating video about your, 25
  dramatic pentad, 22
  fantasy theme analysis and, 23–34
  front and backstage elements to, 23
  Lyotard's "metanarrative" and, 99
  meaning and, 136–37
  social system defining your, 16
  symbolic interaction and, 22–23
Dramatic pentad, 22
Drawing from the Right Side of the Brain (Edwards), 37
Dreyfuss, Richard, 114

E

Edwards, Betty, 37
Effectiveness, communication competence and, 124
Ego (Freudian theory), 30, 31
Ego (Jungian theory), 32
Ego and Mechanisms of Defense (Freud), 32
Electronic age of media, 106
Ellis, Albert, 128
Emotion, cognition vs., 42
Emotional discomfort, communication apprehension and, 117
Empathy, 126
Enlightenment, 99
Entropy, in social systems, 8
Episodes, 58, 59
Esteem needs, 69, 70
Et cetera (critical thinking tool), 50
Ethos, 91
Evaluative attitudes, 41
Event (process) level, in structural differential, 47
Evolution
  creative process and, 11–12
  social, 9–10
Ex concesis, 92
Exercises. *See also* Creative moment
  creating "Coat of Arms," 25
  drawing a picture upside down, 38
  mapping your social system, 14
  motivation, 75
  tree of life sketch, 63
Explicit memory, 41
Explorations in Personality (Murray), 72
Expressives (speech acts), 57
Extensions (argumentation), 92
Extraversion, 33, 81, 82

F

FAB formula for persuasion, 95, 96
The Fabric of Mind (Bergland), 37
Fallacies, logical, 91–93
Families, arguments in, 9
Fantasy themes, 23–24
Father archetype, 33–34
Fears, 114. *See also* Communication apprehension
  defined, 115
  sources of, 115
Feedback loops, 8–9
Feeling, Jungian theory on, 33
Figure-ground relationship, 44
Foucault, Michel, 111
Foundation for Critical Thinking, 50
Franck, Frederick, 62–63
Frankl, Viktor, 62, 66
Freud, Anna, 32
Freud, Sigmund, 30–32, 66
Friedman, Meyers, 80
Front-stage elements in social situations, 23

G

G8 (Group of Eight) countries, 99–100
Gardner, Howard, 35–36
Gardner's multiple intelligences, 35–36
Gawain, Shakti, 66, 71–72, 74, 121
Generalized other, in Mead's theory, 35
General semantics, 46, 48
General Systems Theory, 4
Gerbner, George, 110
Gergen, Kenneth, 84, 85
Gestalt psychology, 44–45
Glasser, William, 66, 70–71
Gleick, James, 29
Goffman, Erving, 22–23
Goldberg, Lewis, 80
Grand narrative, 99
"Grand Old Dialectic" (Thompson), 20–21
Greece, history of rhetoric in, 90
Greenfield, Susan, 42
Guilt, 66–68
Gutenberg, Johannes, 105

H

Hall, Stuart, 110, 111
Hatha yoga, 120
Havingness, 72
Hayakawa, S.I., 47, 48–49
Hegel, Georg, 12
Hierarchies, humans attempting to move up in, 18–19
Hierarchy of needs, Maslow's, 68–70
Homeostasis, 8, 9
Horton Hears a Who (Suess), 5
Humans, Burke's definition of, 16–22
Humor
  in advertising, 96
  as defense mechanism, 32
Huxley, Aldous, 110

Huxley, Thomas, 29
Hyper-reality, 100
Hyphens (critical thinking tool), 50

I

Ichheiser, Gustav, 86
Id (Freudian theory), 30, 31, 32
Identification, 143
  advertising and, 94–96
  persuasion and, 93–94
I-It pattern of interaction, 85
Implicit memory, 41
Impression management, 23
Indexing (critical thinking tool), 50
Indirect speech acts, 57
Individuation (Jungian theory), 34
Inference level, in structural differentiation, 48
Inferences, 49
Information, critical thinking about, 140–41
The Information (Gleick), 29
Inspiration, creative, 74
Institutio Oratoria (Quintilian), 91
Instrumental goals, 124
Interactive model of communication, 2
Interconnectedness, in relationships, 7
Interdependence, in social systems, 7
Interpersonal intelligence, 36
Interpersonal personality, 84–86
Intrapersonal intelligence, 36
Introversion, 33, 81, 82
Intuition, Jungian theory on, 33
Ithaka (Cavafy), 138–39
I-Thou pattern of interaction, 85

J

Jacobson, Edmund, 119
James, William, 44
Jargon, 92
Jung, Carl, 32–33, 72

K

Kabat-Zinn, Jon, 122
Katz, Elihu, 107
Keirsey, David, 84
Kill, the, 68
Knowledge, communication competence and, 125
Korzybski, 40
Korzybski, Alfred, 46–47, 48, 136, 140

L

Language
  Burke's definition of humans and, 16
  "fitting in" function of, 21–22
  meaning and, 56, 57, 59
  order and, 66
  pragmatics and, 56–57
  semantics and, 55
  semiotics and, 55
  symbols and, 16–17
Language and Thought in Action (Hayakawa), 48
"Language games," 99–100
LaPierre, Richard, 42
Law of closure, 44
Law of common fate, 44
Law of continuity, 44
Law of partial inclusion, 5
Law of proximity, 45
Law of similarity, 45
Law of symmetry, 44
Learned attitudes, 41
Left brain, 37
Letting go
  of communication fears, 118–20
  critical awareness and, 141
Linear model of communication, 2
Linguistic context, 55–56
Linguistic intelligence, 36
Listening, 126–27
"Listen to the Mustn'ts" (Silverstein), 18
Literate age of media, 105
Logical fallacies, 91–93
Logical-mathematical intelligence, 36
Logos, 91
Long-term memory, 40
Lyotard, Jean-Francois, 98–99

M

Maiden archetype, 34
Man's Search for Meaning (Frankl), 62, 66
Mantras, 122
MAPs, 136
  attitude, 41–42
  memory, 40–41
  perception, 43–46
Marwell, Gerald, 96–97
Marxist criticism, 111
Maslow, Abraham, 66, 68–70
Maslow's hierarchy of needs, 68–70
Mason, Lisa, 1
McCroskey, James, 114
McLuhan, Marshall, 105, 106
McQuail, Dennis, 107
Mead, George Herbert, 34–35, 78
Meaning, 54–63
  construction of, 136–37
  contextual, 56
  Coordinated Management of Meaning theory, 57–62
  Frankls on, 66
  identifications and, 56–57
  motivation and, 137
  postmodernism and, 98
  pragmatics and, 55–56
  search for, 54, 62
  semantics and, 55
  semiotics and, 55
  speech acts and, 57
  symbolic interaction and, 23
  symbols and, 17
  symbols/referents and, 54–55
The Meaning of Meaning (Ogden/Richards), 54

Media, 104–12
  agenda-setting theory on, 109–10
  as a business, 105
  cultivation perspective on, 110
  effects of, 106–11
  electronic age of, 106
  history of, 105–6
  influence on minding the world, 110–11
  literate age of, 105
  McLuhan's "media is the message" phrase and, 106
  pervasiveness of, 104–5
  photo shoot of your habits with, 112
  as plural, 105, 137
  print age of, 105–6
  serving political and economic interests, 111
  social learning theory and, 108–9
  spiral of silence theory on, 110
  tribal age of, 105
  used to carry the dominant "discourse," 111
  uses-and-gratifications theory on, 107–8
  various relationships with, 137
Meditation, 121–22
"The medium is the message," 106
Memory, 40–41, 42, 43
Metanarrative, 99
Mind
  beyond physical existence, 37
  brain vs., 28–29
  developing within a grander pattern, 136
  freeing the, 13
  Freud's model of, 30–32
  functional view of, 29–30
  Gardner's multiple intelligences and, 35–36
  as information, 29
  Jung's model of, 32–34
  Mead's model of, 34–35
  meaning and, 54
  media and, 109, 110
  as metaphysical, 28
  personality and, 78
  relational ethic and, 139
  as social, 28
  substantial view of, 29
  symbols used to connect, 17
  as transcendent, 28–29
Mind and Nature (Bateson), 30, 140
Mindfulness, 62–63, 122, 142
Models
  of communication, 2–3
  defined, 2
  of mind, 32–35
Monroe, Alan H., 95
Monroe Motivation Sequence, 95
Morgan, Christiana, 72
Morrison, Jim, 113
Mortification, 67
Mother archetype, 33

Motivation, 66–75
　advertising and, 95–96
　communication competence and, 125
　exercise on, 75
　Gawain on, 71–72
　Glasser's choice theory on, 70–71
　letting go of communication fears and, 118
　Maslow's theory on, 68–70
　meaning and, 137
　Murray's theory on, 72–74
　order and, 66–68
　personality and, 137
　spiritual side of creativity and, 74–75
Multiple intelligences, Gardner's, 35–36
Murray, Henry, 66, 72–74
Musical intelligence, 36
Mutatio controversiae, 92
My Big Fat Greek Wedding (film), 115
Myers-Briggs Personality types, 82–84
Mystery, 68

N

Natural intelligence, 36
Nature, humans separated from, 18
Needs
　Glasser's choice theory on, 71
　internal vs. external, 72–73
　Maslow's hierarchy of, 68–70
　psychogenic, 72–74
Negative
　human invention of, 17–18
　internalization of, 30–31
Negative feedback loops, 9
Negentropy, in social systems, 8
Neisser, Ulrich, 43
Neuroticism, 81
Nietzsche, Friedrich, 62, 65, 100
Noelle-Neumann, Elisabeth, 110

O

Object level, in structural differentiation, 47
Odbert, H.S., 79
Ogden, C.K., 54
Open personality type, 81
Order, motivation and, 66–68
Orwell, George, 110
Overgeneralizations, 92

P

Past experiences, attitude formation and, 42
Patterns
　connecting, 140
　cultural, 58
Peale, Norman Vincent, 121
Pearce, W. Barnett, 57
Perception, 43–46
Perfection, 20
Perpetual cycle, Neisser's model of, 43

Personality, 78–87
　Big Five factors (OCEAN), 80–81, 87
　Cattels' factor model, 79–80
　as cognitive, behavioral, relational, and contextual, 86
　factors of, 78–82
　interpersonal, 84–86
　motivation and, 137
　Myers-Briggs types of, 82–84
　overview, 78, 86
　"reading" your, 86
　Type A, 80
　Type B, 80
Persuasion, 90–101
　advertising and, 94–96
　compliance-gaining strategies for, 96–98
　history of rhetoric and, 90–91
　identification and, 93–94
　media and, 104–5
　mind map on persuasive influences, 100–101
　postmodern perspectives on, 98–100
　Schopenhauer's stratagems and, 91–93
The Pessimist's Handbook (Schopenhauer), 91
Phatic communication, 124
The Philosophy of Literary Form (Burke), 56
Physiological needs, 68–69
Plato, 12, 29, 90
Play-and-games stages, 108–9
Positive feedback loops, 8–9
Postman, Neil, 110–11
The Postmodern Condition (Lyotard), 98
Postmodernism
　media and, 104, 111
　perspectives on persuasion, 98–100
Power, in relationships, 6–7
The Power of Now (Tolle), 142
Pragmatics, 55–56
Prägnanz, 44
Preconscious, 30, 31
Predisposed attitudes, 41
Present, living in the, 142–43
Principle of gestalt, 44
Print age of media, 105–6
Progressive muscle relaxation (PMR), 119–20
Projection, 32
Protagoras, 90
Psychogenic needs, 72–74
Purgative guilt cycle, 66–67
Purpose, in dramatic pentad, 22

Q

Quintilian, 91

R

Radio broadcast, *War of the Worlds* (1938), 107
Rational Emotive Behavior Therapy (REBT), 128–29
Reality therapy, 70

Referents, 54, 55
Relational goals, 124
Relational perspective, 139–40
Relationships
　change in, 7
　communication apprehension and, 116
　Coordinated Management of Meaning theory on, 58, 59, 61–62
　feedback loops in, 8–9
　influence of, 137
　interdependence in, 7
　interpersonal personality and, 84–86
　power within, 6–7
　relational perspective and, 139–40
Relaxation
　communication apprehension and, 119–20
　creative process and, 13
Repetition, in advertising, 96
Repression, 32
Retention, in evolution process, 9, 10, 11
Rhetoric, 90–93
Rhetoric (Aristotle), 91
Richards, I.A., 54
Richmond, Virginia, 114
Right brain, 37
Root meanings of words, 55
Rubin, Edgar, 44

S

Safety needs, 69, 70
Schemata, 43, 44
Schmitt, David R., 96–97
Schopenhauer, Arthur, 91–93
Schramm, Wilbur, 2
Science, as grand narrative, 99
Science and Sanity (Korzybski), 46
Searle, John, 57
Secret, the, 68
Seduction of the Innocent (Wertham), 107
Selection, in evolution process, 9, 10, 11
Selective exposure theory on media, 107–8
Self-actualization, 69, 70
Self-assertion, communication competence and, 128–33
Self-esteem, communication apprehension and, 117
Self-monitoring, 117
Self-presentation goals, 124
Semantics, 46, 48, 54, 55
Semiotics, 55
Sensation, Jungian theory on, 33
"Shadow" (Jungian theory), 34
Shannon, Claude, 2
Short-term memory, 40
Silva Mind Control, 121
Silverstein, Shel, 18
Simulacrum, 100
Situational communication apprehension, 115
Situational context, 56
Smith, Adam, 99

Social composure, 125
Social confirmation, 125
Social construction of reality, 16, 23–24, 59, 98
Social evolution, 9–10
Social experience, 125
Social interaction, drama of, 16–25
Social learning theory, 108–109
Social needs, 69
Social reality, creating your, 136–44
Social systems
    boundaries of, 5–6
    dramas and, 16, 20, 24, 136
    as dynamic, 7
    evolving, 9–10
    explained, 3–4
    homeostasis in, 8
    interdependence in, 7
    mapping exercise, 14
    meaning and, 54, 56–57
    purgative guilt cycle and, 66–67
    relationships between people in, 6–7
    social order and, 66–67
    stochastic process in, 10–11
    subsystems in, 4–5
Socrates, 27, 90
Sophists, 90
Soul, 29
Spatial intelligence, 36
Speech acts, theory of, 57
Spiral of silence theory, 110
Spiritual intelligence, 36
Steps to an Ecology of Mind (Bateson), 11
Stochastic process, 10–11
Story. *See* Drama
Structural differential, 46, 47–48, 50–51
Substantial view of mind, 29
Subsystems, 4–5
   interdependent, 7

Sullivan, Harry Stack, 84, 85
Superego (Freudian theory), 30, 31, 32
Symbolic convergence theory, 23
Symbolic interaction, 22–23
Symbol-making, 16–17
Symbol-misusing, 17
Symbols, meaning making and, 54
Symbol-using, 27
Systems. *See* Social systems
Systems diagram, 4

T

Technological determinism, 106
Technology
    cultural change and communication, 106
    media impact and, 110, 111
    misrepresentation of reality and, 140–41
    separation from nature and, 18
Thinking
    emotion vs., 42
    Jungian theory on, 33
Tisias, 90
Tolle, Eckhart, 142
Toulmin, Stephen, 91
Tragic frame of rejection, 141
Traitlike communication apprehension, 114
Transactional model of communication, 3
Transcendence, 68
Tree of Being, 143
Tree of life, sketching, 63
Tribal age of media, 105
Trickster archetype, 34
True self, 86
Tucker, Ray, 128, 130, 133
Type A personality, 80
Type B personality, 80

U

Ultimate identification, 140
Unconscious, the, 30, 31, 32–34
Uses-and-gratifications theory on media, 107

V

Variation, in evolution process, 9, 10, 11
Victimage, 67
VIPS formula for persuasion, 95
Visualization, 120–21
Von Bertalanffy, Ludwig, 4

W

The War of the Worlds radio broadcast, 107
Wealth of Nations (Smith), 99
Weaver, Warren, 2
Weick, Karl, 141
Weiner, Norbert, 2
Welles, Orson, 107
Wells, H.G., 107
Wertham, Frederick, 107
What About Bob? (film), 114
Wherever You Go, There You Are (Kabat-Zinn), 122
Words, meaning and, 54–57

Y

Yin & yang dialectic, 12, 13
Yoga, 120

Z

The Zen of Seeing: Seeing/Drawing as Meditation (Franck), 63
Zen practice, 62–63
Ziglar, Zig, 75, 89